SPELL CHECKERS™

VOLUME 3

An Oni Press Publication

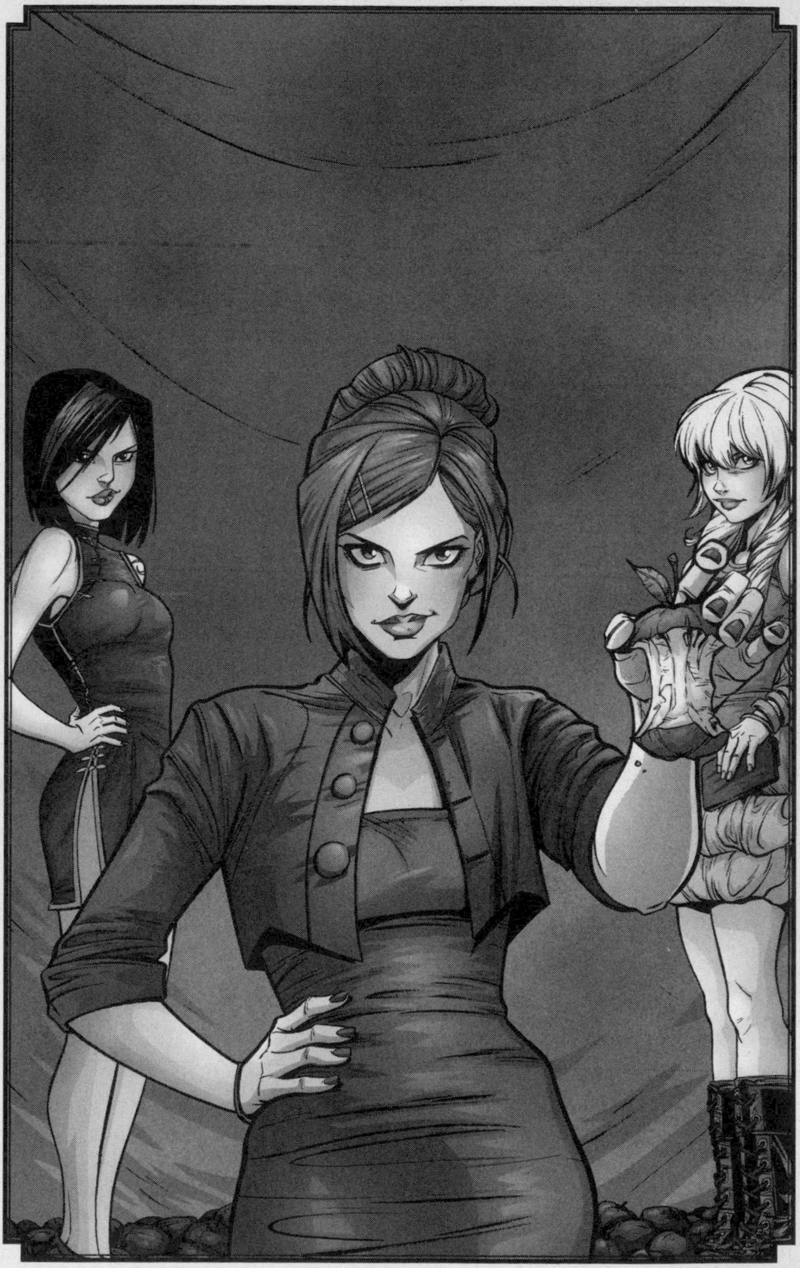

SPELL CHECKERS

Volume 3: Careless Whisper

written by
Jamie S. Rich

illustrated by
Nicolas Hitori De

flashbacks and cover
illustrated by
Joëlle Jones

cover colored by
Warren Wucinich

lettered by
Warren Wucinich

designed by
Keith A. Wood

edited by
Jill Beaton

Oni Press, Inc.

publisher, Joe Nozemack

editor in chief, James Lucas Jones

art director, Keith Wood

director of publicity, John Schork

director of sales, Cheyenne Allott

editor, Jill Beaton

editor, Charlie Chu

graphic designer, Jason Storey

digital prepress lead, Troy Look

administrative assistant, Robin Herrera

Oni Press Inc.
1305 SE Martin Luther King Jr. Blvd.
Suite A
Portland, OR 97214

www.onipress.com

First Edition: October 2013

ISBN: 978-1-62010-094-3
eISBN: 978-1-62010-107-0
Library of Congress Control Number: 2013937932

1 3 5 7 9 10 8 6 4 2

Printed in the U.S.A.

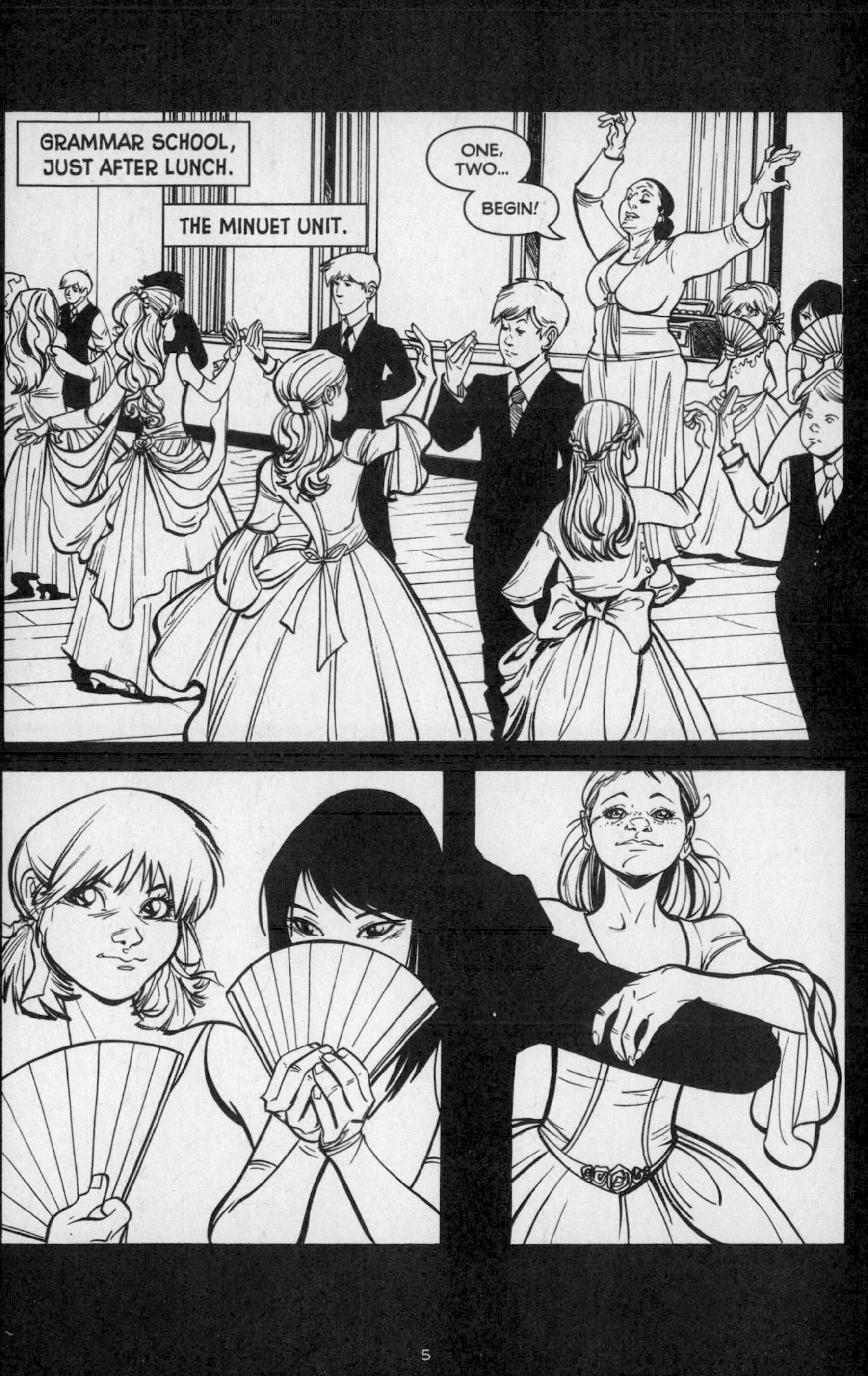
GRAMMAR SCHOOL,
JUST AFTER LUNCH.
THE MINUET UNIT.
ONE,
TWO...
BEGIN!

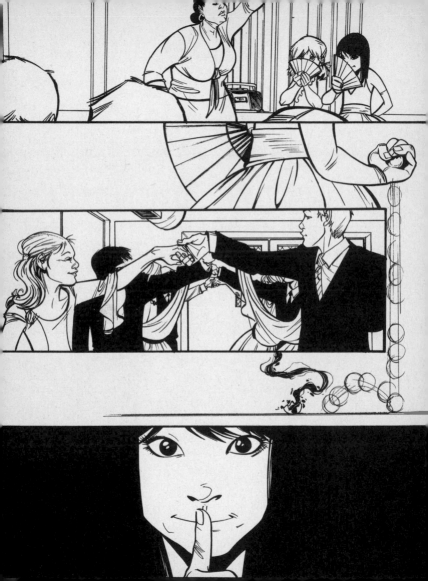

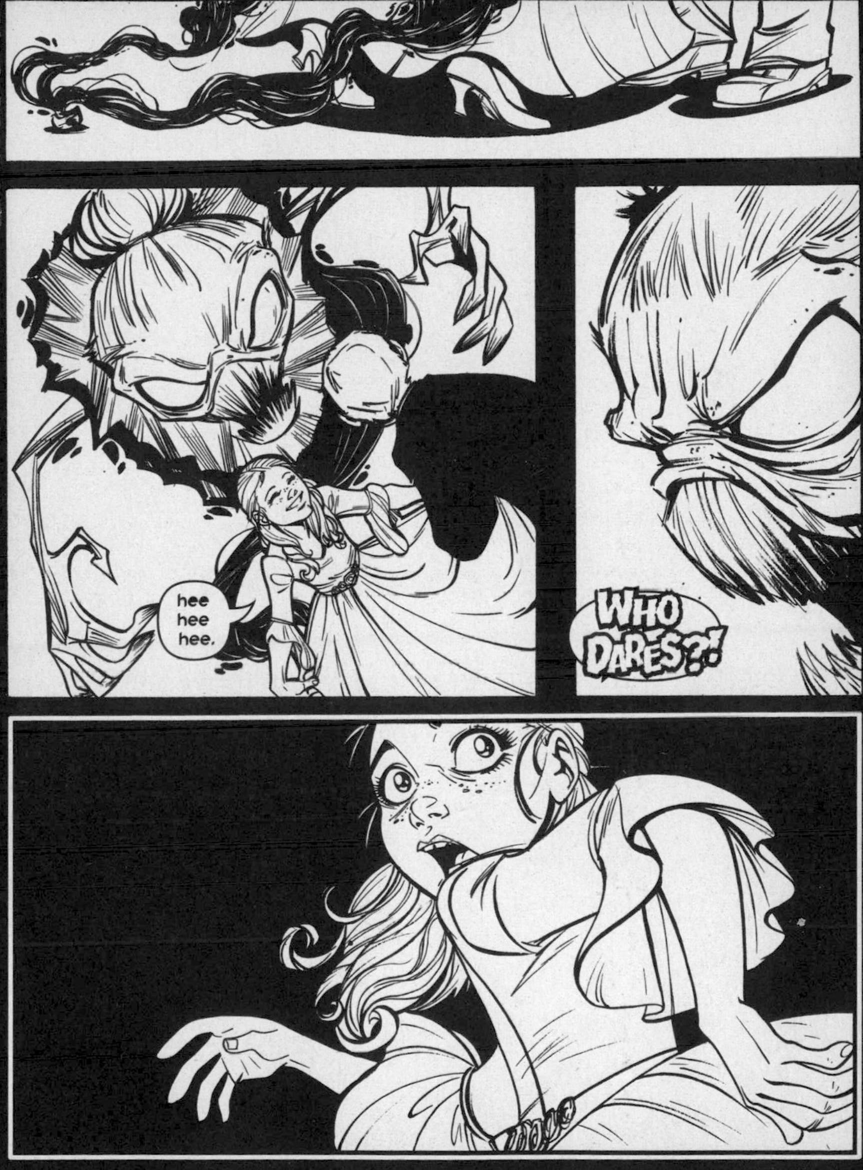
hee hee hee.
WHO DARES?!

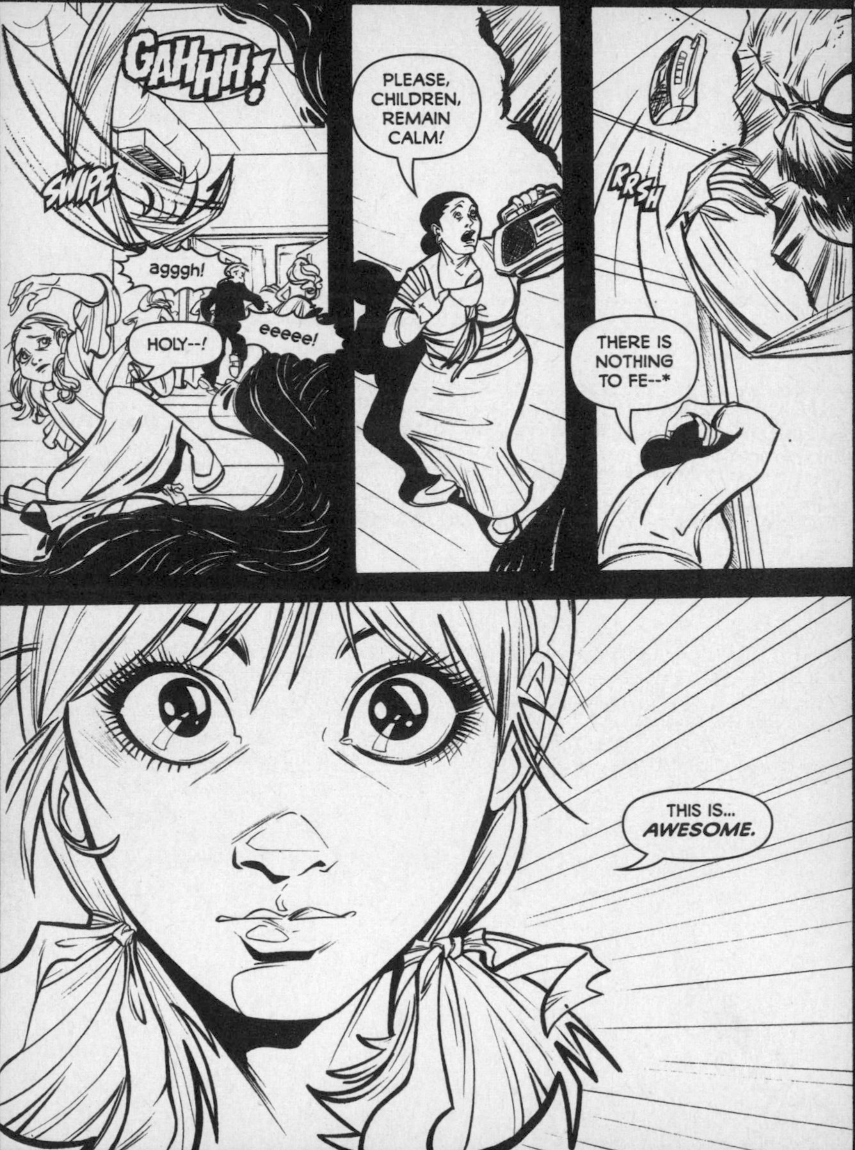
GAHHH!
SWIPE
agggh!
HOLY--!
eeeee!
PLEASE, CHILDREN, REMAIN CALM!
KRSH
THERE IS NOTHING TO FE--*
THIS IS... AWESOME.

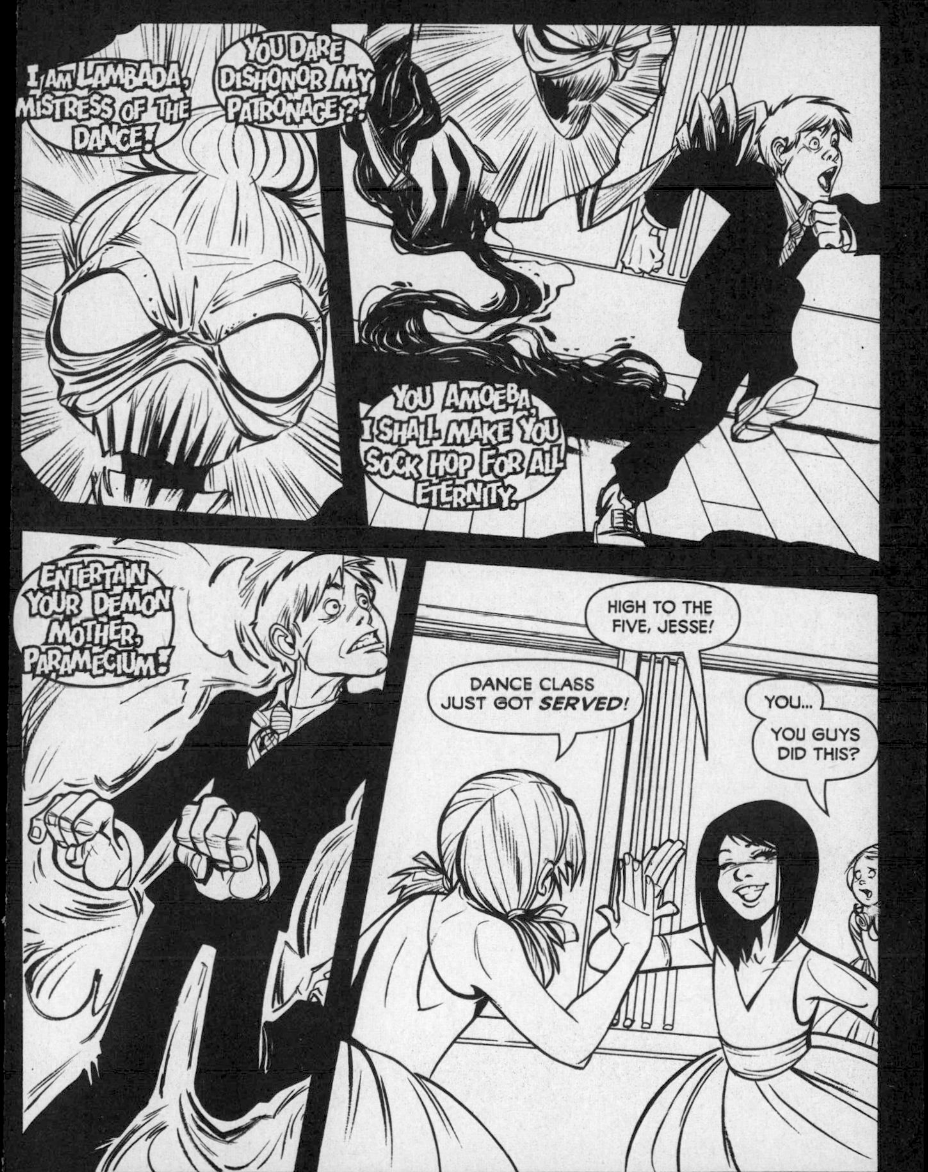
I AM LAMBADA, MISTRESS OF THE DANCE!
YOU DARE DISHONOR MY PATRONAGE?!
YOU AMOEBA, I SHALL MAKE YOU SOCK HOP FOR ALL ETERNITY.
ENTERTAIN YOUR DEMON MOTHER, PARAMECIUM!
HIGH TO THE FIVE, JESSE!
DANCE CLASS JUST GOT SERVED!
YOU...
YOU GUYS DID THIS?

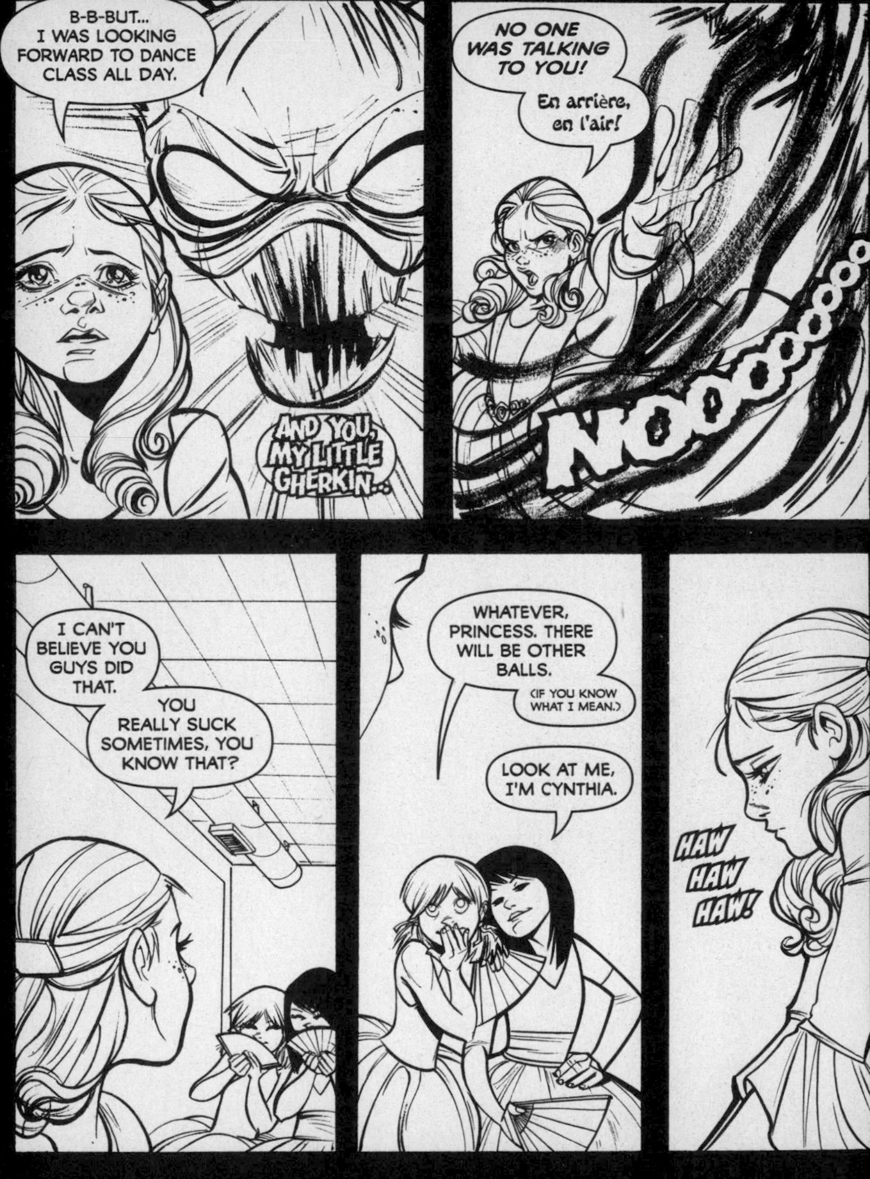
B-B-BUT... I WAS LOOKING FORWARD TO DANCE CLASS ALL DAY.
AND YOU, MY LITTLE GHERKIN...
NO ONE WAS TALKING TO YOU!
En arrière, en l'air!
NOOOOOOOOO
I CAN'T BELIEVE YOU GUYS DID THAT.
YOU REALLY SUCK SOMETIMES, YOU KNOW THAT?
WHATEVER, PRINCESS. THERE WILL BE OTHER BALLS.
(IF YOU KNOW WHAT I MEAN.)
LOOK AT ME, I'M CYNTHIA.
HAW HAW HAW!

Chapter 1
"Say You'll Go"

I

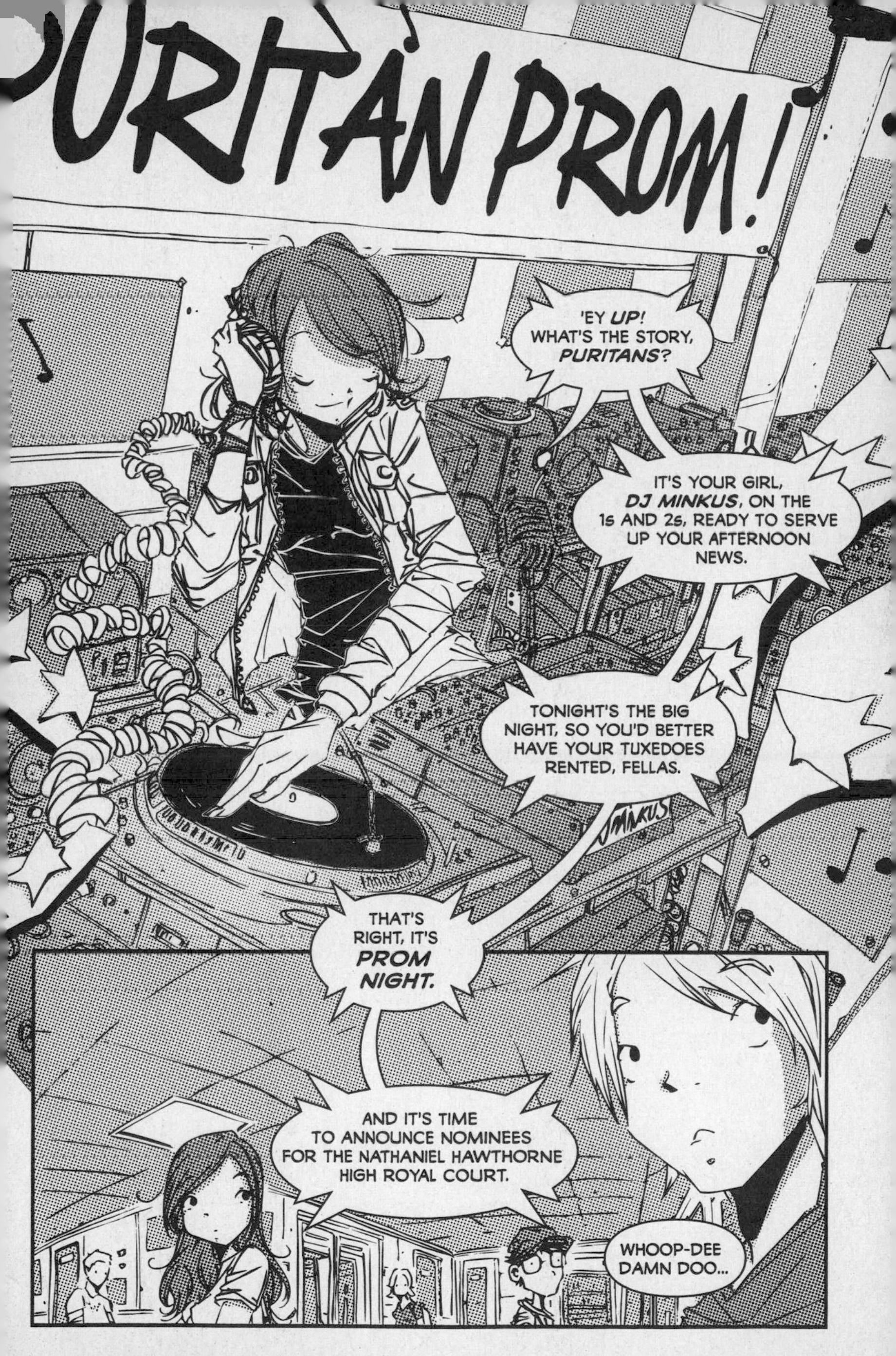
PURITAN PROM!
'EY UP! WHAT'S THE STORY, PURITANS?
IT'S YOUR GIRL, DJ MINKUS, ON THE 1s AND 2s, READY TO SERVE UP YOUR AFTERNOON NEWS.
TONIGHT'S THE BIG NIGHT, SO YOU'D BETTER HAVE YOUR TUXEDOES RENTED, FELLAS.
MINKUS
THAT'S RIGHT, IT'S PROM NIGHT.
AND IT'S TIME TO ANNOUNCE NOMINEES FOR THE NATHANIEL HAWTHORNE HIGH ROYAL COURT.
WHOOP-DEE DAMN DOO...

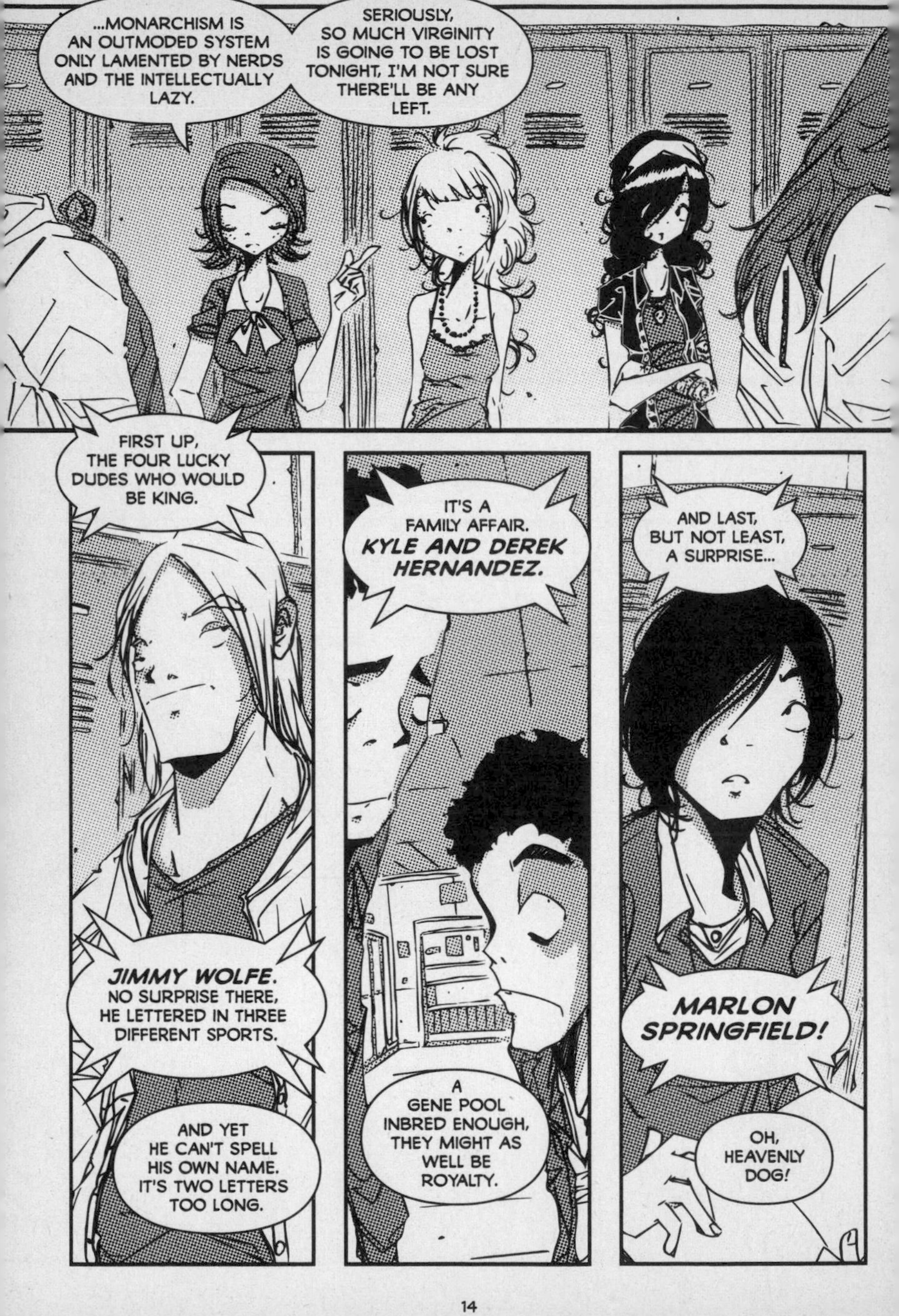
...MONARCHISM IS AN OUTMODED SYSTEM ONLY LAMENTED BY NERDS AND THE INTELLECTUALLY LAZY.
SERIOUSLY, SO MUCH VIRGINITY IS GOING TO BE LOST TONIGHT, I'M NOT SURE THERE'LL BE ANY LEFT.
FIRST UP, THE FOUR LUCKY DUDES WHO WOULD BE KING.
JIMMY WOLFE. NO SURPRISE THERE, HE LETTERED IN THREE DIFFERENT SPORTS.
AND YET HE CAN'T SPELL HIS OWN NAME. IT'S TWO LETTERS TOO LONG.
IT'S A FAMILY AFFAIR. KYLE AND DEREK HERNANDEZ.
A GENE POOL INBRED ENOUGH, THEY MIGHT AS WELL BE ROYALTY.
AND LAST, BUT NOT LEAST, A SURPRISE...
MARLON SPRINGFIELD!
OH, HEAVENLY DOG!

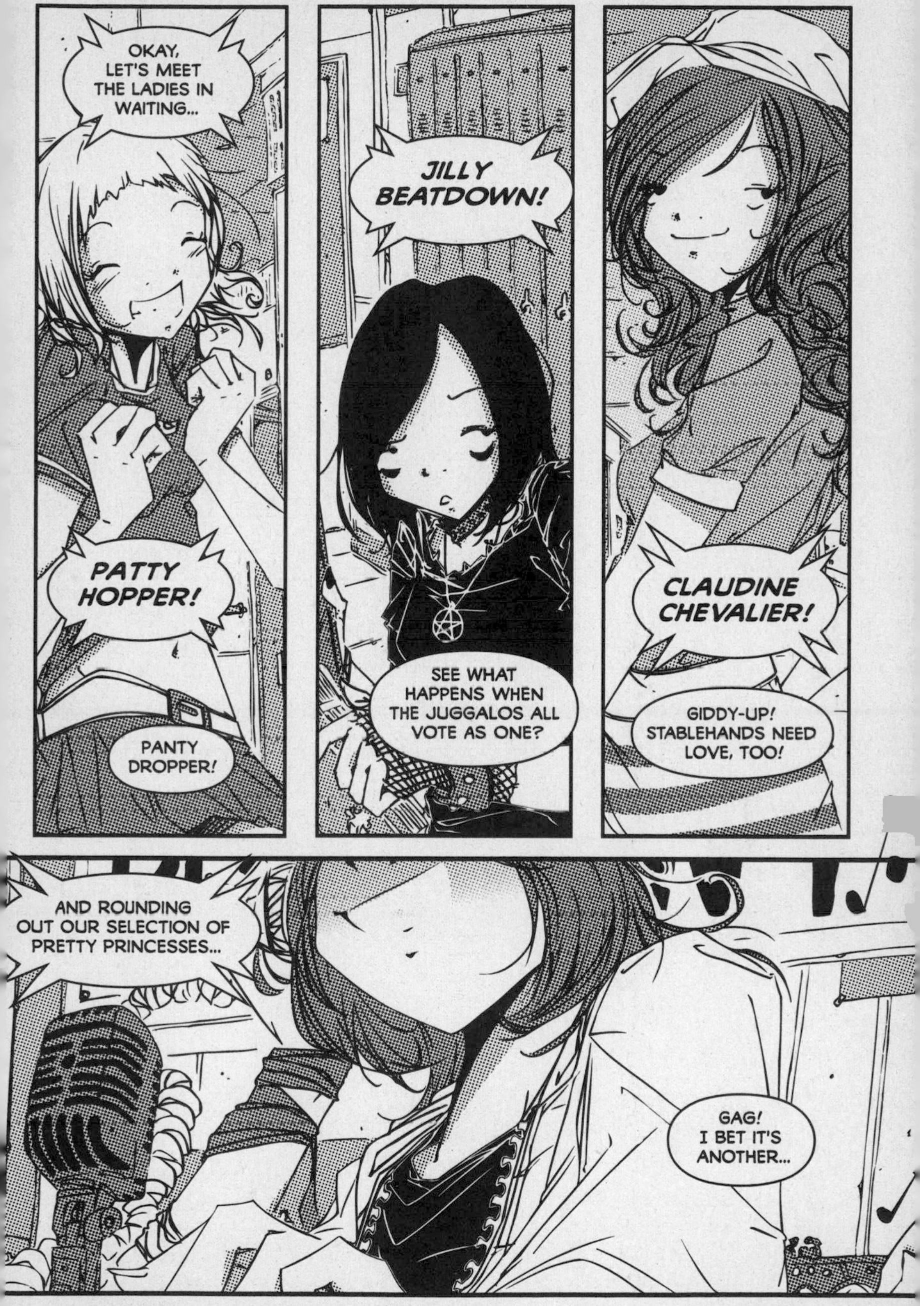
OKAY, LET'S MEET THE LADIES IN WAITING...
PATTY HOPPER!
PANTY DROPPER!
JILLY BEATDOWN!
SEE WHAT HAPPENS WHEN THE JUGGALOS ALL VOTE AS ONE?
CLAUDINE CHEVALIER!
GIDDY-UP! STABLEHANDS NEED LOVE, TOO!
AND ROUNDING OUT OUR SELECTION OF PRETTY PRINCESSES...
GAG! I BET IT'S ANOTHER...

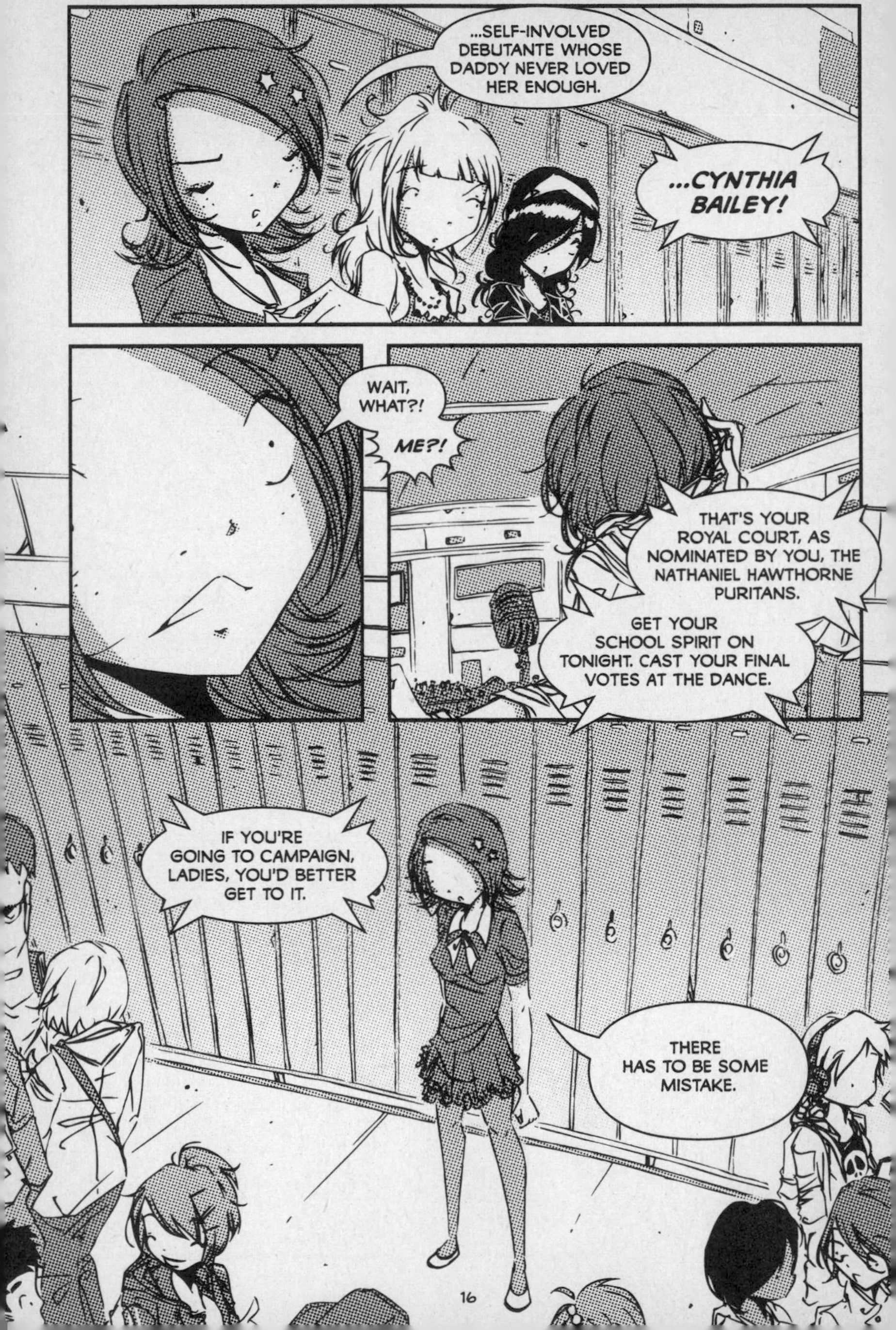
...SELF-INVOLVED DEBUTANTE WHOSE DADDY NEVER LOVED HER ENOUGH.
...CYNTHIA BAILEY!
WAIT, WHAT?!
ME?!
THAT'S YOUR ROYAL COURT, AS NOMINATED BY YOU, THE NATHANIEL HAWTHORNE PURITANS.
GET YOUR SCHOOL SPIRIT ON TONIGHT. CAST YOUR FINAL VOTES AT THE DANCE.
IF YOU'RE GOING TO CAMPAIGN, LADIES, YOU'D BETTER GET TO IT.
THERE HAS TO BE SOME MISTAKE.

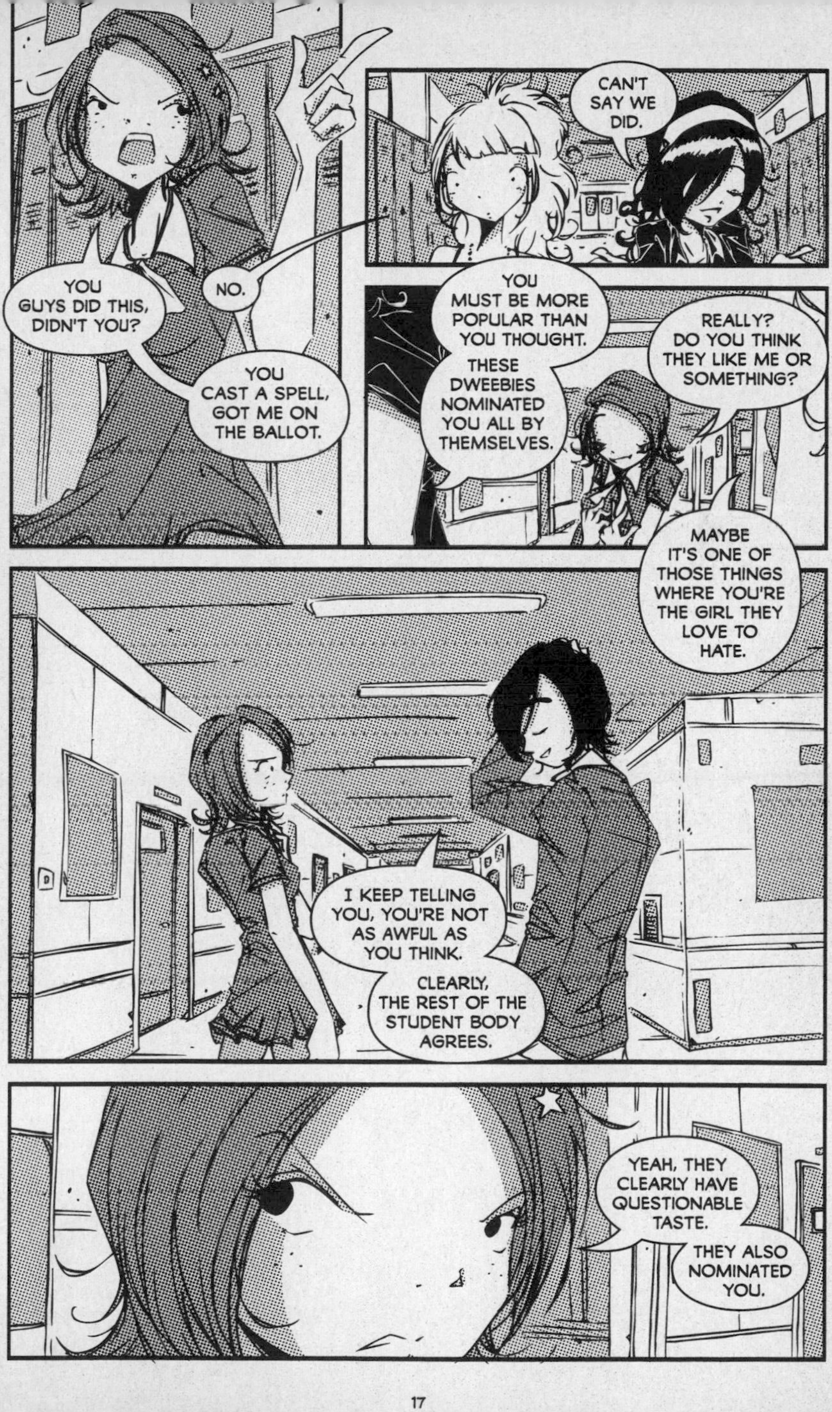
YOU GUYS DID THIS, DIDN'T YOU?
NO.
YOU CAST A SPELL, GOT ME ON THE BALLOT.
CAN'T SAY WE DID.
YOU MUST BE MORE POPULAR THAN YOU THOUGHT.
THESE DWEEBIES NOMINATED YOU ALL BY THEMSELVES.
REALLY? DO YOU THINK THEY LIKE ME OR SOMETHING?
MAYBE IT'S ONE OF THOSE THINGS WHERE YOU'RE THE GIRL THEY LOVE TO HATE.
I KEEP TELLING YOU, YOU'RE NOT AS AWFUL AS YOU THINK.
CLEARLY, THE REST OF THE STUDENT BODY AGREES.
YEAH, THEY CLEARLY HAVE QUESTIONABLE TASTE.
THEY ALSO NOMINATED YOU.

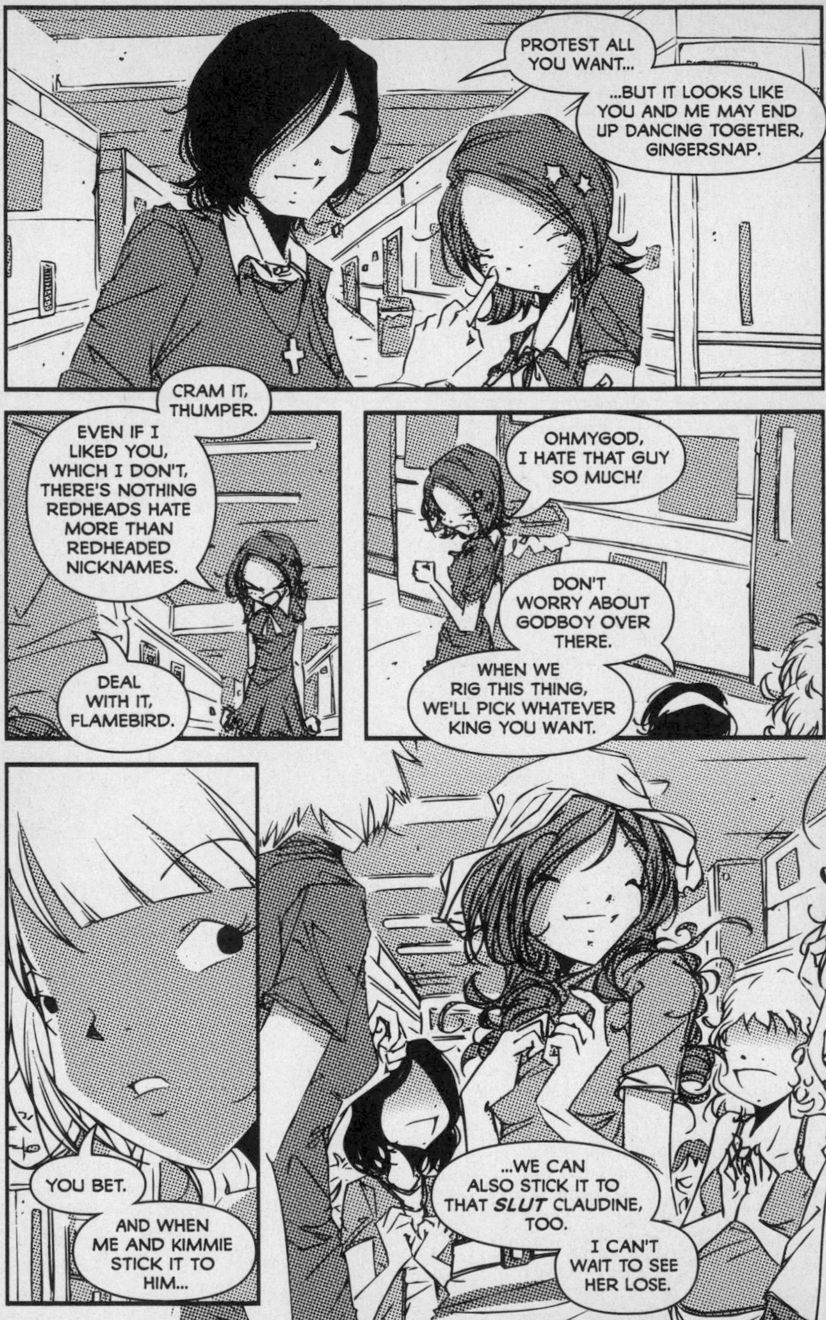
PROTEST ALL YOU WANT...
...BUT IT LOOKS LIKE YOU AND ME MAY END UP DANCING TOGETHER, GINGERSNAP.
CRAM IT, THUMPER.
EVEN IF I LIKED YOU, WHICH I DON'T, THERE'S NOTHING REDHEADS HATE MORE THAN REDHEADED NICKNAMES.
DEAL WITH IT, FLAMEBIRD.
OHMYGOD, I HATE THAT GUY SO MUCH!
DON'T WORRY ABOUT GODBOY OVER THERE.
WHEN WE RIG THIS THING, WE'LL PICK WHATEVER KING YOU WANT.
YOU BET.
AND WHEN ME AND KIMMIE STICK IT TO HIM...
...WE CAN ALSO STICK IT TO THAT *SLUT* CLAUDINE, TOO.
I CAN'T WAIT TO SEE HER LOSE.

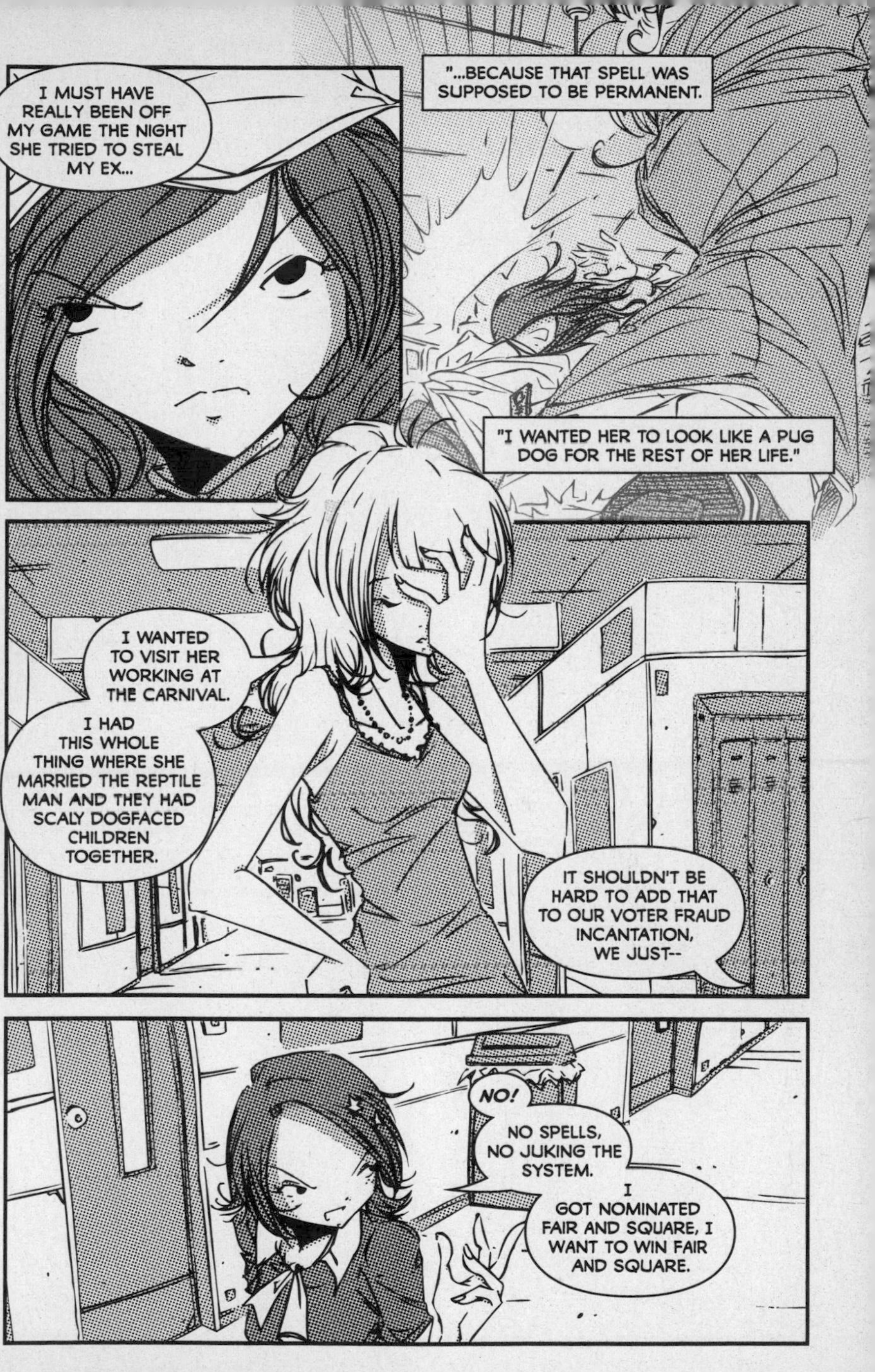
I MUST HAVE REALLY BEEN OFF MY GAME THE NIGHT SHE TRIED TO STEAL MY EX...
"...BECAUSE THAT SPELL WAS SUPPOSED TO BE PERMANENT.
"I WANTED HER TO LOOK LIKE A PUG DOG FOR THE REST OF HER LIFE."
I WANTED TO VISIT HER WORKING AT THE CARNIVAL.
I HAD THIS WHOLE THING WHERE SHE MARRIED THE REPTILE MAN AND THEY HAD SCALY DOGFACED CHILDREN TOGETHER.
IT SHOULDN'T BE HARD TO ADD THAT TO OUR VOTER FRAUD INCANTATION, WE JUST--
NO!
NO SPELLS, NO JUKING THE SYSTEM.
I GOT NOMINATED FAIR AND SQUARE, I WANT TO WIN FAIR AND SQUARE.

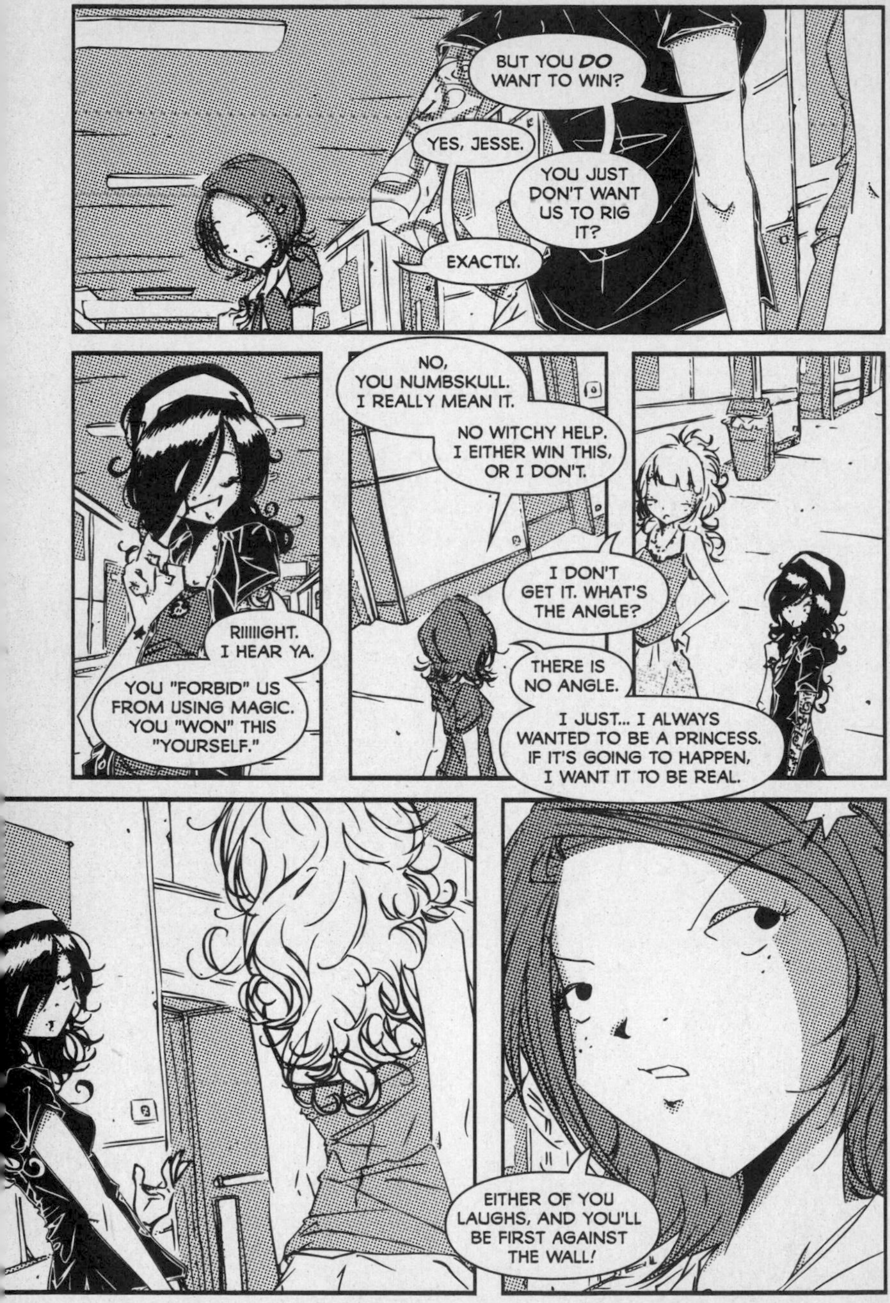
BUT YOU *DO* WANT TO WIN?
YES, JESSE.
YOU JUST DON'T WANT US TO RIG IT?
EXACTLY.
RIIIIIGHT. I HEAR YA.
YOU "FORBID" US FROM USING MAGIC. YOU "WON" THIS "YOURSELF."
NO, YOU NUMBSKULL. I REALLY MEAN IT.
NO WITCHY HELP. I EITHER WIN THIS, OR I DON'T.
I DON'T GET IT. WHAT'S THE ANGLE?
THERE IS NO ANGLE.
I JUST... I ALWAYS WANTED TO BE A PRINCESS. IF IT'S GOING TO HAPPEN, I WANT IT TO BE REAL.
EITHER OF YOU LAUGHS, AND YOU'LL BE FIRST AGAINST THE WALL!

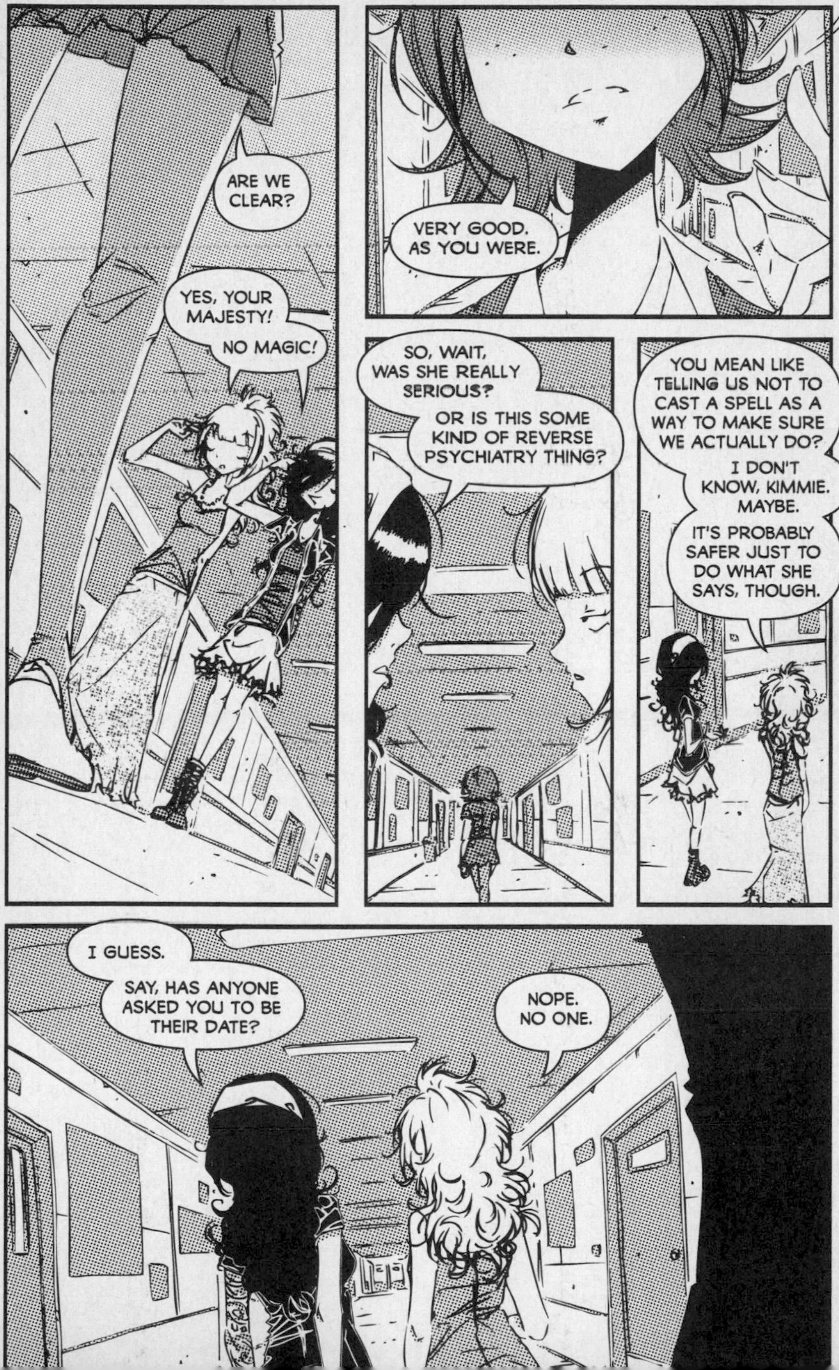
ARE WE CLEAR?
YES, YOUR MAJESTY!
NO MAGIC!
VERY GOOD. AS YOU WERE.
SO, WAIT, WAS SHE REALLY SERIOUS?
OR IS THIS SOME KIND OF REVERSE PSYCHIATRY THING?
YOU MEAN LIKE TELLING US NOT TO CAST A SPELL AS A WAY TO MAKE SURE WE ACTUALLY DO?
I DON'T KNOW, KIMMIE. MAYBE.
IT'S PROBABLY SAFER JUST TO DO WHAT SHE SAYS, THOUGH.
I GUESS.
SAY, HAS ANYONE ASKED YOU TO BE THEIR DATE?
NOPE. NO ONE.

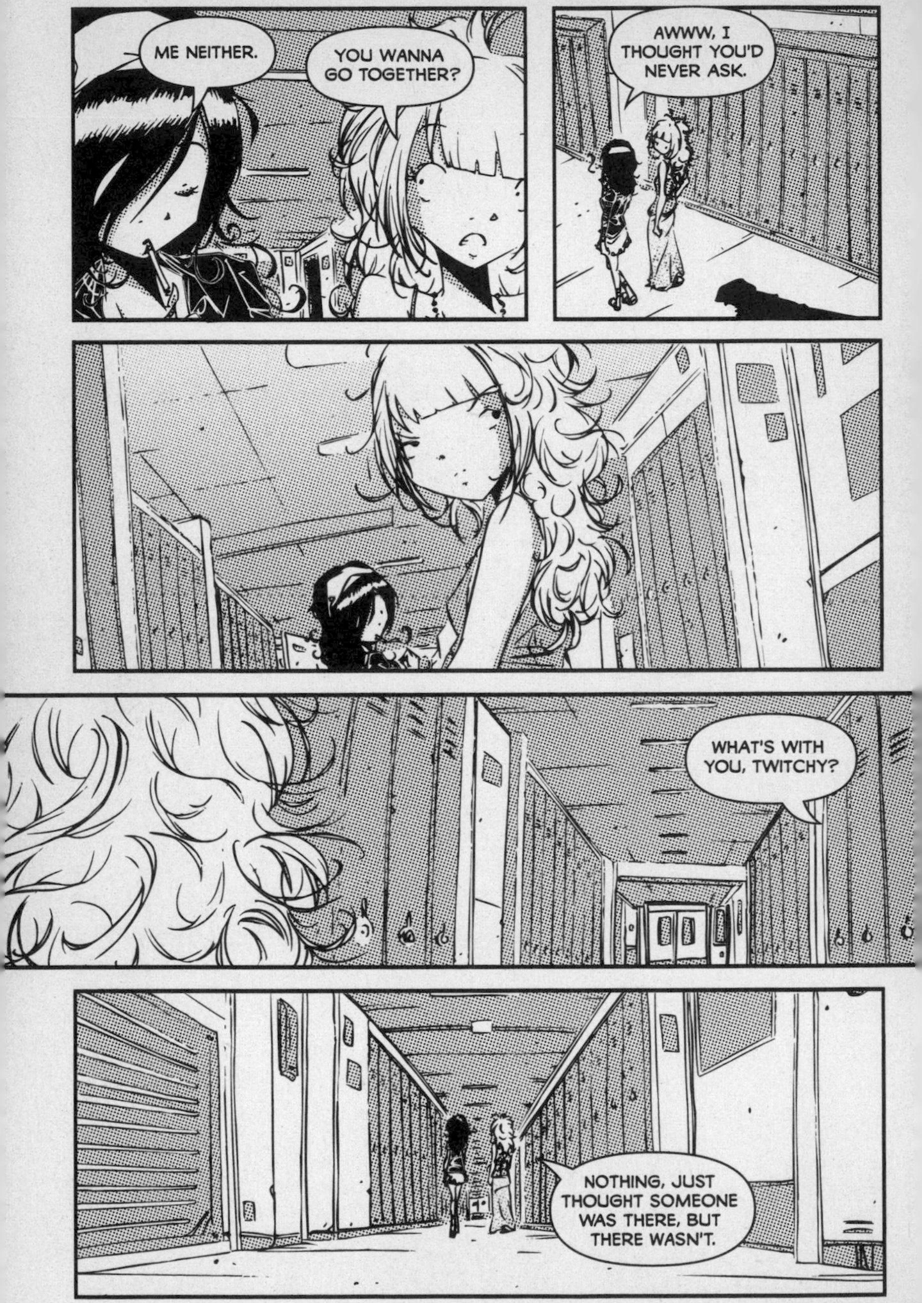
ME NEITHER.
YOU WANNA GO TOGETHER?
AWWW, I THOUGHT YOU'D NEVER ASK.
WHAT'S WITH YOU, TWITCHY?
NOTHING, JUST THOUGHT SOMEONE WAS THERE, BUT THERE WASN'T.

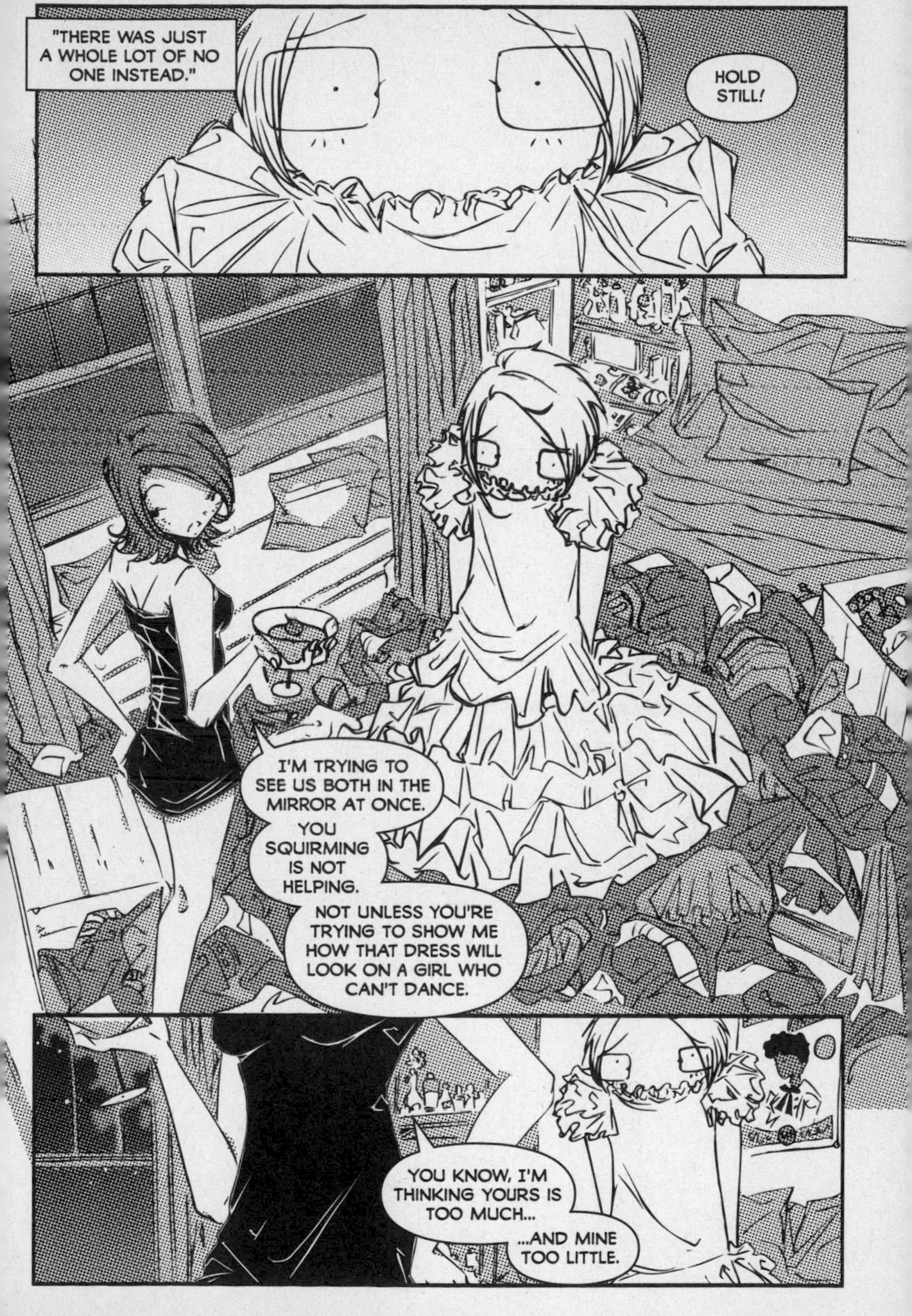

"THERE WAS JUST A WHOLE LOT OF NO ONE INSTEAD."
HOLD STILL!
I'M TRYING TO SEE US BOTH IN THE MIRROR AT ONCE.
YOU SQUIRMING IS NOT HELPING.
NOT UNLESS YOU'RE TRYING TO SHOW ME HOW THAT DRESS WILL LOOK ON A GIRL WHO CAN'T DANCE.
YOU KNOW, I'M THINKING YOURS IS TOO MUCH...
...AND MINE TOO LITTLE.

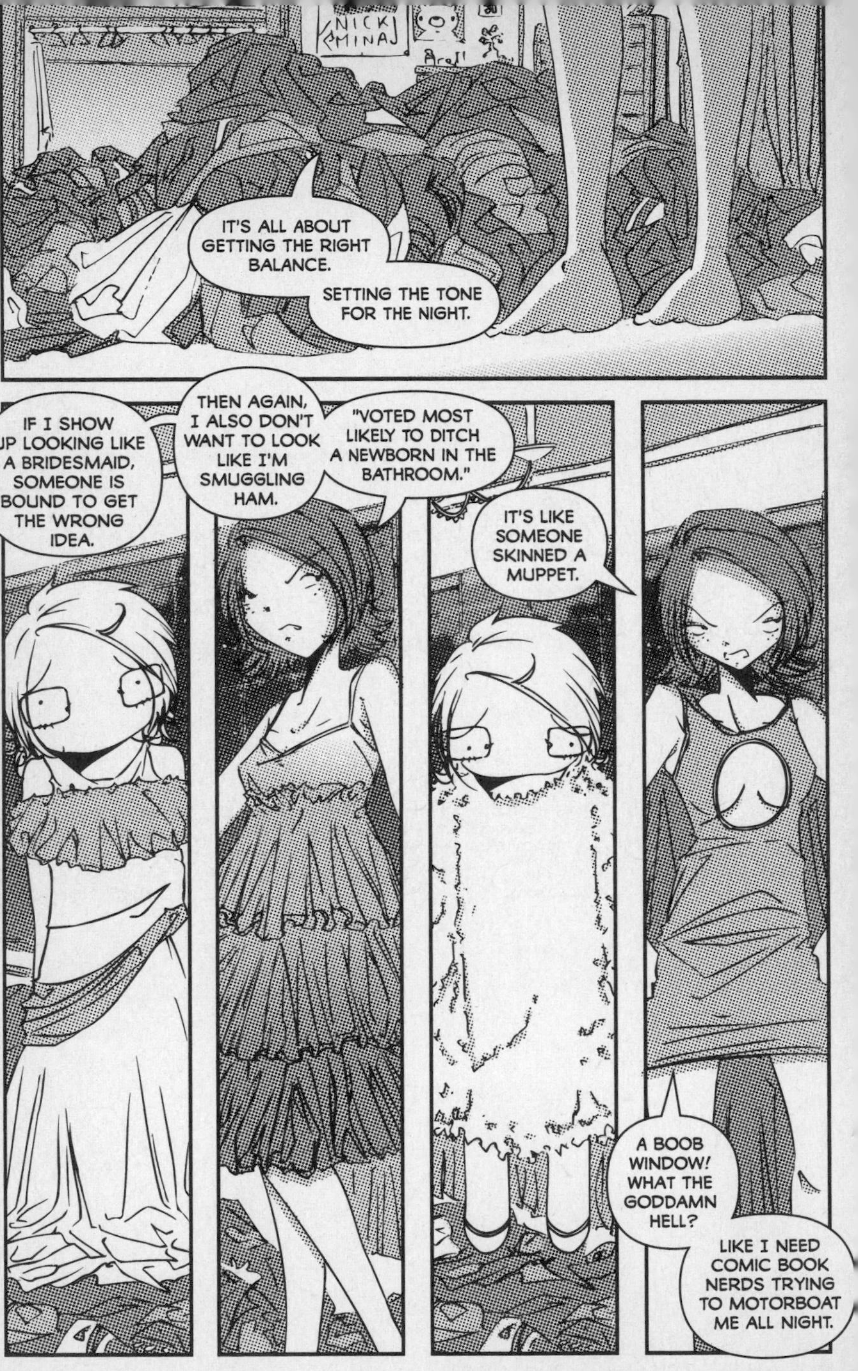
NICKI MINAJ
IT'S ALL ABOUT GETTING THE RIGHT BALANCE.
SETTING THE TONE FOR THE NIGHT.
IF I SHOW UP LOOKING LIKE A BRIDESMAID, SOMEONE IS BOUND TO GET THE WRONG IDEA.
THEN AGAIN, I ALSO DON'T WANT TO LOOK LIKE I'M SMUGGLING HAM.
"VOTED MOST LIKELY TO DITCH A NEWBORN IN THE BATHROOM."
IT'S LIKE SOMEONE SKINNED A MUPPET.
A BOOB WINDOW! WHAT THE GODDAMN HELL?
LIKE I NEED COMIC BOOK NERDS TRYING TO MOTORBOAT ME ALL NIGHT.

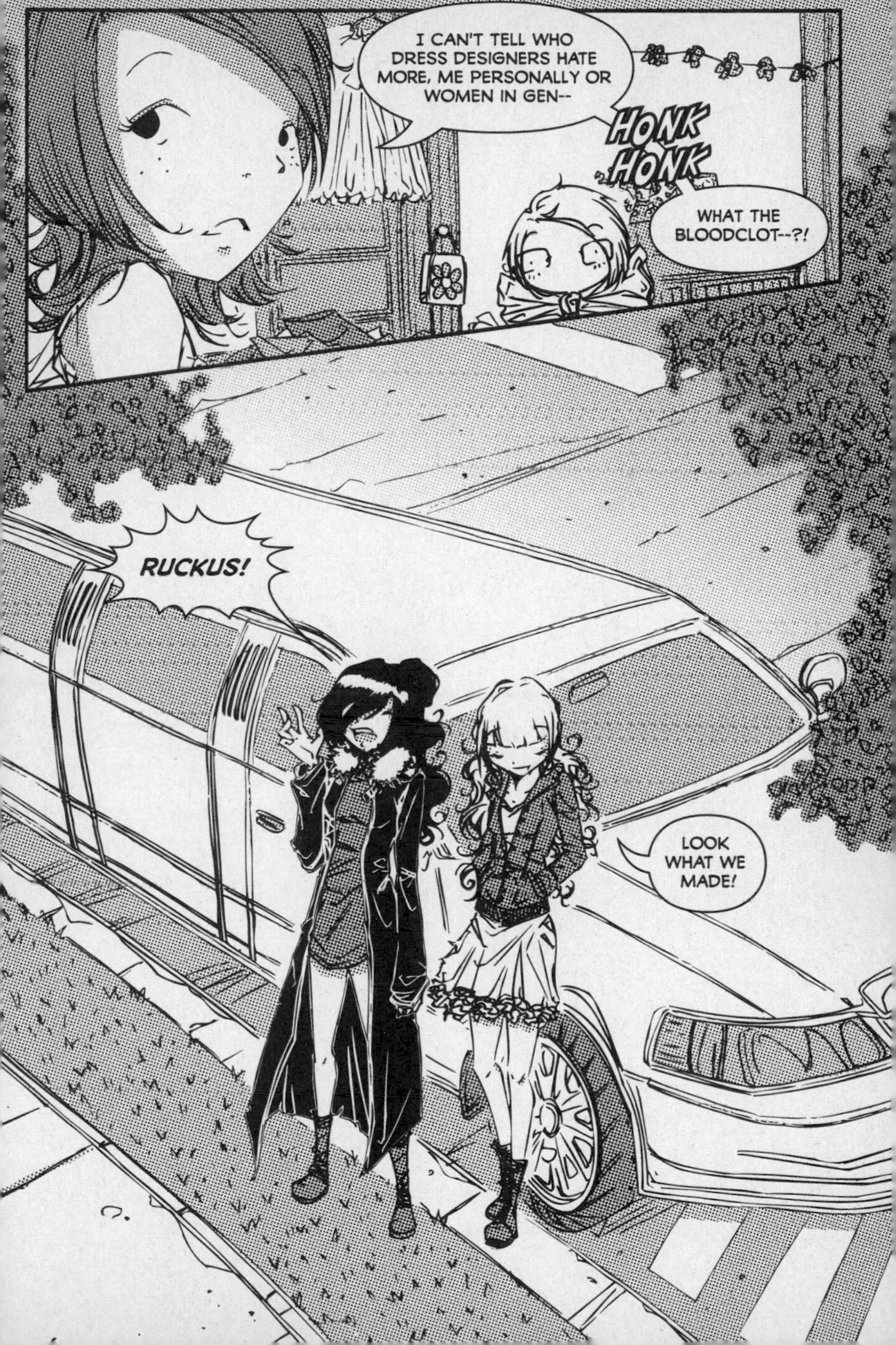
I CAN'T TELL WHO DRESS DESIGNERS HATE MORE, ME PERSONALLY OR WOMEN IN GEN--
HONK HONK
WHAT THE BLOODCLOT--?!
RUCKUS!
LOOK WHAT WE MADE!

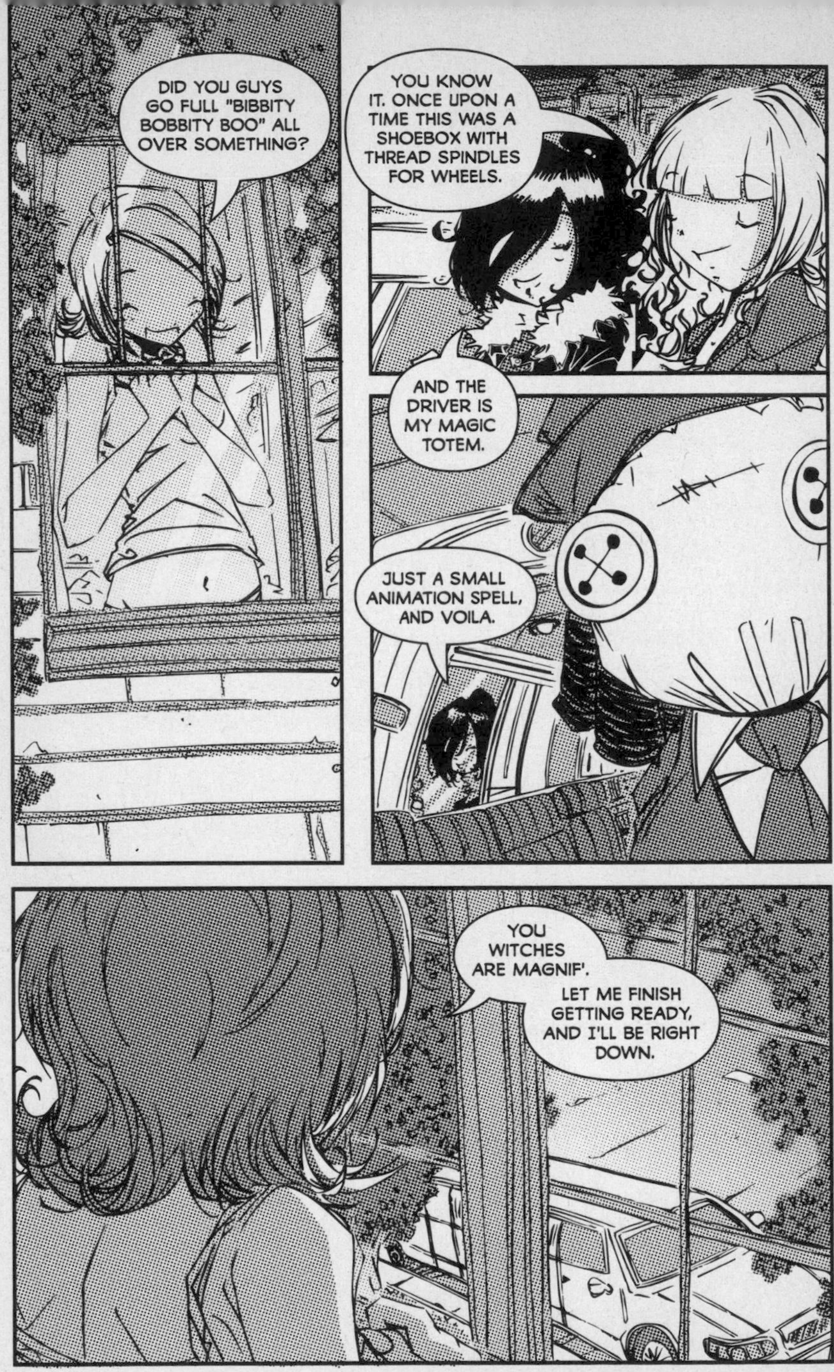
DID YOU GUYS GO FULL "BIBBITY BOBBITY BOO" ALL OVER SOMETHING?
YOU KNOW IT. ONCE UPON A TIME THIS WAS A SHOEBOX WITH THREAD SPINDLES FOR WHEELS.
AND THE DRIVER IS MY MAGIC TOTEM.
JUST A SMALL ANIMATION SPELL, AND VOILA.
YOU WITCHES ARE MAGNIF'.
LET ME FINISH GETTING READY, AND I'LL BE RIGHT DOWN.

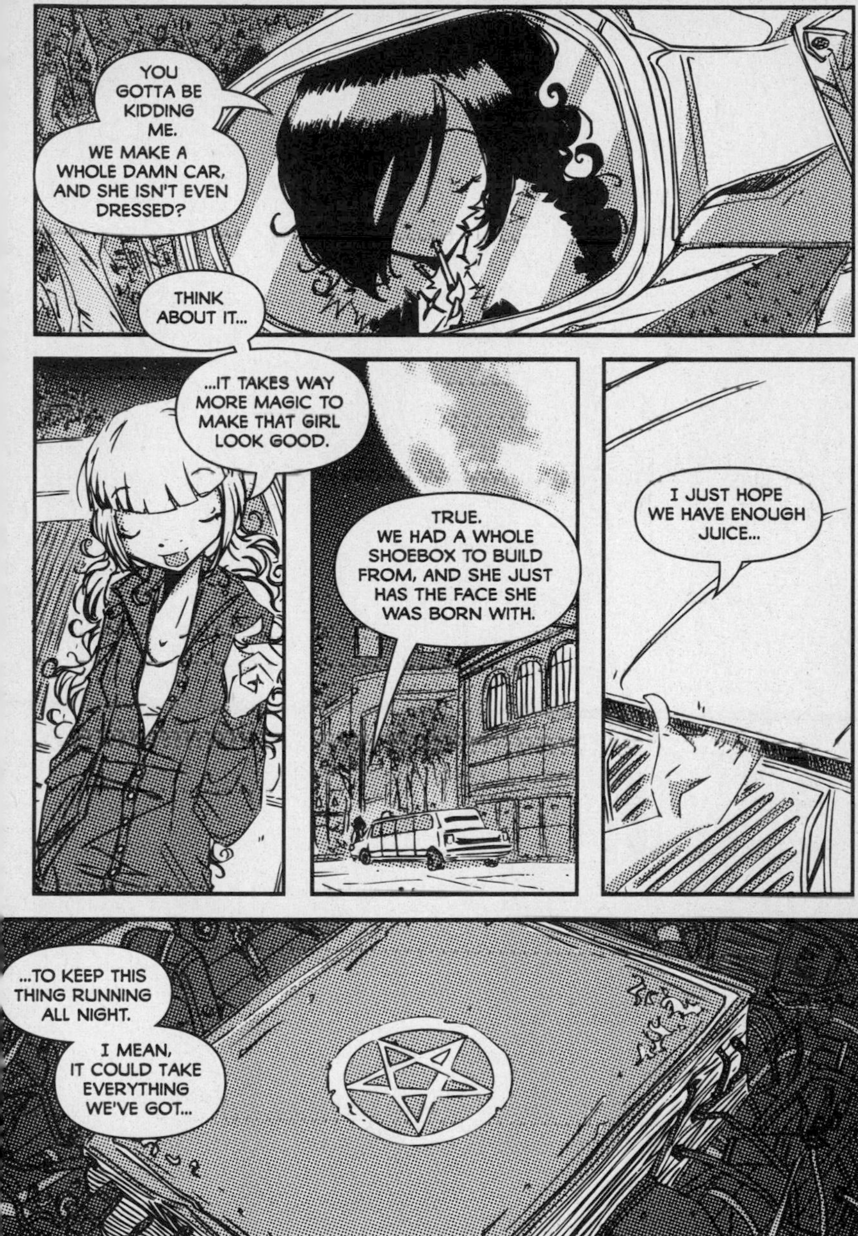
YOU GOTTA BE KIDDING ME.
WE MAKE A WHOLE DAMN CAR, AND SHE ISN'T EVEN DRESSED?
THINK ABOUT IT...
...IT TAKES WAY MORE MAGIC TO MAKE THAT GIRL LOOK GOOD.
TRUE.
WE HAD A WHOLE SHOEBOX TO BUILD FROM, AND SHE JUST HAS THE FACE SHE WAS BORN WITH.
I JUST HOPE WE HAVE ENOUGH JUICE...
...TO KEEP THIS THING RUNNING ALL NIGHT.
I MEAN, IT COULD TAKE EVERYTHING WE'VE GOT...

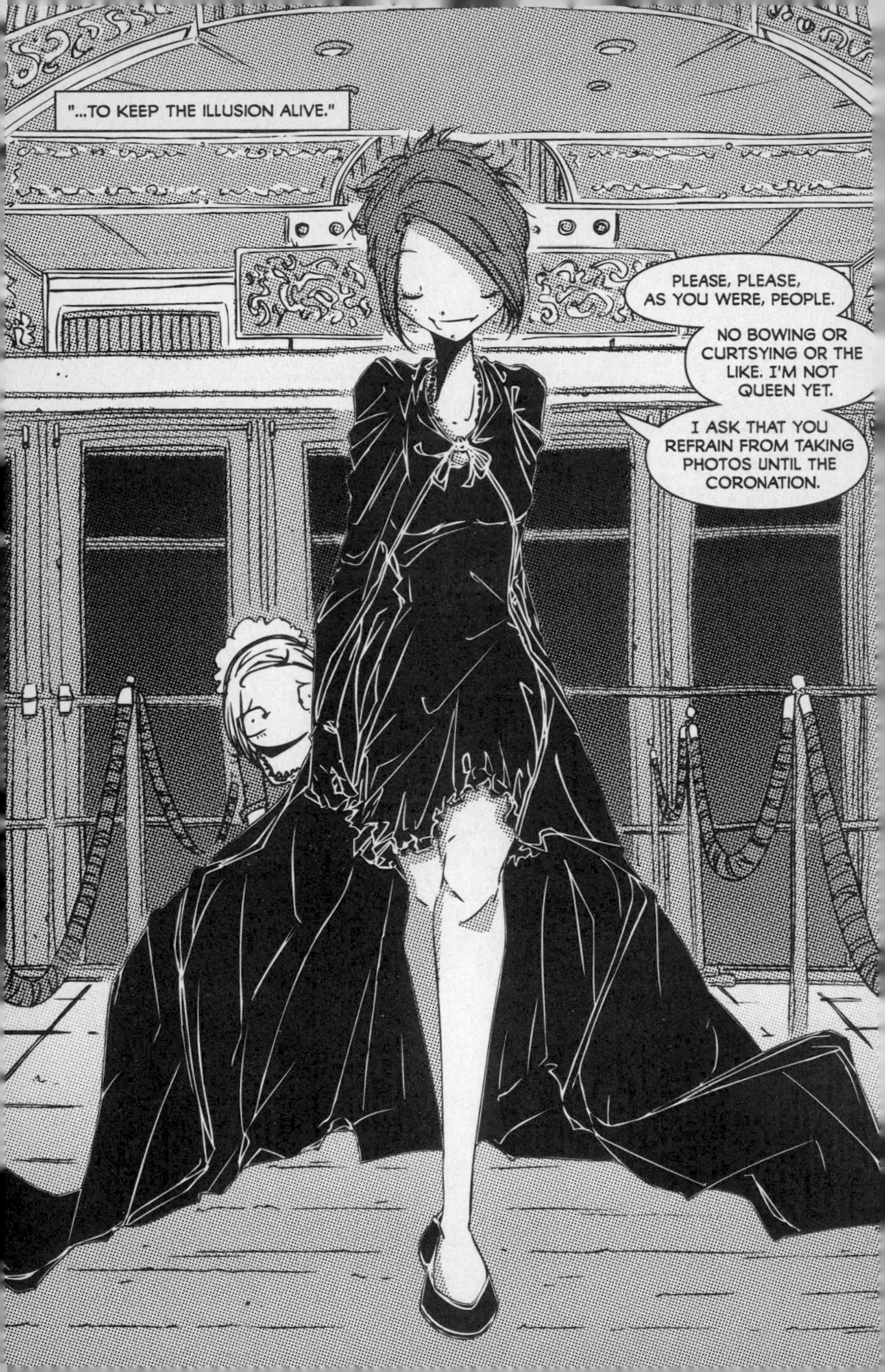
"...TO KEEP THE ILLUSION ALIVE."
PLEASE, PLEASE, AS YOU WERE, PEOPLE.
NO BOWING OR CURTSYING OR THE LIKE. I'M NOT QUEEN YET.
I ASK THAT YOU REFRAIN FROM TAKING PHOTOS UNTIL THE CORONATION.

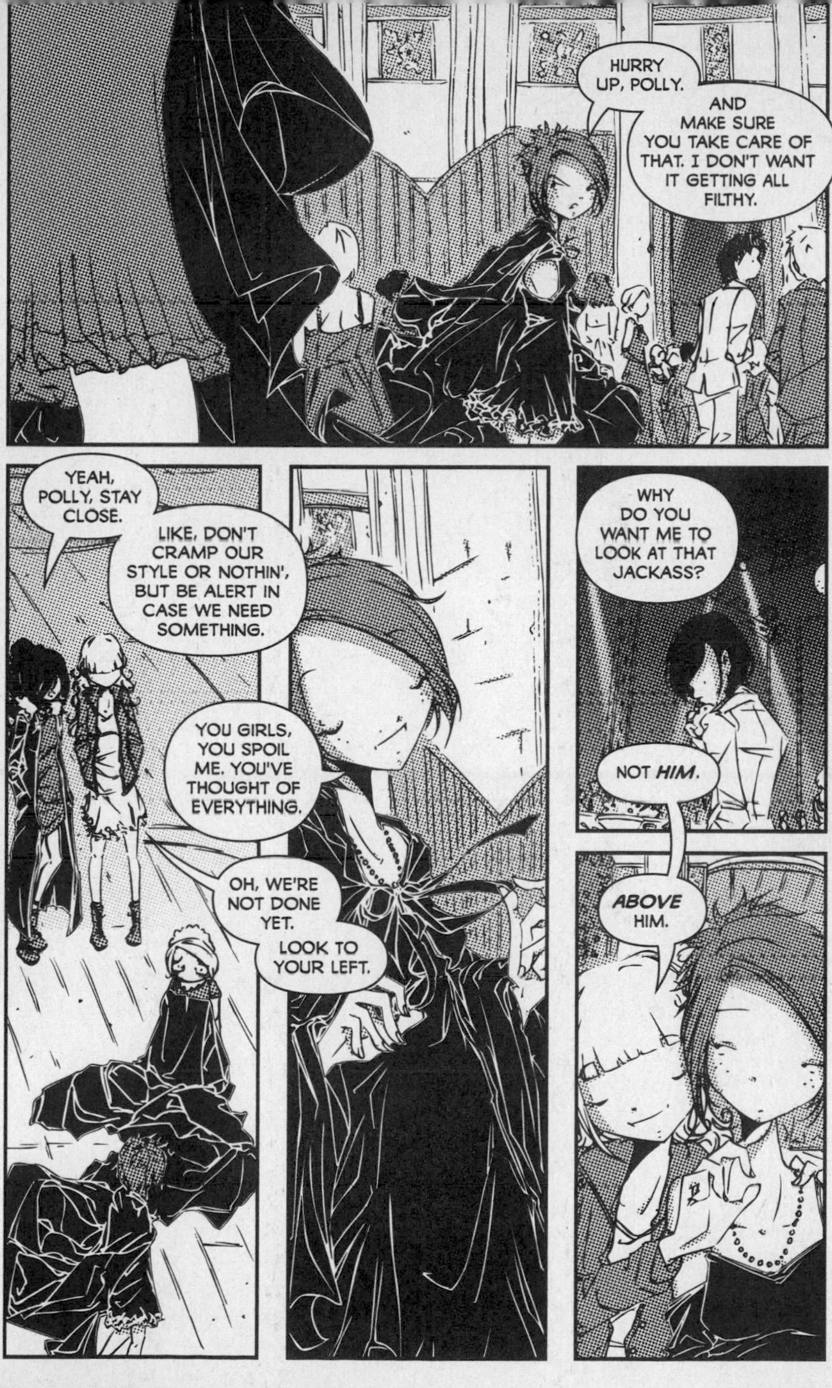
HURRY UP, POLLY.
AND MAKE SURE YOU TAKE CARE OF THAT. I DON'T WANT IT GETTING ALL FILTHY.
YEAH, POLLY, STAY CLOSE.
LIKE, DON'T CRAMP OUR STYLE OR NOTHIN', BUT BE ALERT IN CASE WE NEED SOMETHING.
YOU GIRLS, YOU SPOIL ME. YOU'VE THOUGHT OF EVERYTHING.
OH, WE'RE NOT DONE YET.
LOOK TO YOUR LEFT.
WHY DO YOU WANT ME TO LOOK AT THAT JACKASS?
NOT HIM.
ABOVE HIM.

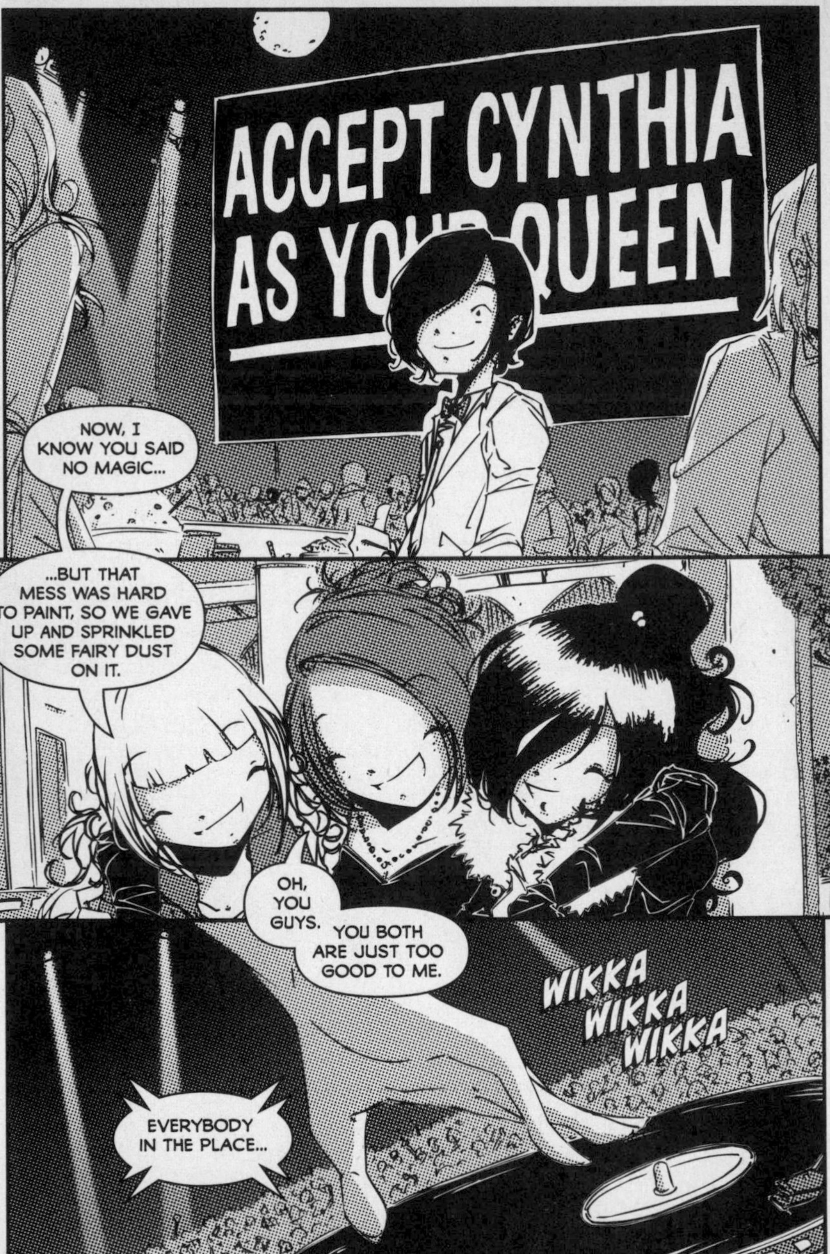
ACCEPT CYNTHIA AS YOUR QUEEN
NOW, I KNOW YOU SAID NO MAGIC...
...BUT THAT MESS WAS HARD TO PAINT, SO WE GAVE UP AND SPRINKLED SOME FAIRY DUST ON IT.
OH, YOU GUYS.
YOU BOTH ARE JUST TOO GOOD TO ME.
WIKKA WIKKA WIKKA
EVERYBODY IN THE PLACE...

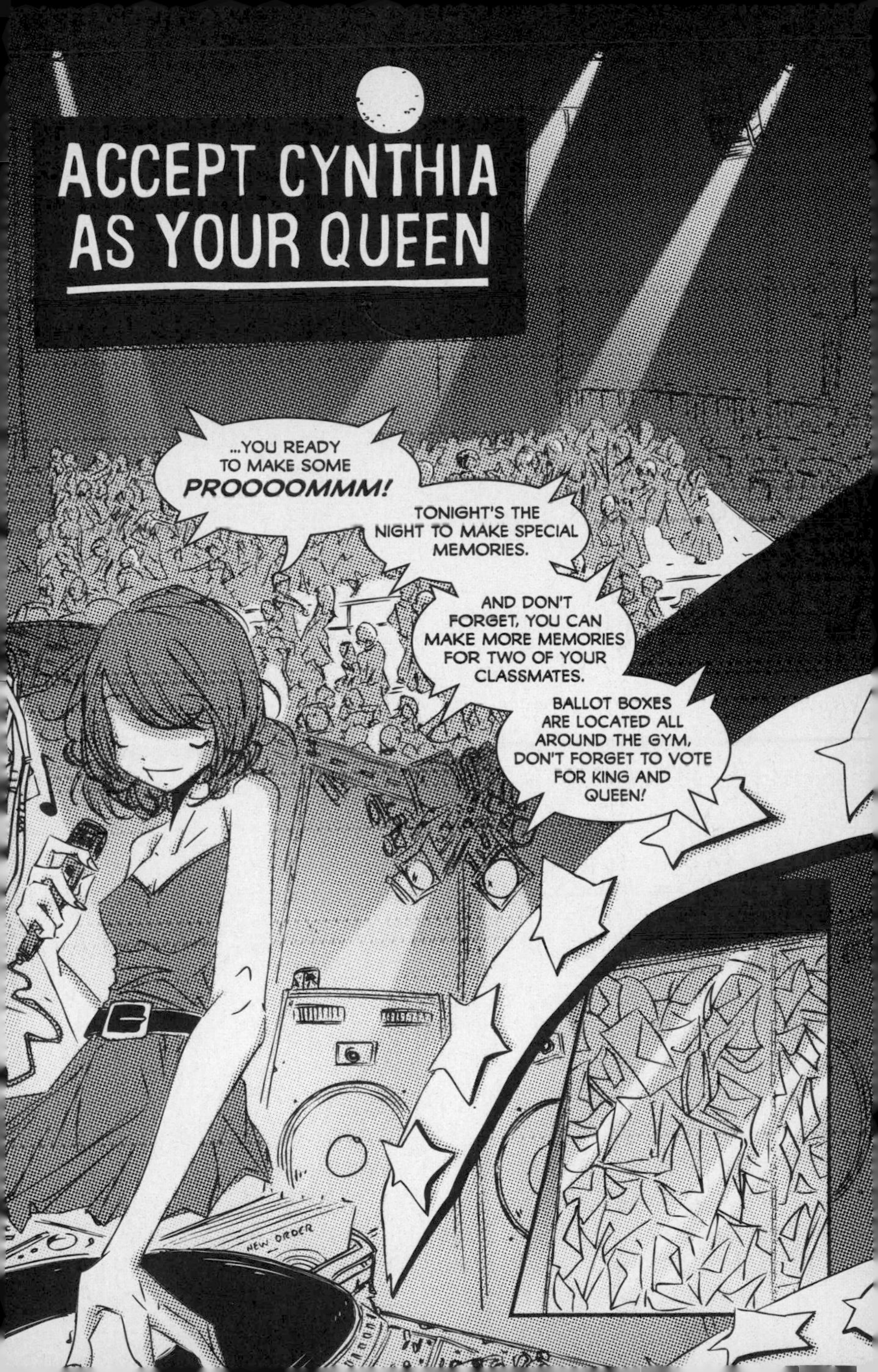
ACCEPT CYNTHIA AS YOUR QUEEN
...YOU READY TO MAKE SOME PROOOOMMM!
TONIGHT'S THE NIGHT TO MAKE SPECIAL MEMORIES.
AND DON'T FORGET, YOU CAN MAKE MORE MEMORIES FOR TWO OF YOUR CLASSMATES.
BALLOT BOXES ARE LOCATED ALL AROUND THE GYM, DON'T FORGET TO VOTE FOR KING AND QUEEN!
NEW ORDER

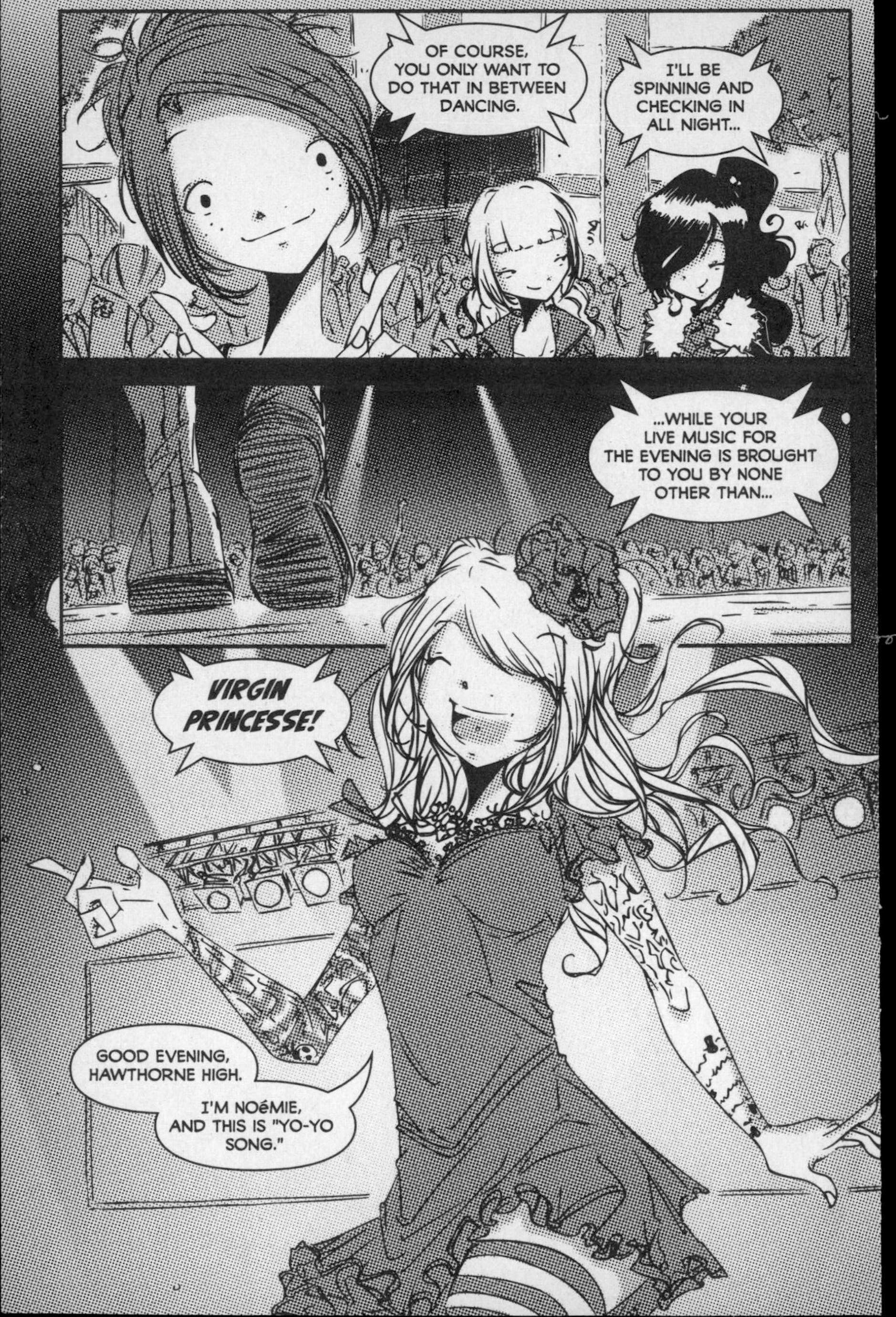
OF COURSE, YOU ONLY WANT TO DO THAT IN BETWEEN DANCING.
I'LL BE SPINNING AND CHECKING IN ALL NIGHT...
...WHILE YOUR LIVE MUSIC FOR THE EVENING IS BROUGHT TO YOU BY NONE OTHER THAN...
VIRGIN PRINCESSE!
GOOD EVENING, HAWTHORNE HIGH.
I'M NOéMIE, AND THIS IS "YO-YO SONG."

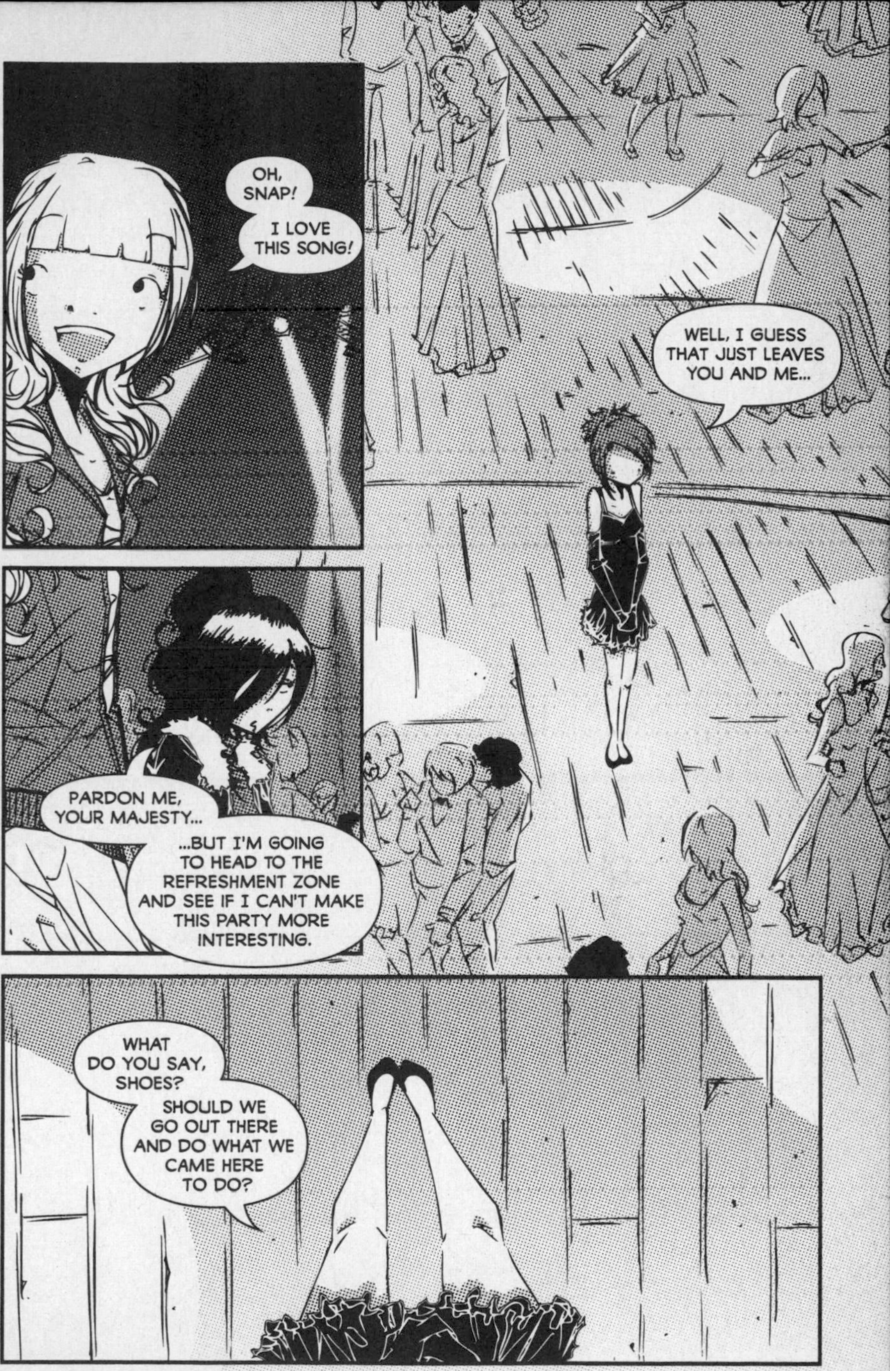
OH, SNAP!
I LOVE THIS SONG!
WELL, I GUESS THAT JUST LEAVES YOU AND ME...
PARDON ME, YOUR MAJESTY...
...BUT I'M GOING TO HEAD TO THE REFRESHMENT ZONE AND SEE IF I CAN'T MAKE THIS PARTY MORE INTERESTING.
WHAT DO YOU SAY, SHOES?
SHOULD WE GO OUT THERE AND DO WHAT WE CAME HERE TO DO?

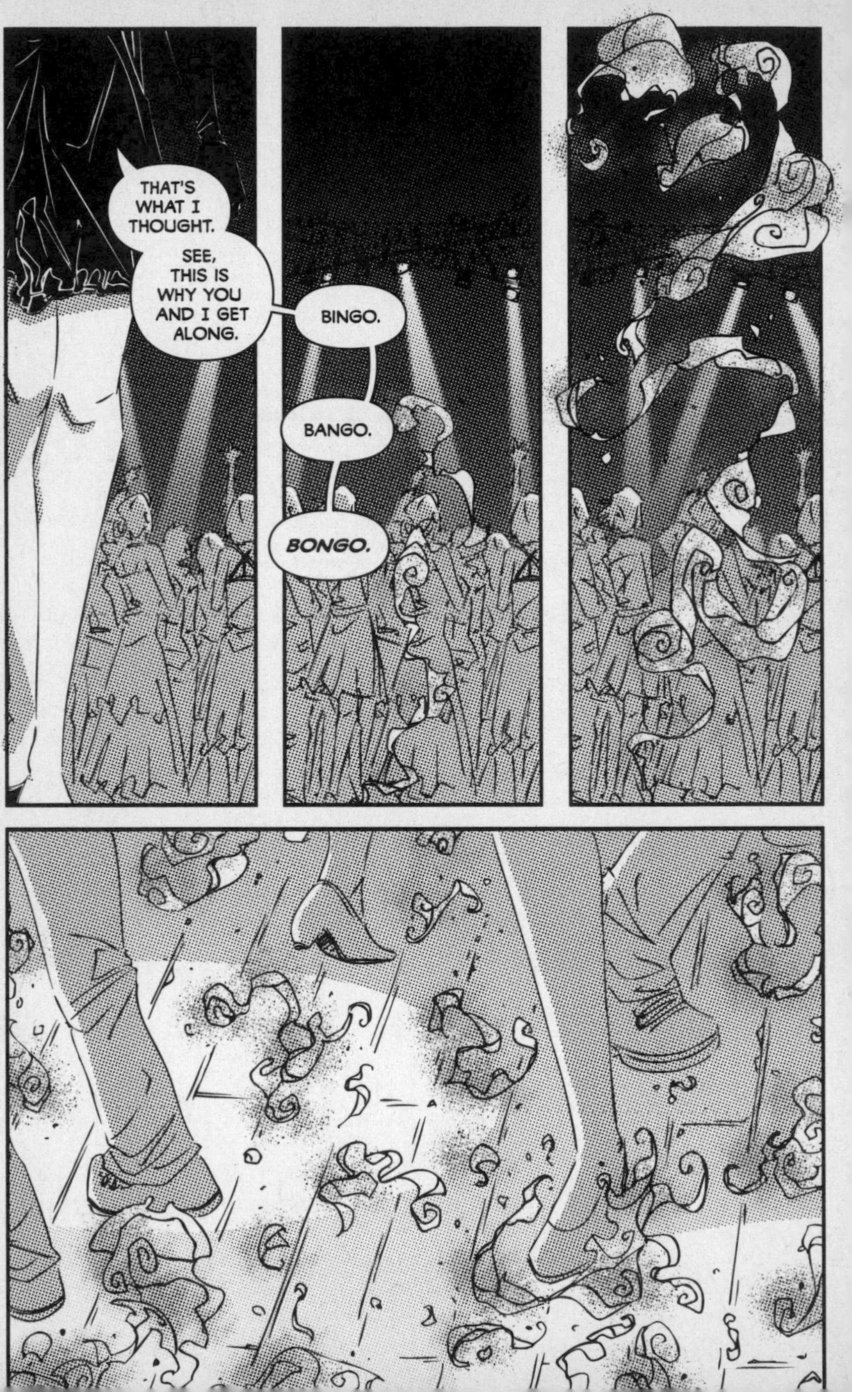
THAT'S WHAT I THOUGHT.
SEE, THIS IS WHY YOU AND I GET ALONG.
BINGO.
BANGO.
BONGO.

Chapter 2
"Jesse, Are You Listening?"

2

Visit Minkus at minkusgavein.tumblr.com
or on Twitter @minkus.

Visit Noémie Allard and Virgin Princesse at
https://www.facebook.com/pages/Virgin-Princesse/8606479651

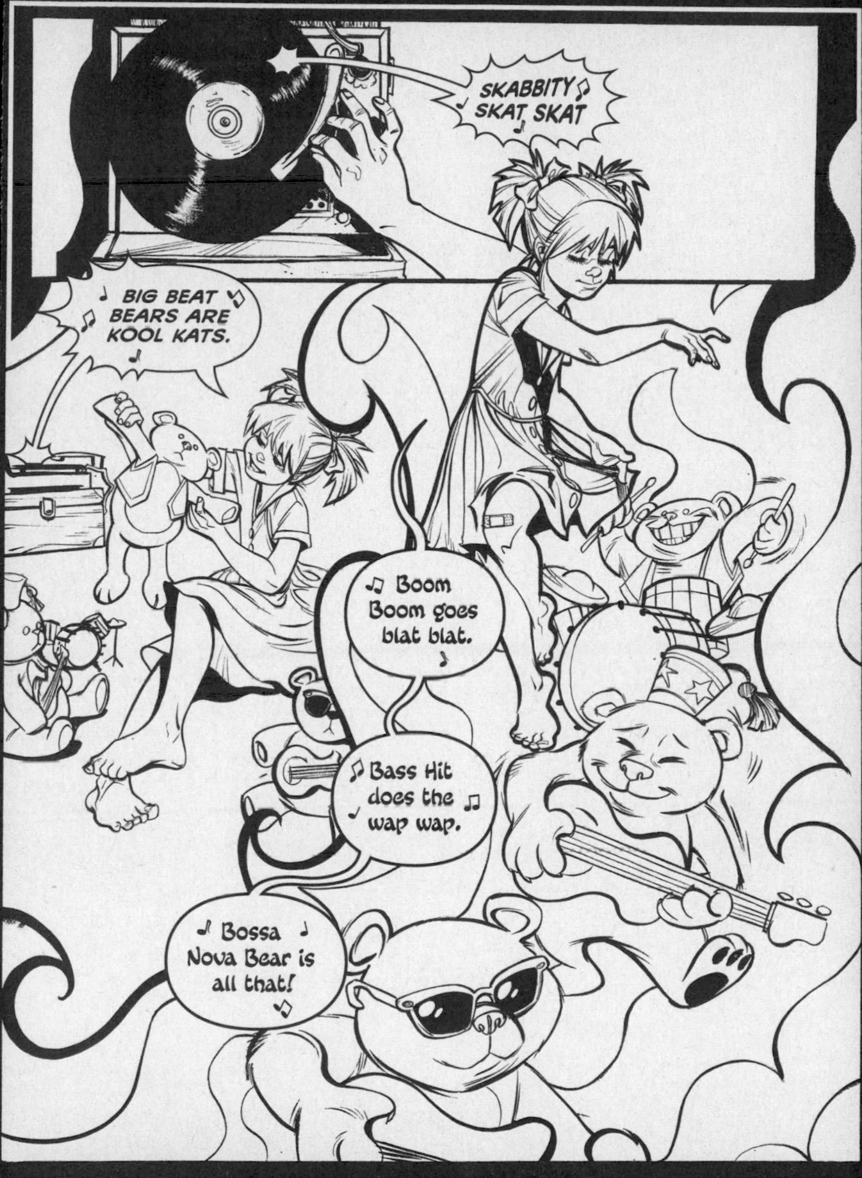
SKABBITY SKAT SKAT
BIG BEAT BEARS ARE KOOL KATS.
Boom Boom goes blat blat.
Bass Hit does the wap wap.
Bossa Nova Bear is all that!

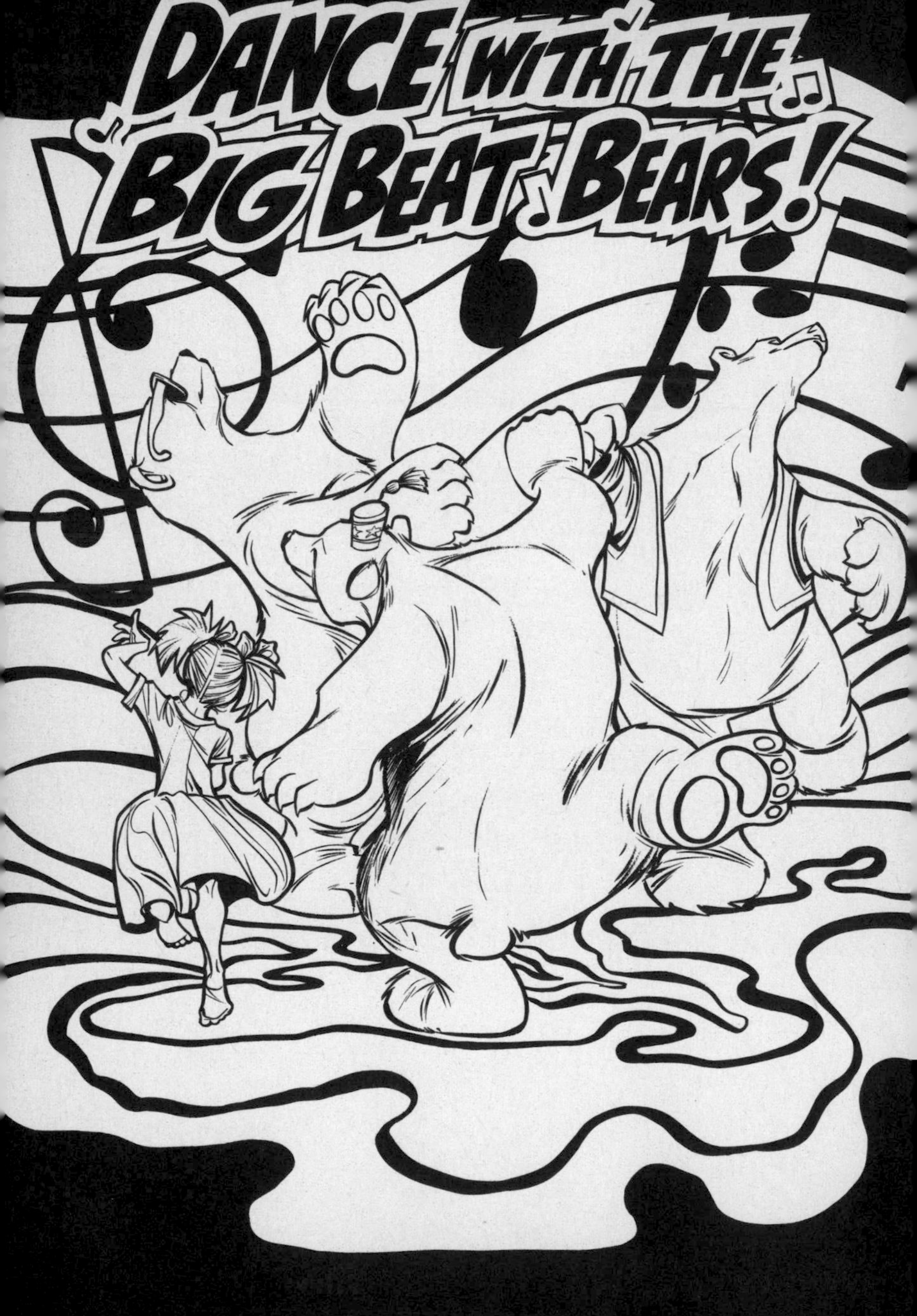
DANCE WITH THE
BIG BEAT BEARS!

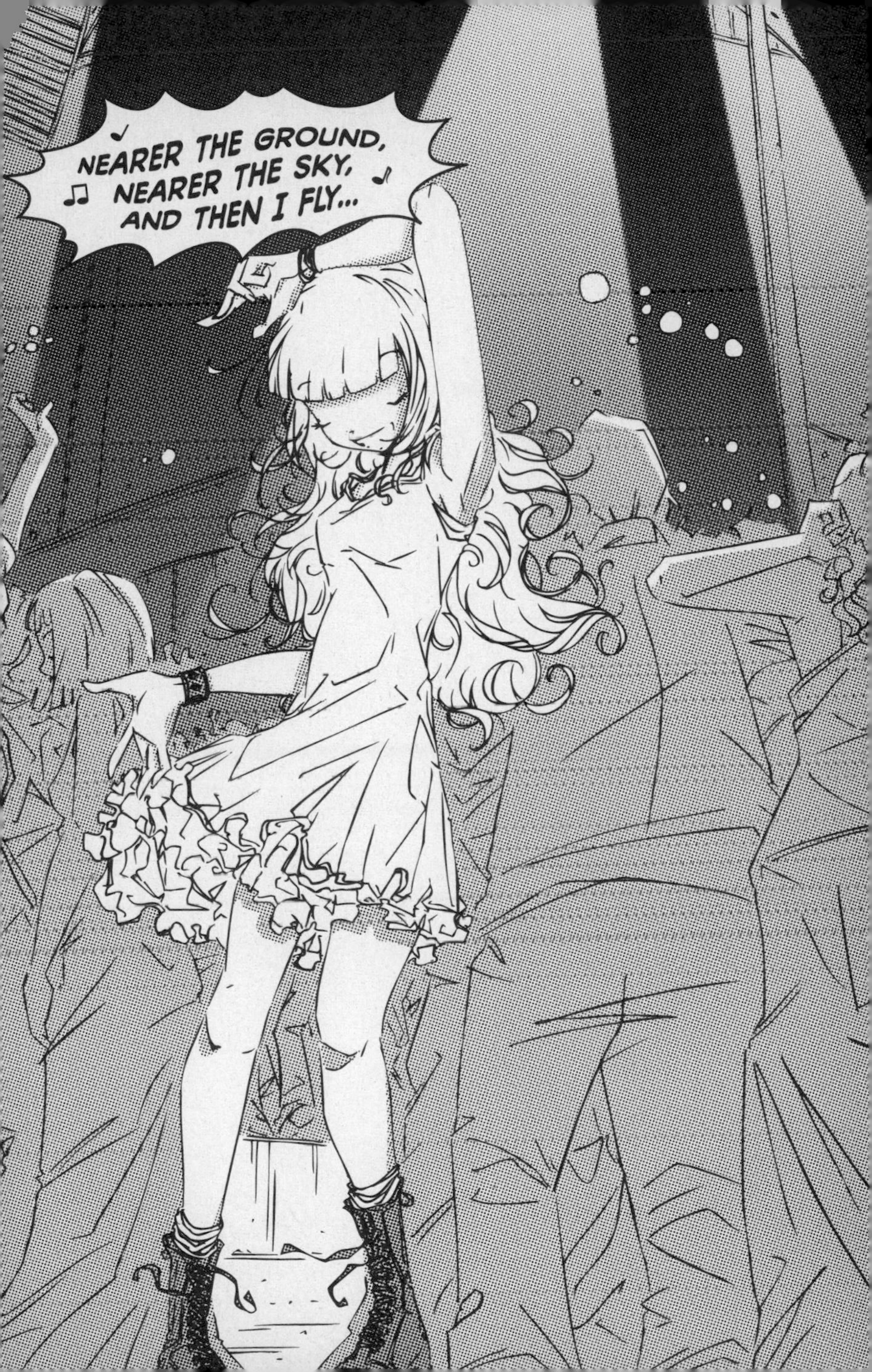
NEARER THE GROUND, NEARER THE SKY, AND THEN I FLY...

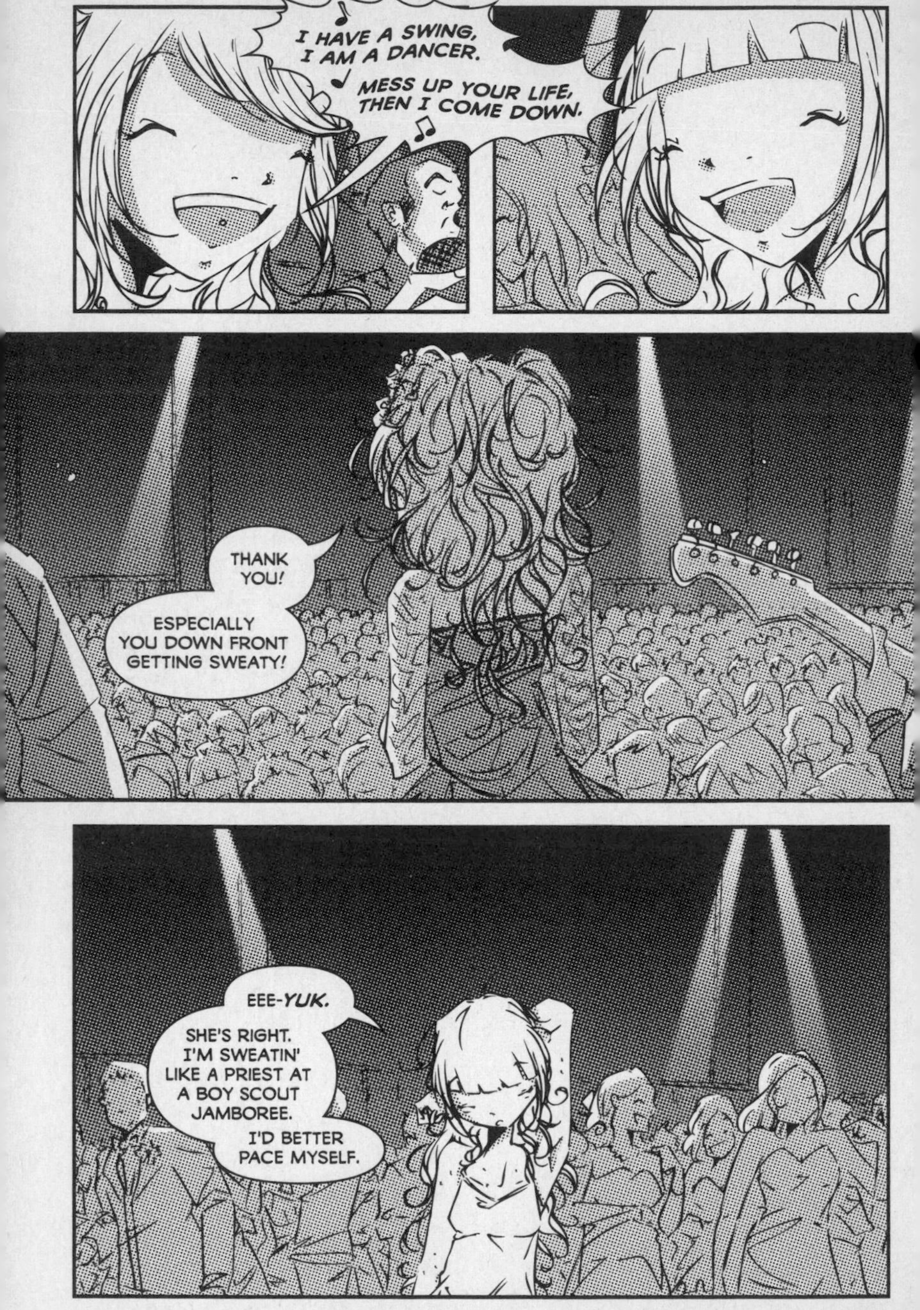
I HAVE A SWING, I AM A DANCER.
MESS UP YOUR LIFE, THEN I COME DOWN.
THANK YOU!
ESPECIALLY YOU DOWN FRONT GETTING SWEATY!
EEE-*YUK.*
SHE'S RIGHT. I'M SWEATIN' LIKE A PRIEST AT A BOY SCOUT JAMBOREE.
I'D BETTER PACE MYSELF.

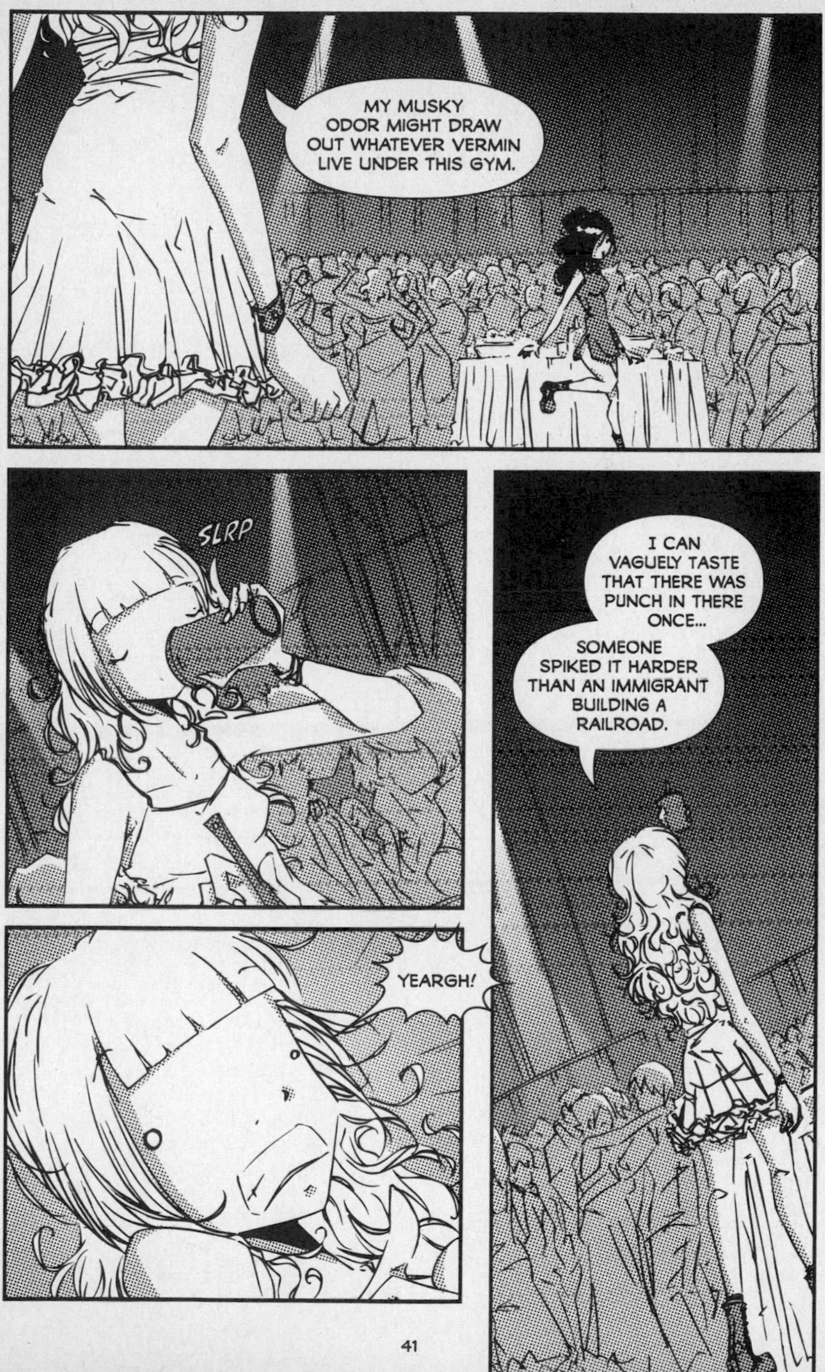
MY MUSKY ODOR MIGHT DRAW OUT WHATEVER VERMIN LIVE UNDER THIS GYM.
SLRP
I CAN VAGUELY TASTE THAT THERE WAS PUNCH IN THERE ONCE...
SOMEONE SPIKED IT HARDER THAN AN IMMIGRANT BUILDING A RAILROAD.
YEARGH!

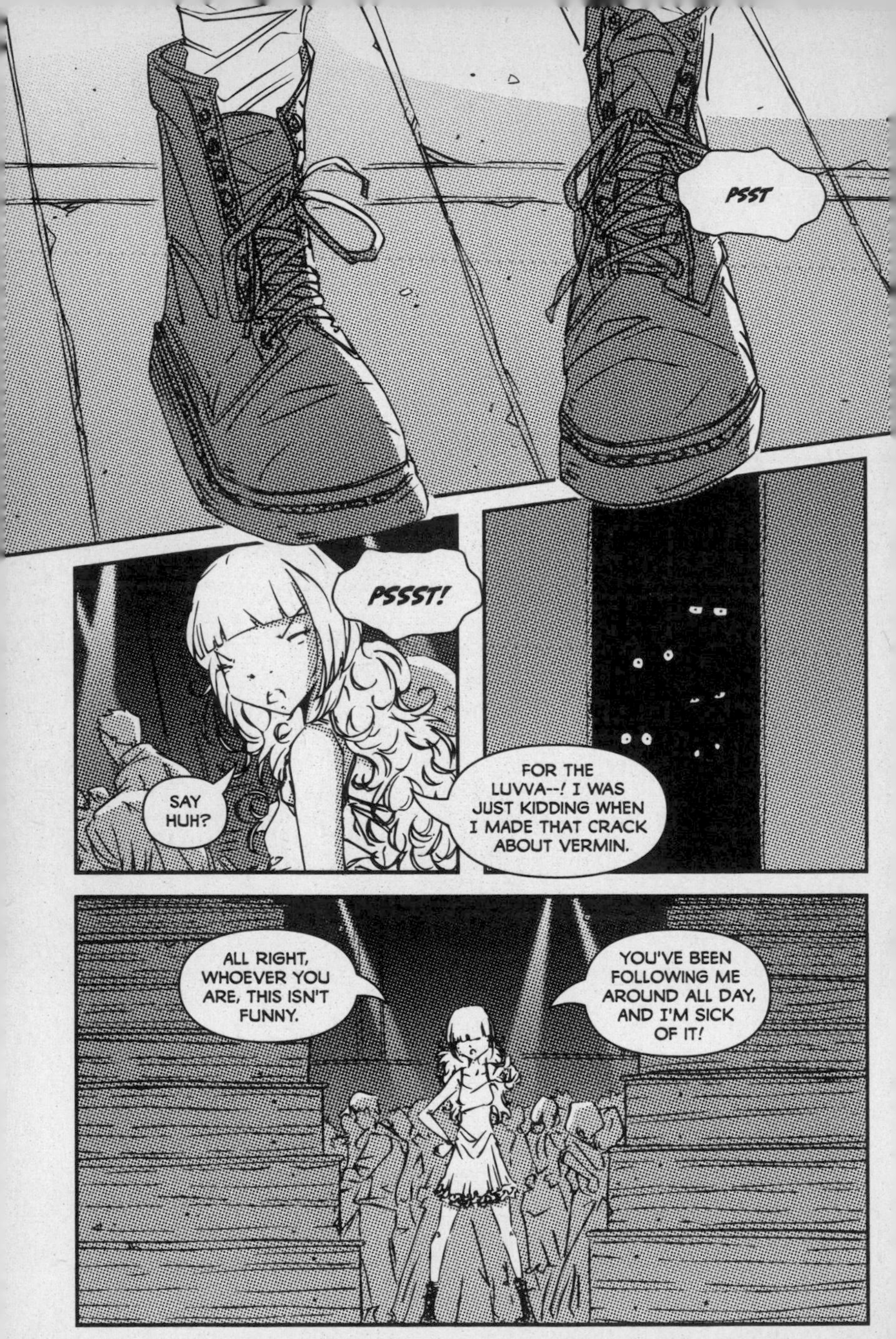
PSST
PSSST!
SAY HUH?
FOR THE LUVVA--! I WAS JUST KIDDING WHEN I MADE THAT CRACK ABOUT VERMIN.
ALL RIGHT, WHOEVER YOU ARE, THIS ISN'T FUNNY.
YOU'VE BEEN FOLLOWING ME AROUND ALL DAY, AND I'M SICK OF IT!

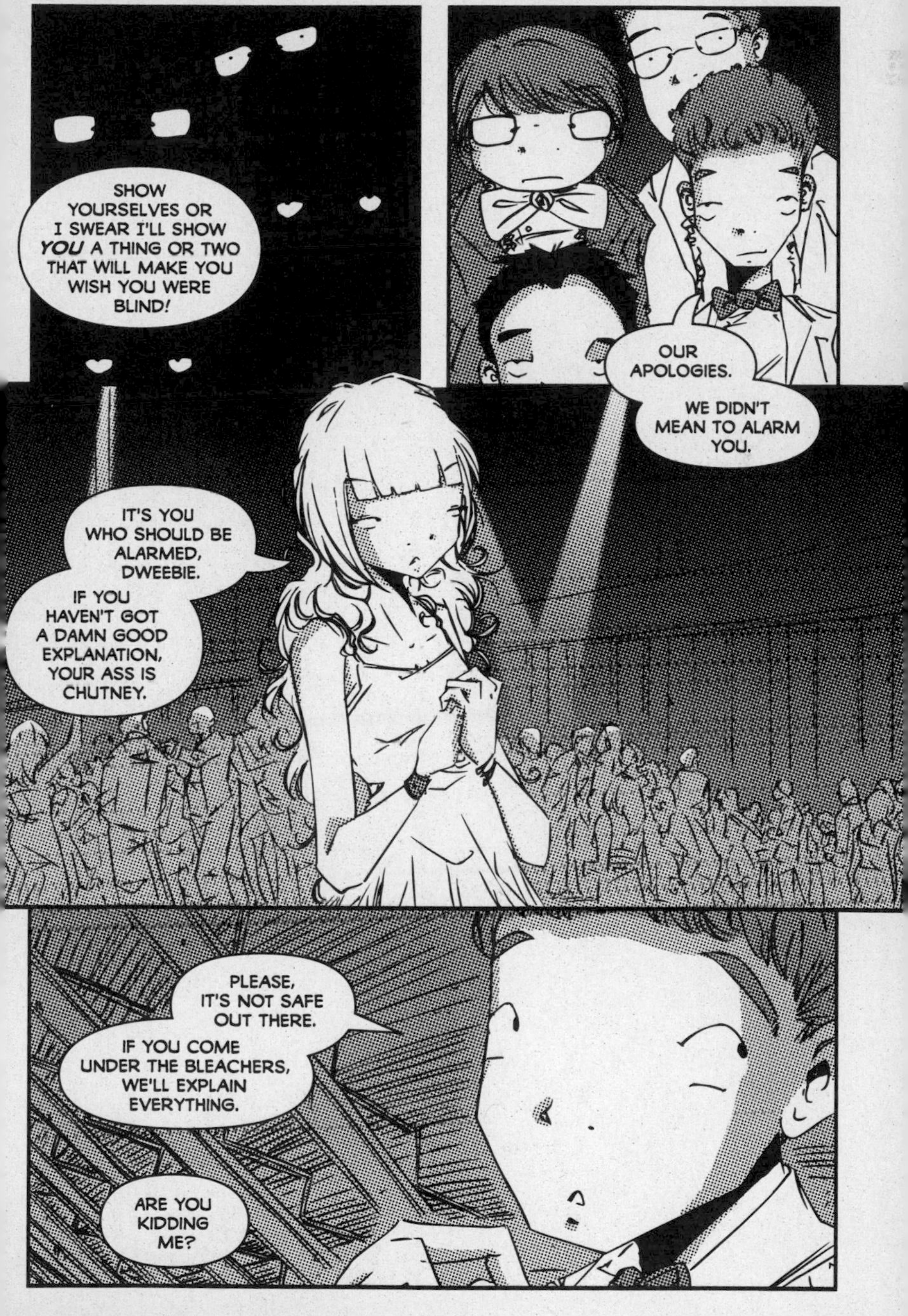
SHOW YOURSELVES OR I SWEAR I'LL SHOW *YOU* A THING OR TWO THAT WILL MAKE YOU WISH YOU WERE BLIND!
OUR APOLOGIES.
WE DIDN'T MEAN TO ALARM YOU.
IT'S YOU WHO SHOULD BE ALARMED, DWEEBIE.
IF YOU HAVEN'T GOT A DAMN GOOD EXPLANATION, YOUR ASS IS CHUTNEY.
PLEASE, IT'S NOT SAFE OUT THERE.
IF YOU COME UNDER THE BLEACHERS, WE'LL EXPLAIN EVERYTHING.
ARE YOU KIDDING ME?

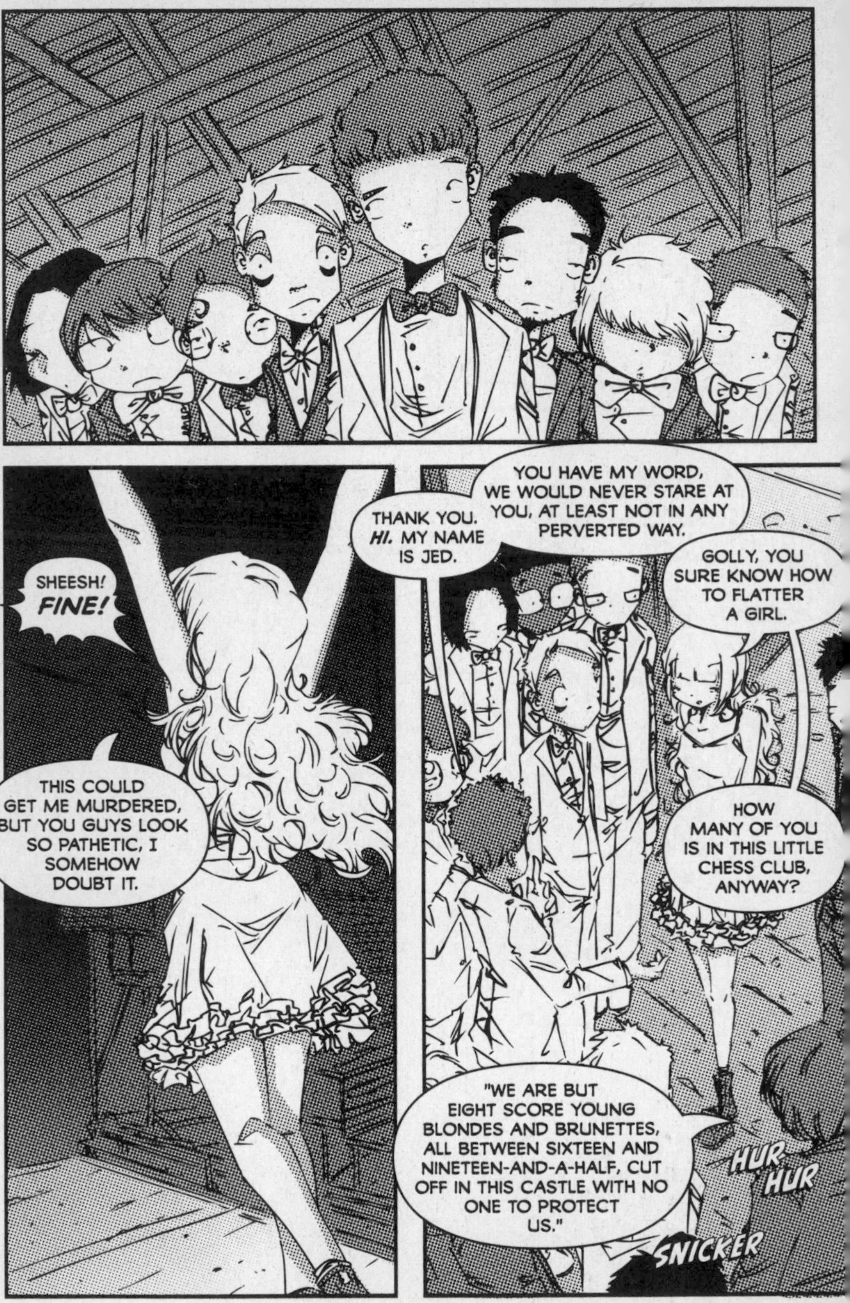
SHEESH! *FINE!*
THIS COULD GET ME MURDERED, BUT YOU GUYS LOOK SO PATHETIC, I SOMEHOW DOUBT IT.
THANK YOU. *HI.* MY NAME IS JED.
YOU HAVE MY WORD, WE WOULD NEVER STARE AT YOU, AT LEAST NOT IN ANY PERVERTED WAY.
GOLLY, YOU SURE KNOW HOW TO FLATTER A GIRL.
HOW MANY OF YOU IS IN THIS LITTLE CHESS CLUB, ANYWAY?
"WE ARE BUT EIGHT SCORE YOUNG BLONDES AND BRUNETTES, ALL BETWEEN SIXTEEN AND NINETEEN-AND-A-HALF, CUT OFF IN THIS CASTLE WITH NO ONE TO PROTECT US."
HUR HUR
SNICKER

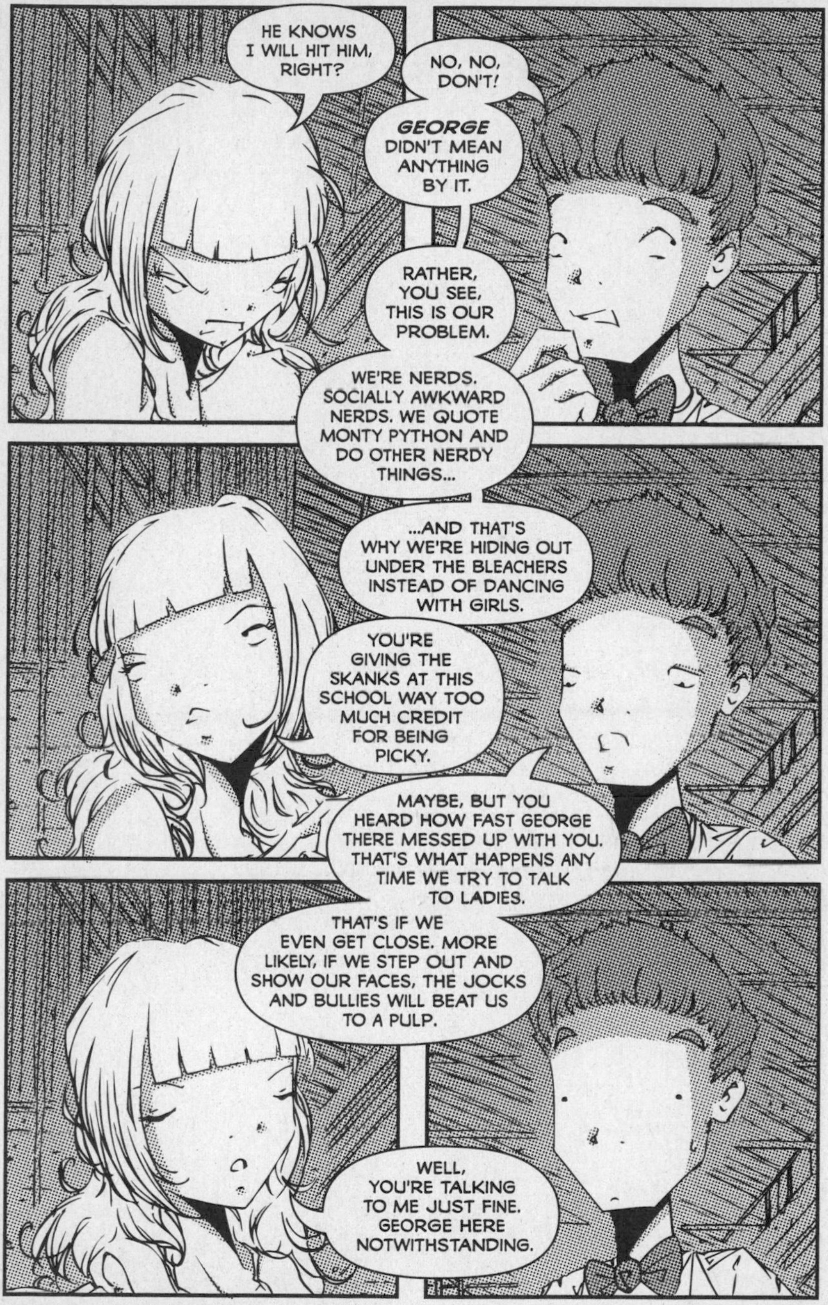
HE KNOWS I WILL HIT HIM, RIGHT?
NO, NO, DON'T!
GEORGE DIDN'T MEAN ANYTHING BY IT.
RATHER, YOU SEE, THIS IS OUR PROBLEM.
WE'RE NERDS. SOCIALLY AWKWARD NERDS. WE QUOTE MONTY PYTHON AND DO OTHER NERDY THINGS...
...AND THAT'S WHY WE'RE HIDING OUT UNDER THE BLEACHERS INSTEAD OF DANCING WITH GIRLS.
YOU'RE GIVING THE SKANKS AT THIS SCHOOL WAY TOO MUCH CREDIT FOR BEING PICKY.
MAYBE, BUT YOU HEARD HOW FAST GEORGE THERE MESSED UP WITH YOU. THAT'S WHAT HAPPENS ANY TIME WE TRY TO TALK TO LADIES.
THAT'S IF WE EVEN GET CLOSE. MORE LIKELY, IF WE STEP OUT AND SHOW OUR FACES, THE JOCKS AND BULLIES WILL BEAT US TO A PULP.
WELL, YOU'RE TALKING TO ME JUST FINE. GEORGE HERE NOTWITHSTANDING.

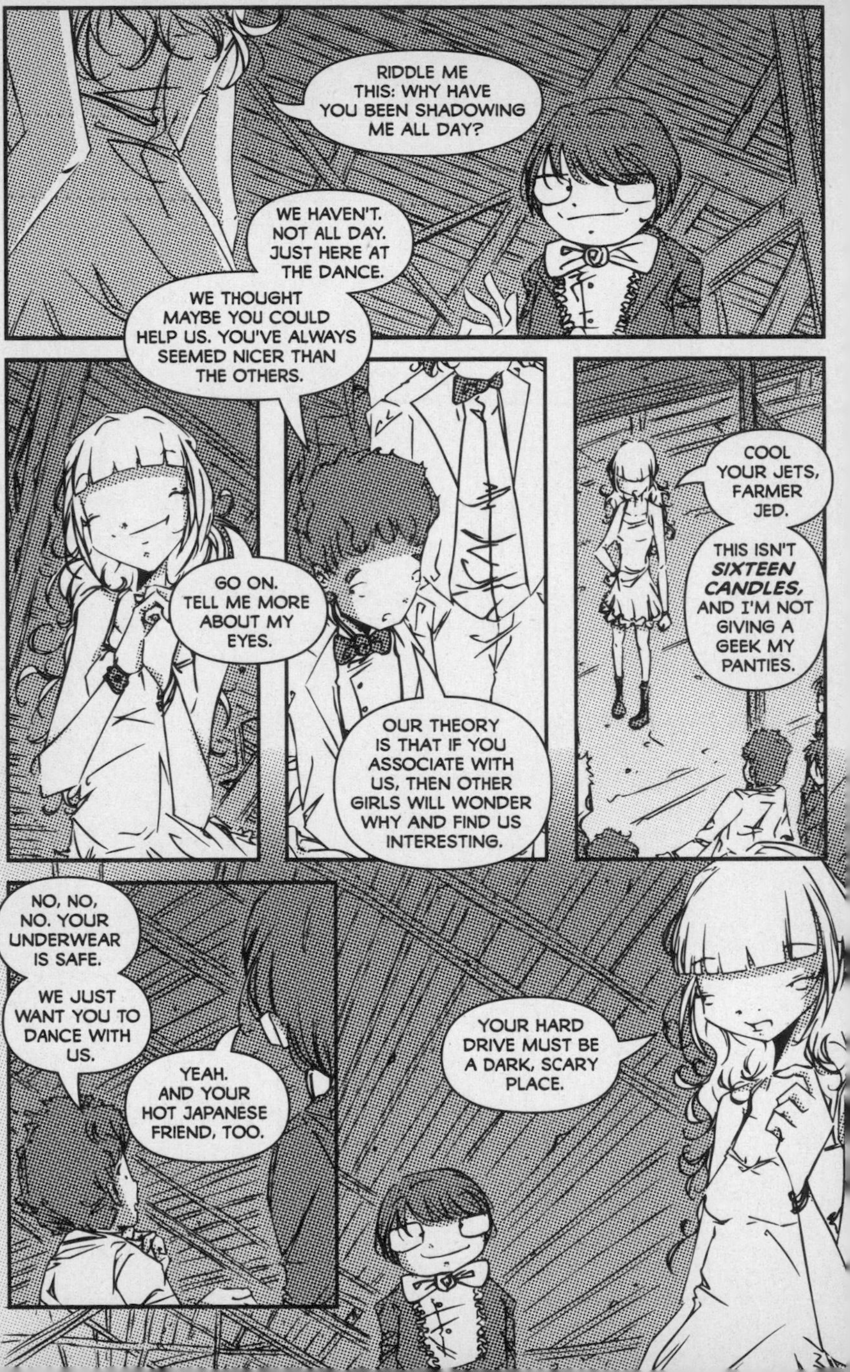
RIDDLE ME THIS: WHY HAVE YOU BEEN SHADOWING ME ALL DAY?
WE HAVEN'T. NOT ALL DAY. JUST HERE AT THE DANCE.
WE THOUGHT MAYBE YOU COULD HELP US. YOU'VE ALWAYS SEEMED NICER THAN THE OTHERS.
GO ON. TELL ME MORE ABOUT MY EYES.
OUR THEORY IS THAT IF YOU ASSOCIATE WITH US, THEN OTHER GIRLS WILL WONDER WHY AND FIND US INTERESTING.
COOL YOUR JETS, FARMER JED.
THIS ISN'T ***SIXTEEN CANDLES,*** AND I'M NOT GIVING A GEEK MY PANTIES.
NO, NO, NO. YOUR UNDERWEAR IS SAFE.
WE JUST WANT YOU TO DANCE WITH US.
YEAH. AND YOUR HOT JAPANESE FRIEND, TOO.
YOUR HARD DRIVE MUST BE A DARK, SCARY PLACE.

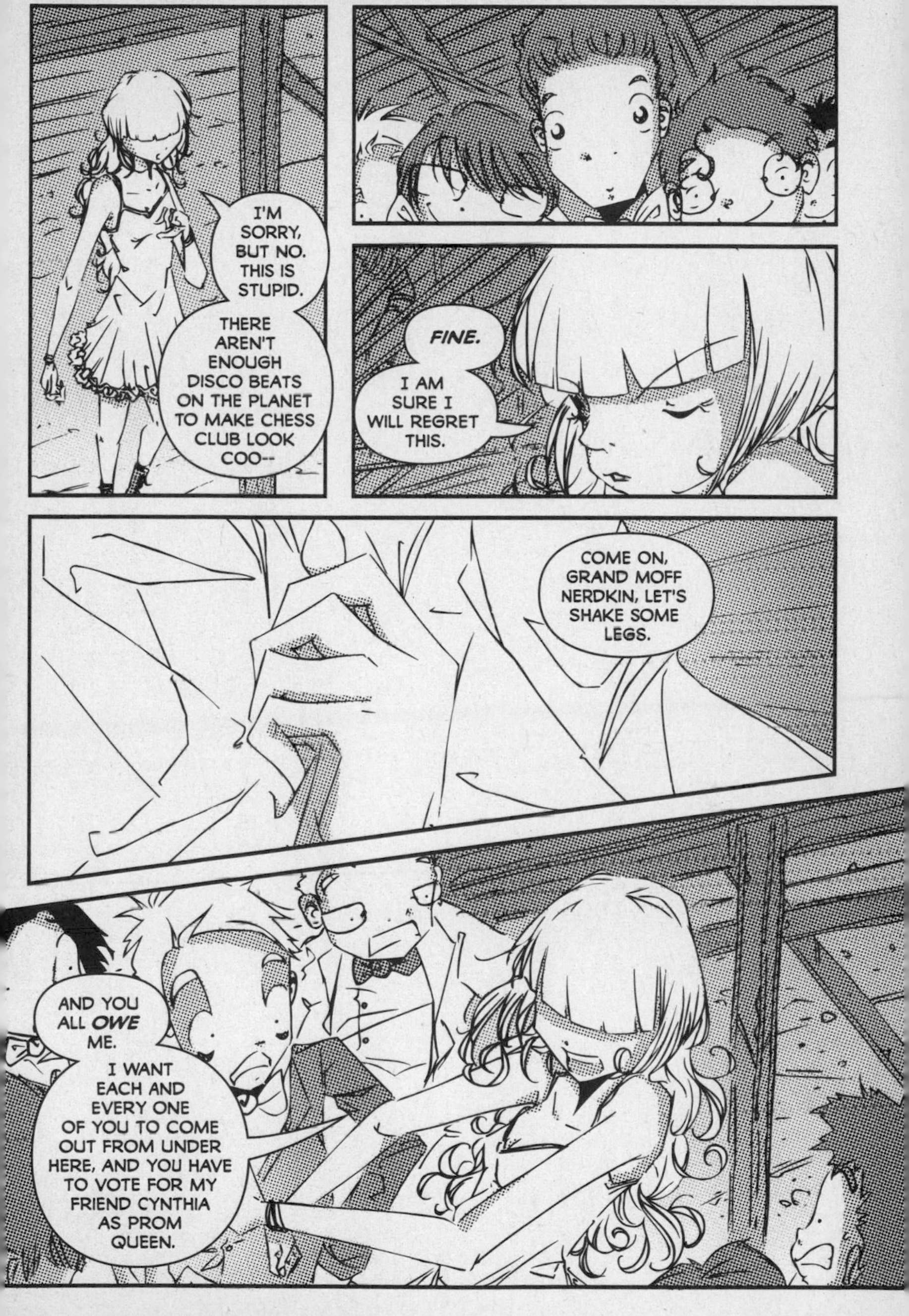
I'M SORRY, BUT NO. THIS IS STUPID.
THERE AREN'T ENOUGH DISCO BEATS ON THE PLANET TO MAKE CHESS CLUB LOOK COO--
FINE.
I AM SURE I WILL REGRET THIS.
COME ON, GRAND MOFF NERDKIN, LET'S SHAKE SOME LEGS.
AND YOU ALL OWE ME.
I WANT EACH AND EVERY ONE OF YOU TO COME OUT FROM UNDER HERE, AND YOU HAVE TO VOTE FOR MY FRIEND CYNTHIA AS PROM QUEEN.

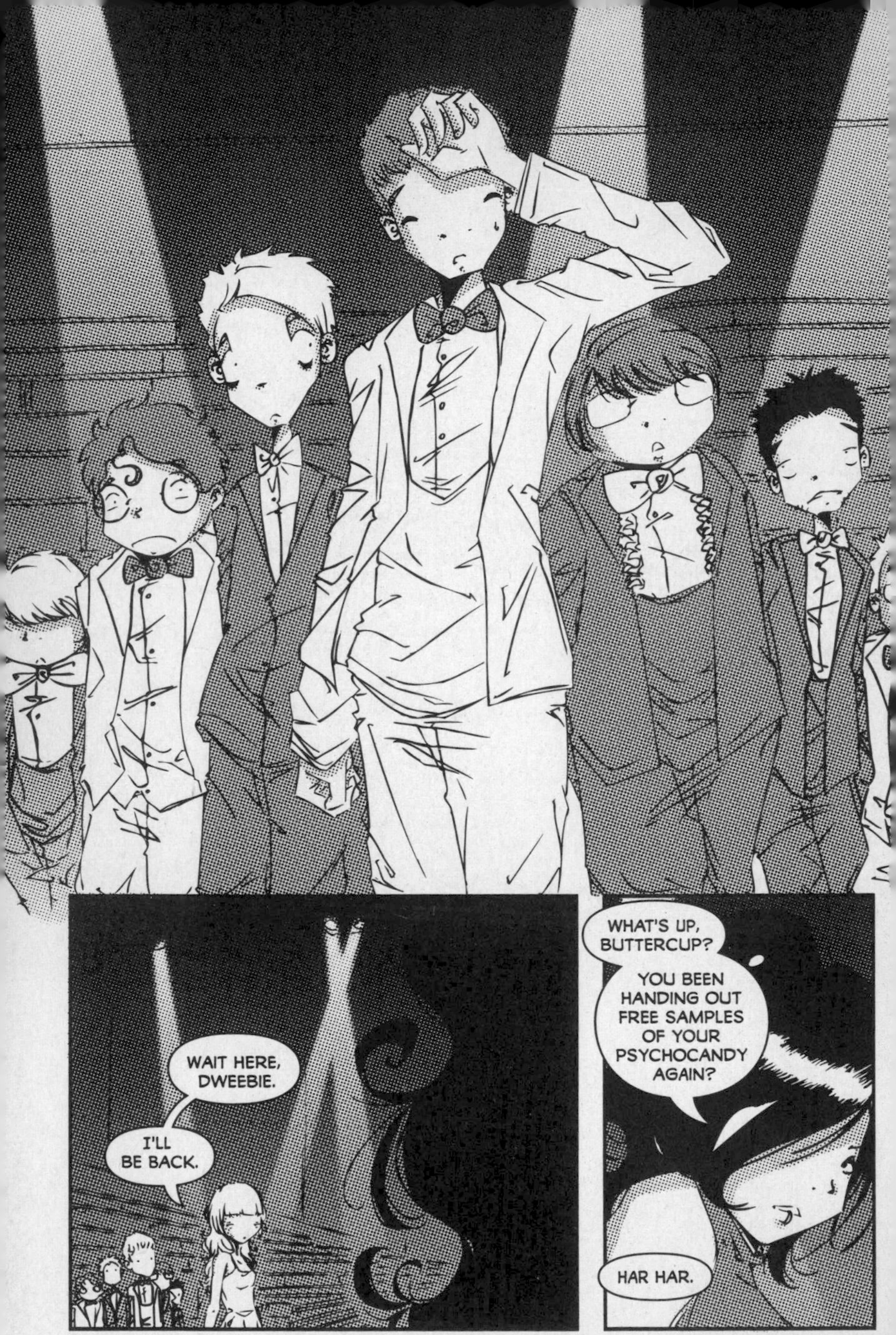
WAIT HERE, DWEEBIE.
I'LL BE BACK.
WHAT'S UP, BUTTERCUP?
YOU BEEN HANDING OUT FREE SAMPLES OF YOUR PSYCHOCANDY AGAIN?
HAR HAR.

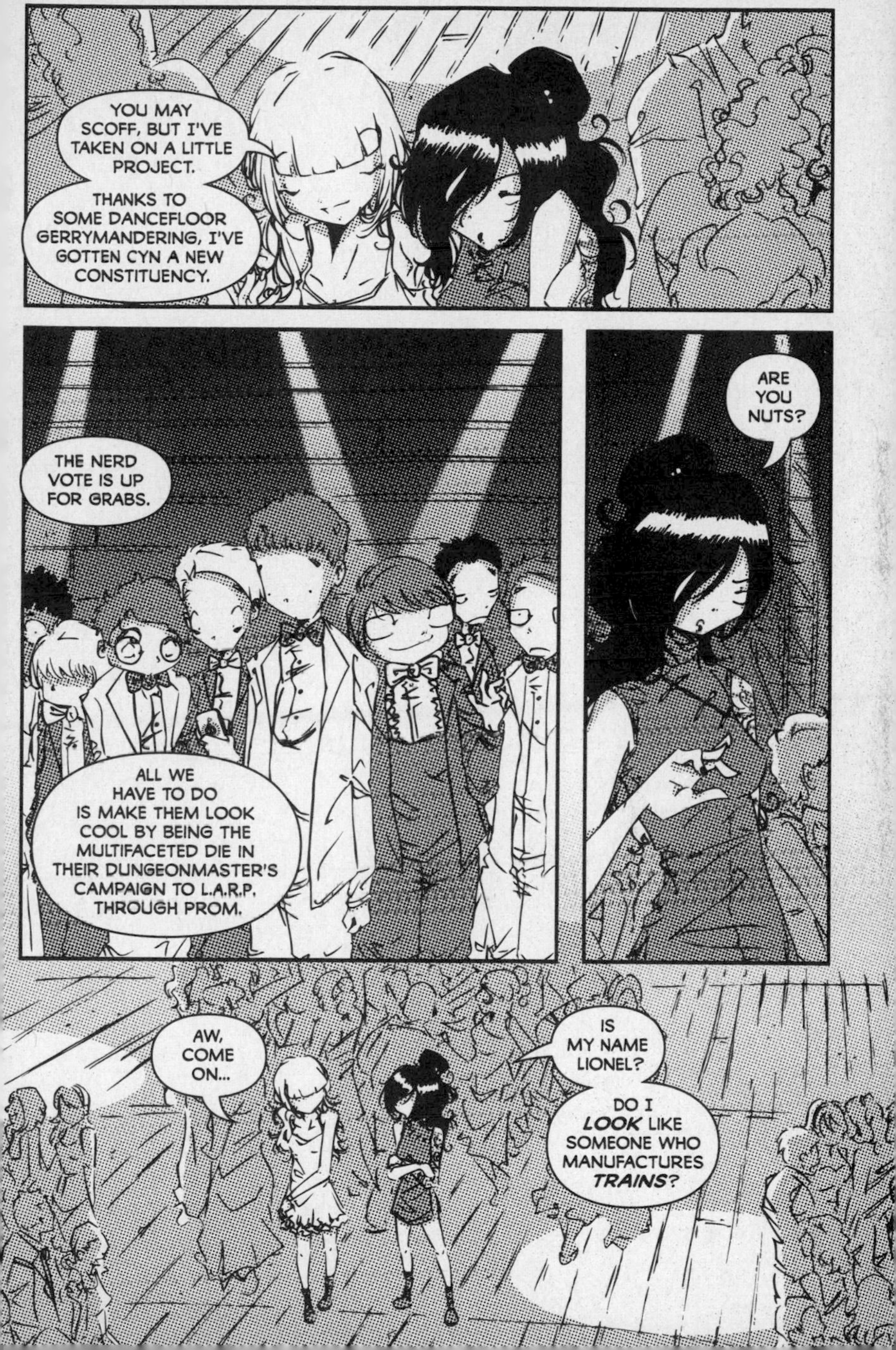
YOU MAY SCOFF, BUT I'VE TAKEN ON A LITTLE PROJECT.
THANKS TO SOME DANCEFLOOR GERRYMANDERING, I'VE GOTTEN CYN A NEW CONSTITUENCY.
THE NERD VOTE IS UP FOR GRABS.
ALL WE HAVE TO DO IS MAKE THEM LOOK COOL BY BEING THE MULTIFACETED DIE IN THEIR DUNGEONMASTER'S CAMPAIGN TO L.A.R.P. THROUGH PROM.
ARE YOU NUTS?
AW, COME ON...
IS MY NAME LIONEL?
DO I LOOK LIKE SOMEONE WHO MANUFACTURES TRAINS?

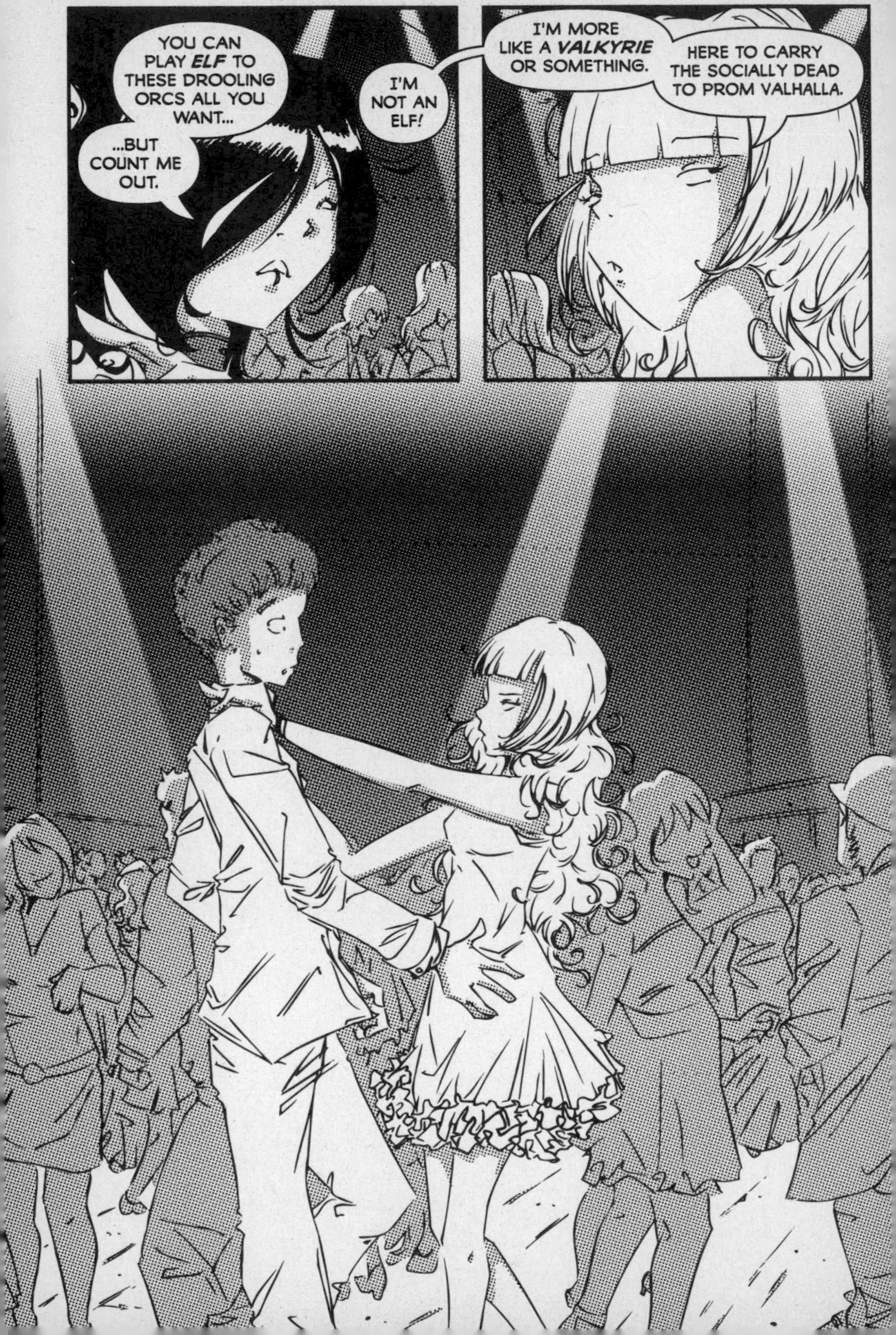

YOU CAN PLAY ELF TO THESE DROOLING ORCS ALL YOU WANT...
...BUT COUNT ME OUT.
I'M NOT AN ELF!
I'M MORE LIKE A VALKYRIE OR SOMETHING.
HERE TO CARRY THE SOCIALLY DEAD TO PROM VALHALLA.

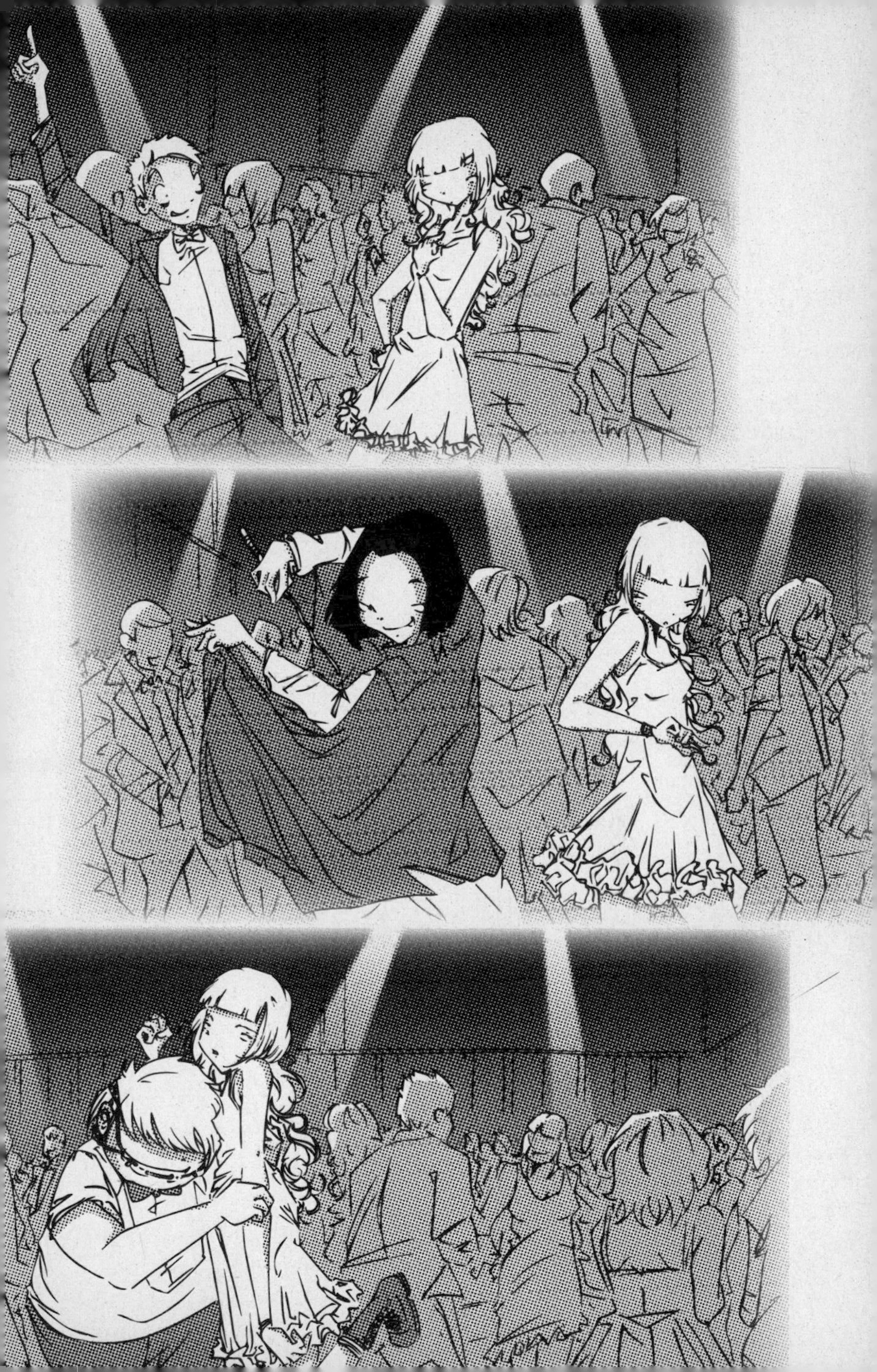

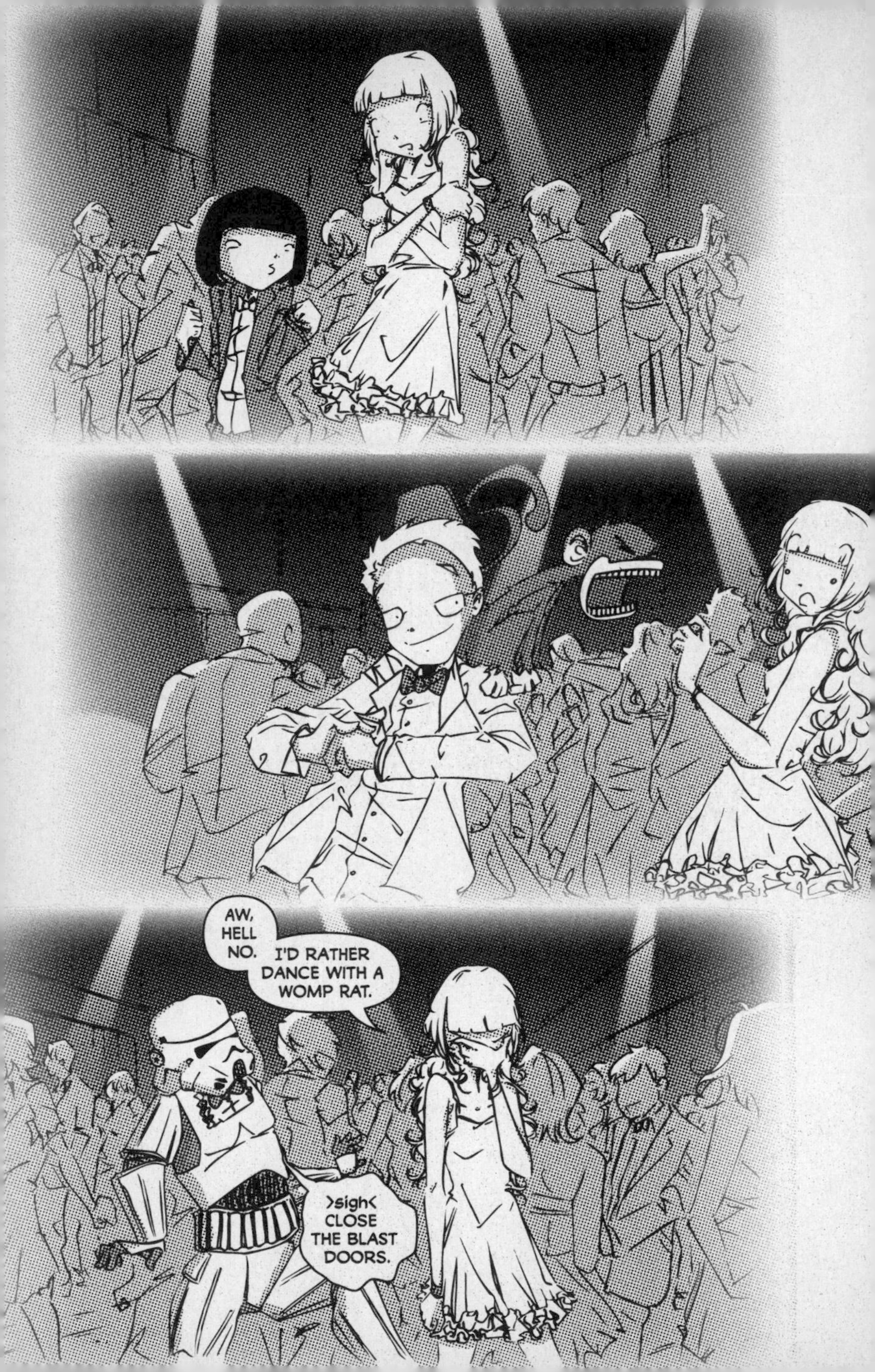
AW, HELL NO.
I'D RATHER DANCE WITH A WOMP RAT.
>sigh< CLOSE THE BLAST DOORS.

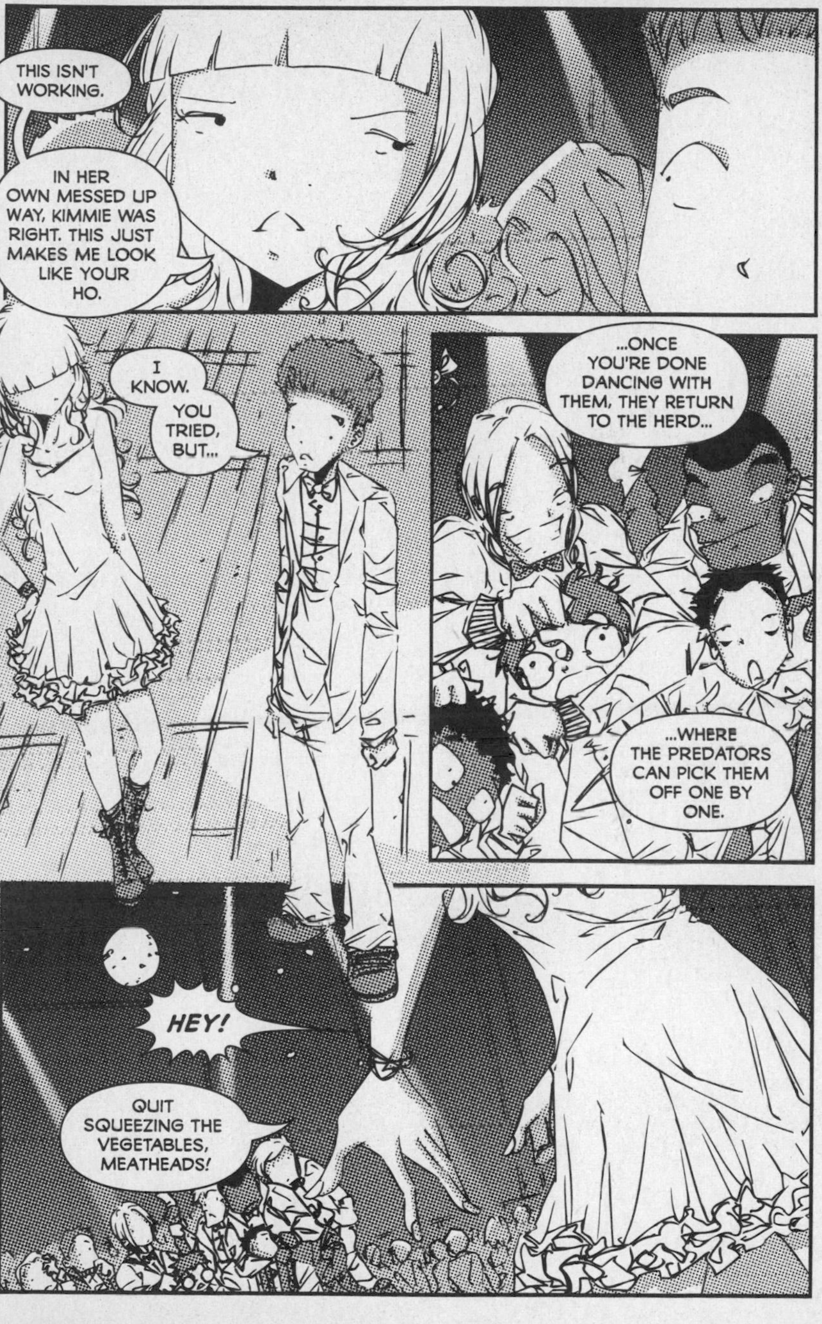
THIS ISN'T WORKING.
IN HER OWN MESSED UP WAY, KIMMIE WAS RIGHT. THIS JUST MAKES ME LOOK LIKE YOUR HO.
I KNOW.
YOU TRIED, BUT...
...ONCE YOU'RE DONE DANCING WITH THEM, THEY RETURN TO THE HERD...
...WHERE THE PREDATORS CAN PICK THEM OFF ONE BY ONE.
HEY!
QUIT SQUEEZING THE VEGETABLES, MEATHEADS!

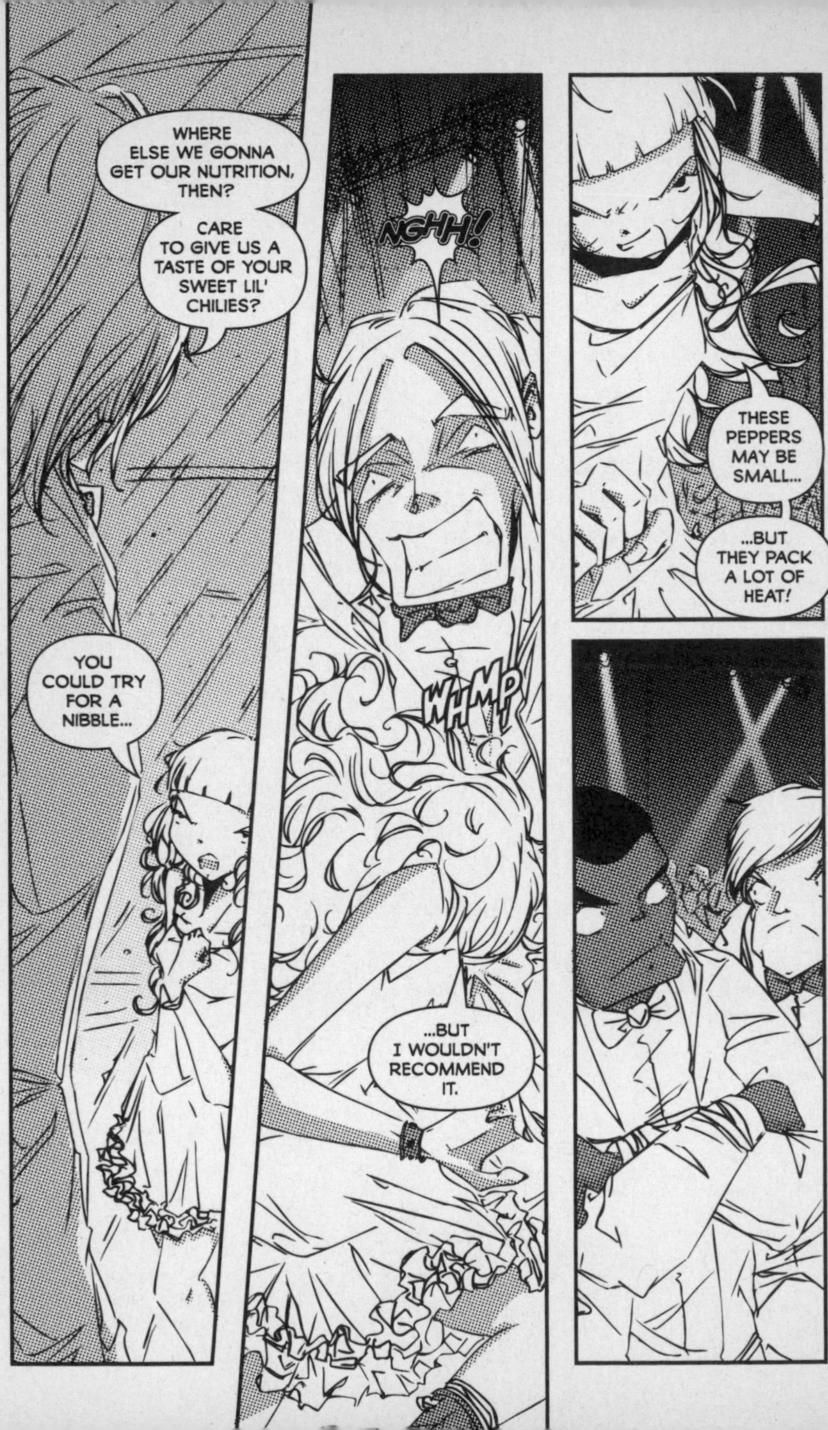
WHERE ELSE WE GONNA GET OUR NUTRITION, THEN?
CARE TO GIVE US A TASTE OF YOUR SWEET LIL' CHILIES?
YOU COULD TRY FOR A NIBBLE...
NGHH!
WHMP
...BUT I WOULDN'T RECOMMEND IT.
THESE PEPPERS MAY BE SMALL...
...BUT THEY PACK A LOT OF HEAT!

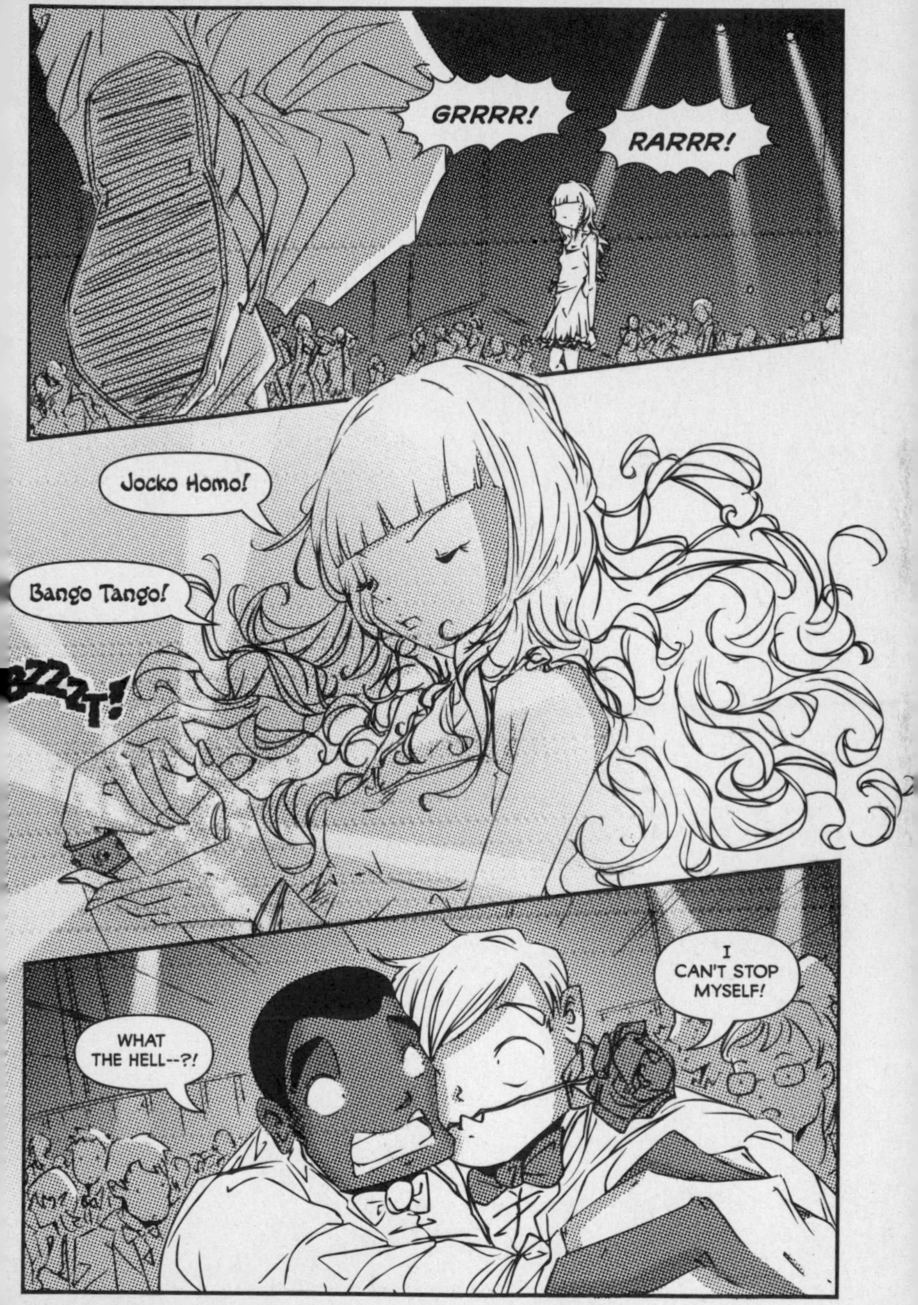
GRRRR!
RARRR!
Jocko Homo!
Bango Tango!
BZZZT!
I CAN'T STOP MYSELF!
WHAT THE HELL--?!

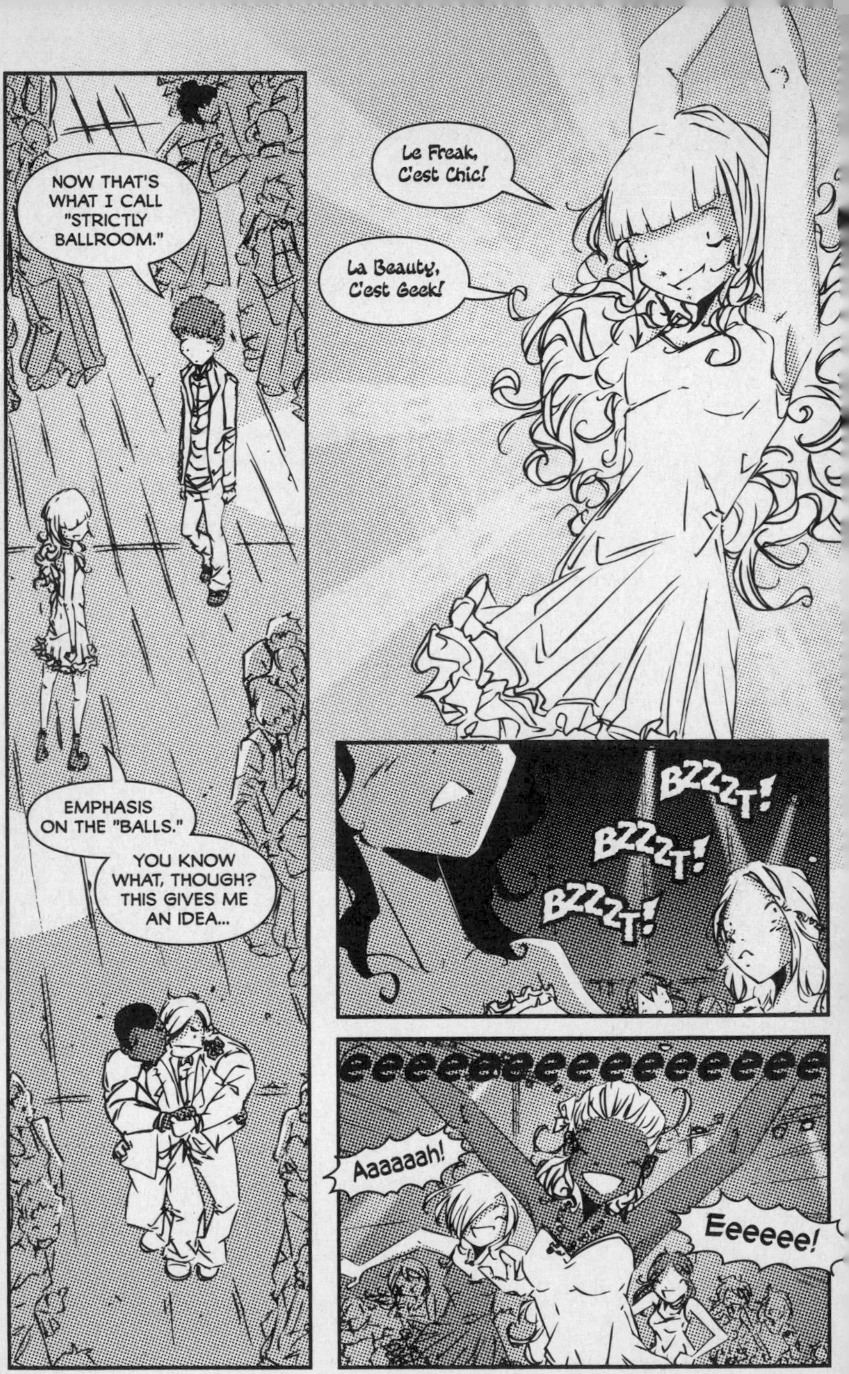
NOW THAT'S WHAT I CALL "STRICTLY BALLROOM."
Le Freak, C'est Chic!
La Beauty, C'est Geek!
EMPHASIS ON THE "BALLS."
YOU KNOW WHAT, THOUGH? THIS GIVES ME AN IDEA...
BZZZZT!
BZZZZT!
BZZZZT!
eeeeeeeeeeeeeeeeeee
Aaaaaah!
Eeeeee!

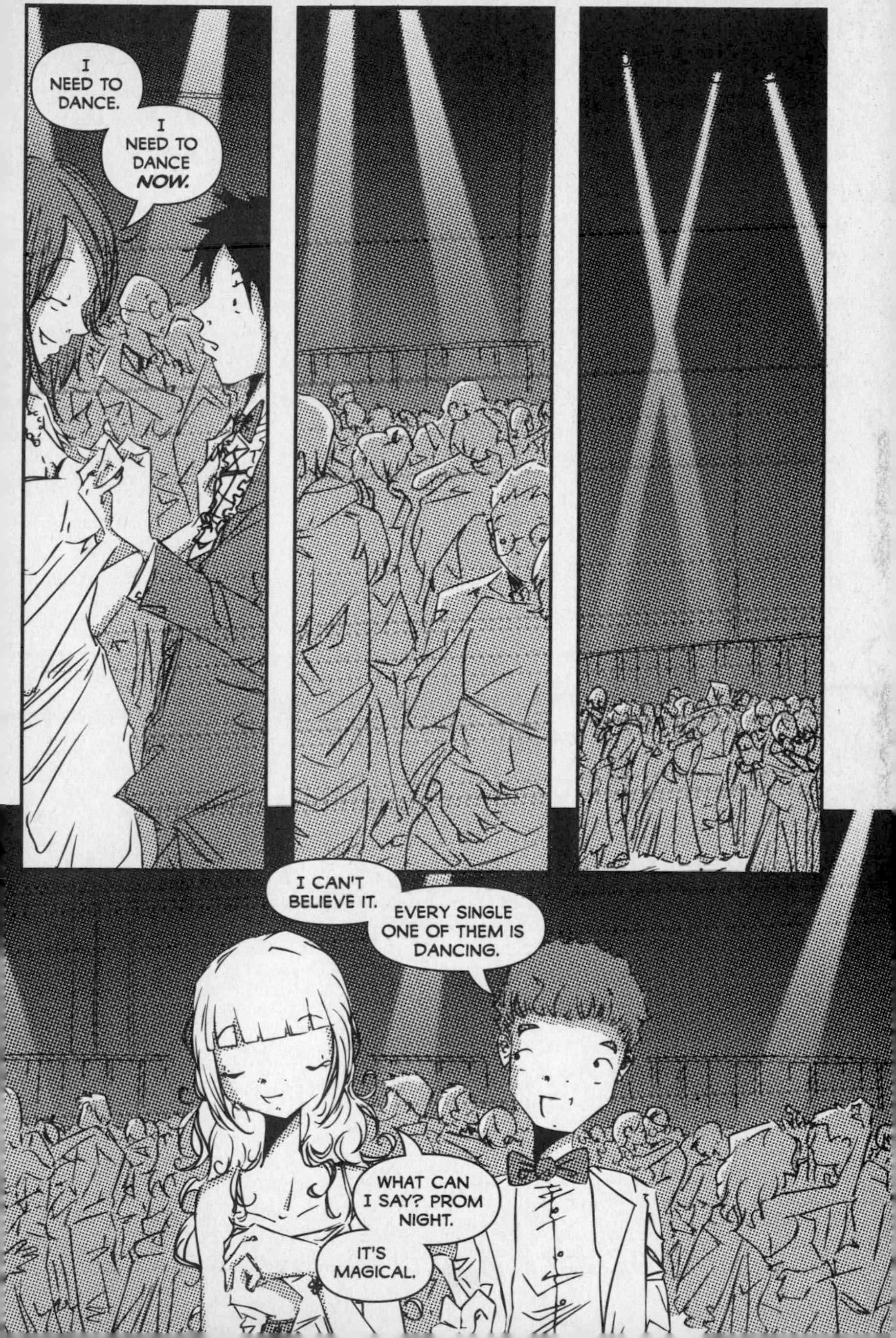

I NEED TO DANCE.
I NEED TO DANCE *NOW.*
I CAN'T BELIEVE IT.
EVERY SINGLE ONE OF THEM IS DANCING.
WHAT CAN I SAY? PROM NIGHT.
IT'S MAGICAL.

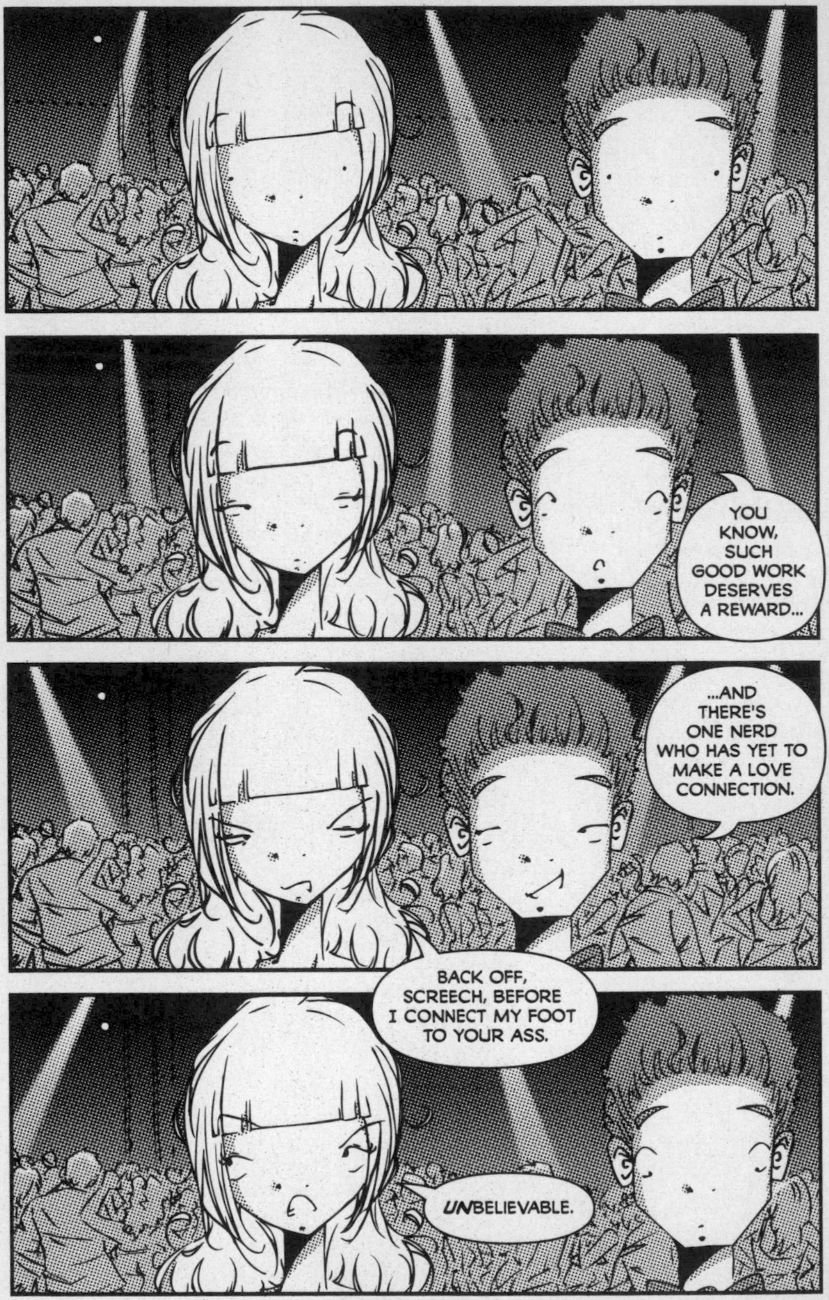
YOU KNOW, SUCH GOOD WORK DESERVES A REWARD...
...AND THERE'S ONE NERD WHO HAS YET TO MAKE A LOVE CONNECTION.
BACK OFF, SCREECH, BEFORE I CONNECT MY FOOT TO YOUR ASS.
UNBELIEVABLE.

Chapter 3
"Ahh, Cindy B, What's It Gonna Be?"

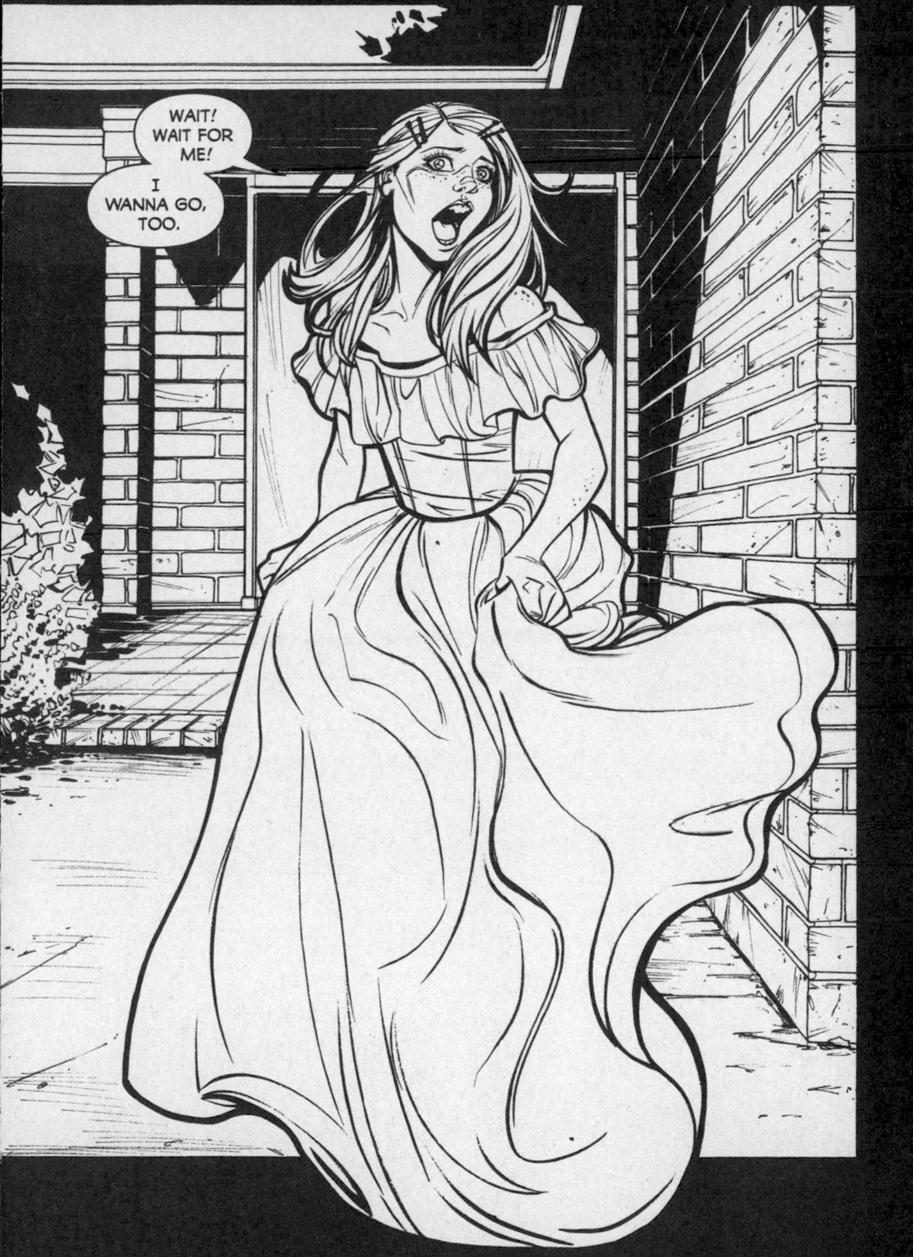
WAIT! WAIT FOR ME!
I WANNA GO, TOO.

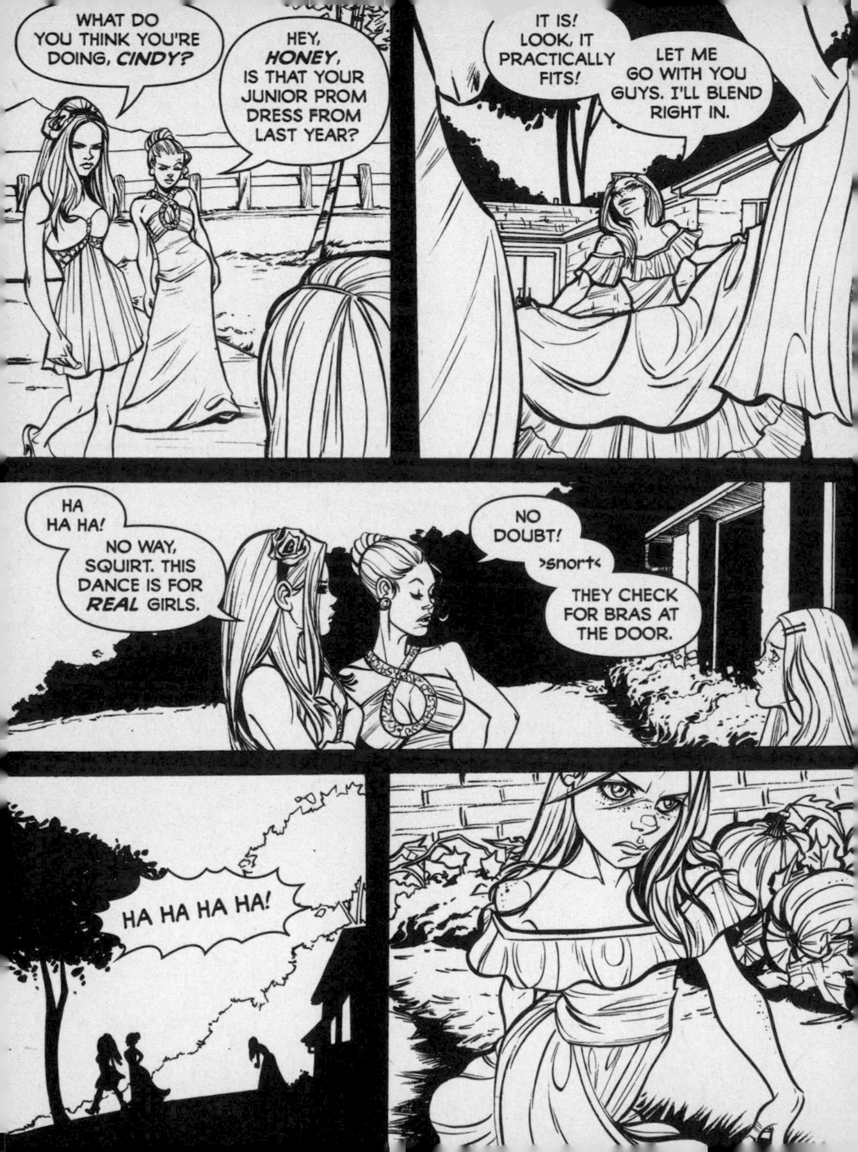
WHAT DO YOU THINK YOU'RE DOING, *CINDY?*
HEY, ***HONEY***, IS THAT YOUR JUNIOR PROM DRESS FROM LAST YEAR?
IT IS! LOOK, IT PRACTICALLY FITS!
LET ME GO WITH YOU GUYS. I'LL BLEND RIGHT IN.
HA HA HA!
NO WAY, SQUIRT. THIS DANCE IS FOR ***REAL*** GIRLS.
NO DOUBT!
>snort<
THEY CHECK FOR BRAS AT THE DOOR.
HA HA HA HA!

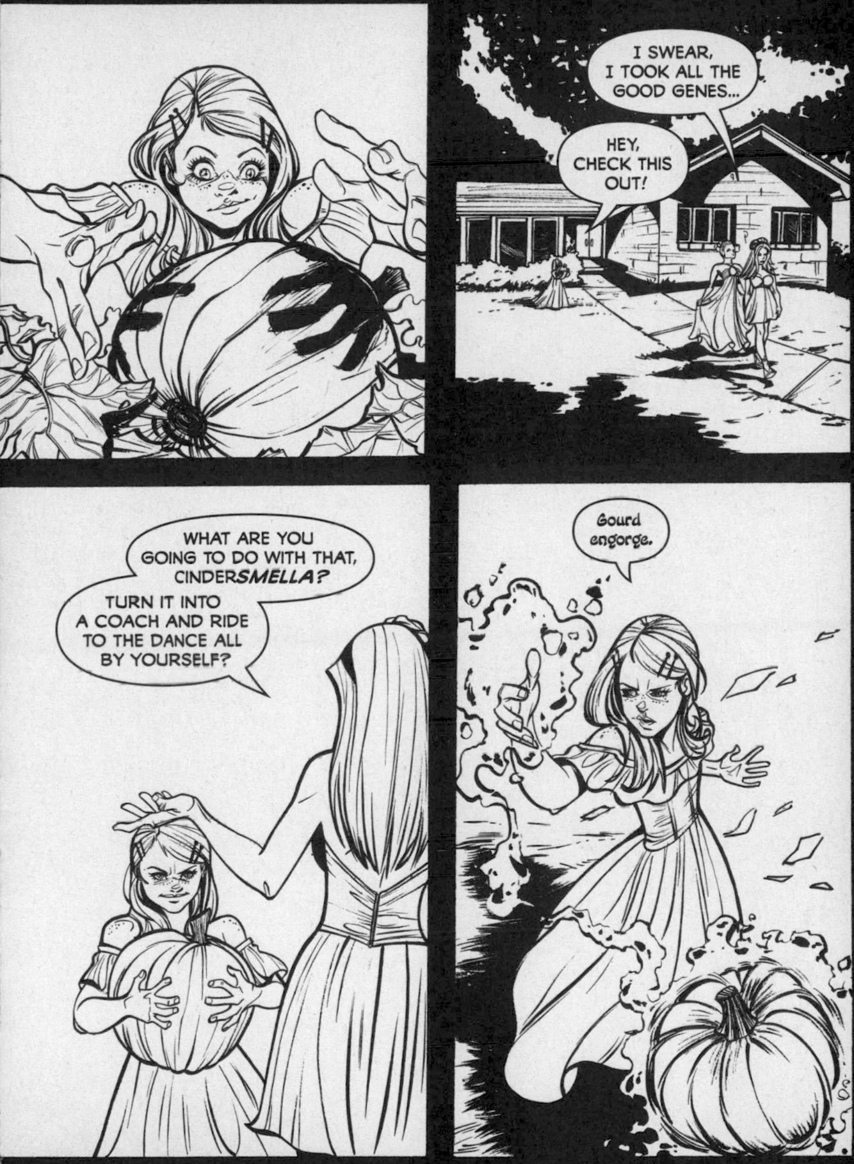
I SWEAR, I TOOK ALL THE GOOD GENES...
HEY, CHECK THIS OUT!
WHAT ARE YOU GOING TO DO WITH THAT, CINDER*SMELLA?*
TURN IT INTO A COACH AND RIDE TO THE DANCE ALL BY YOURSELF?
Gourd engorge.

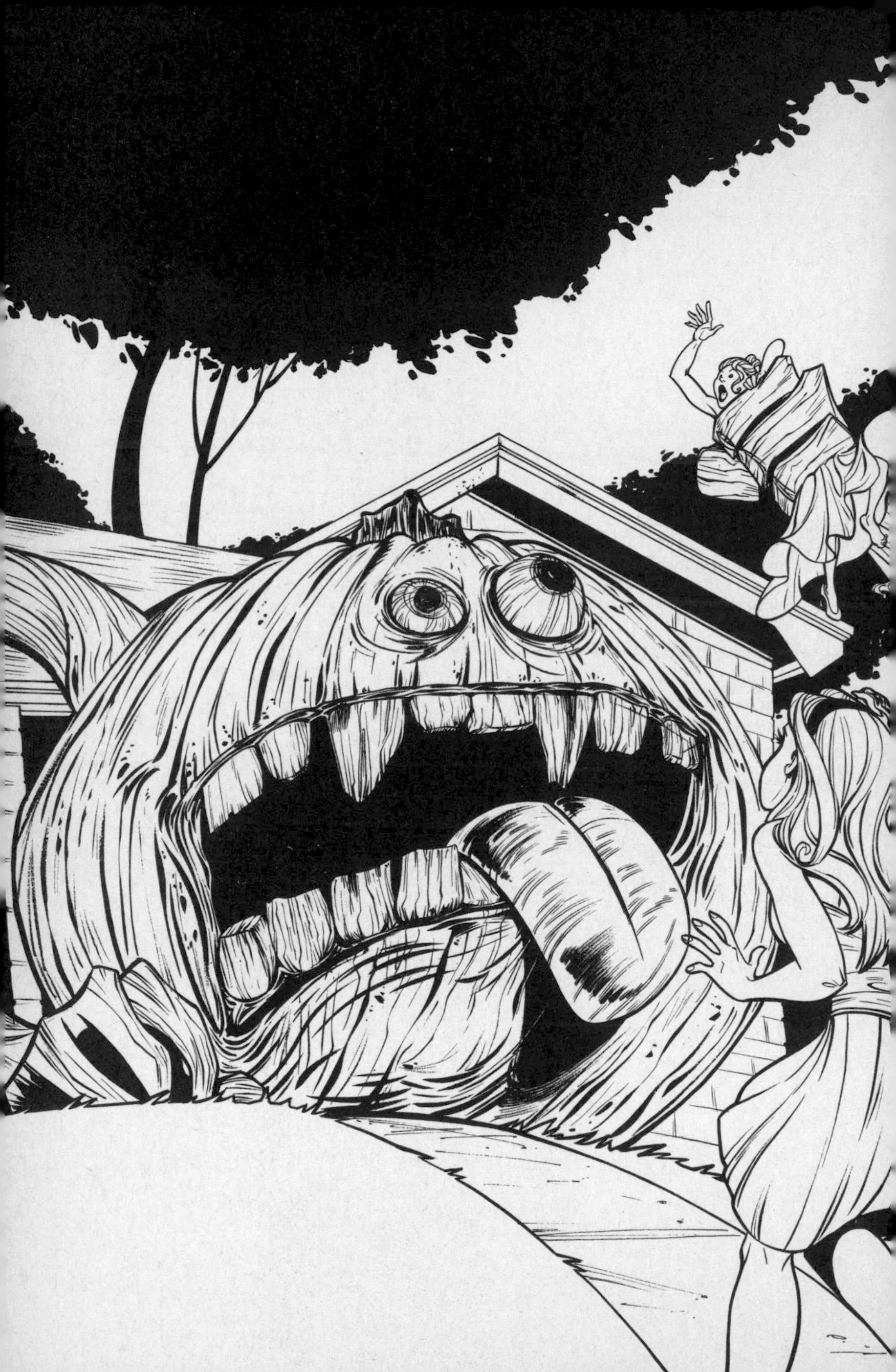

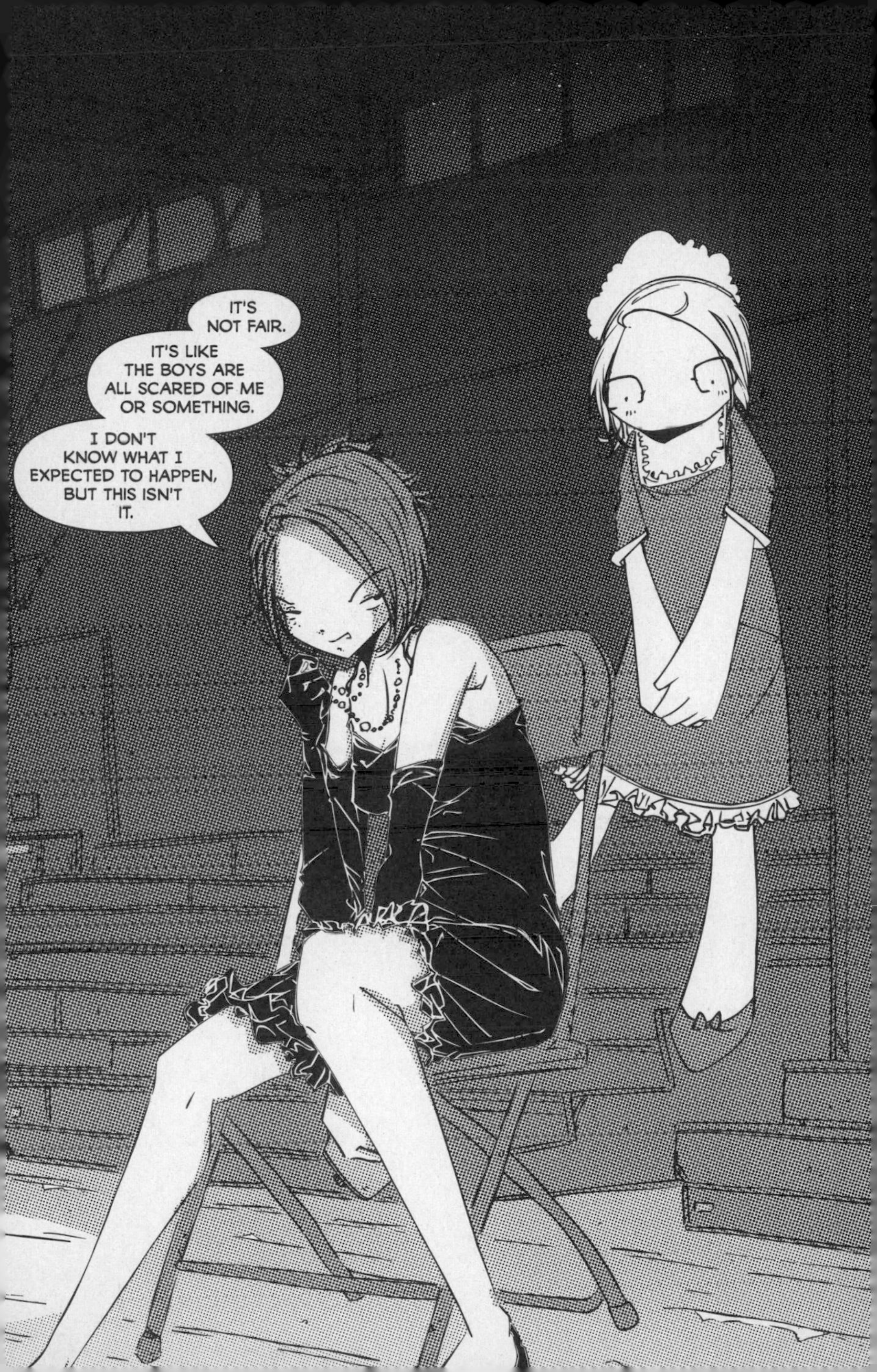
IT'S NOT FAIR.
IT'S LIKE THE BOYS ARE ALL SCARED OF ME OR SOMETHING.
I DON'T KNOW WHAT I EXPECTED TO HAPPEN, BUT THIS ISN'T IT.

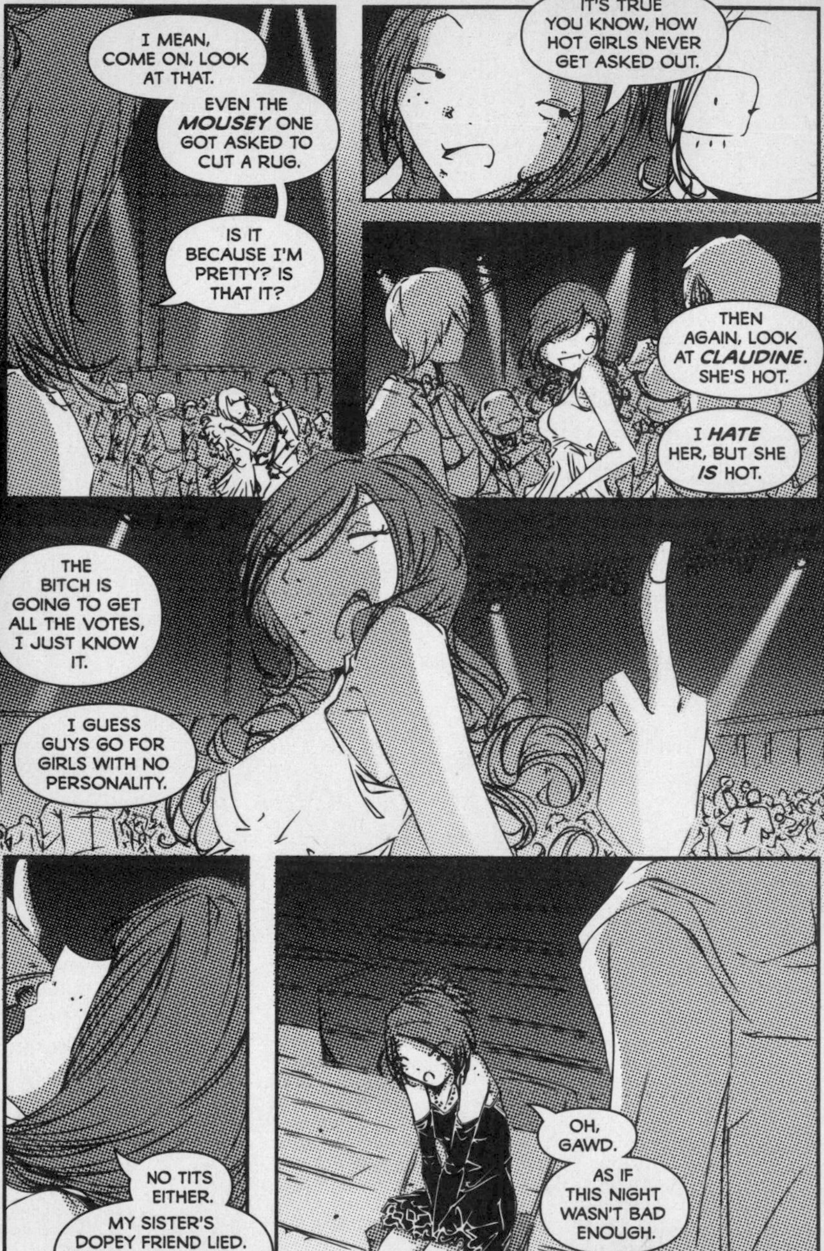
I MEAN, COME ON, LOOK AT THAT.
EVEN THE *MOUSEY* ONE GOT ASKED TO CUT A RUG.
IS IT BECAUSE I'M PRETTY? IS THAT IT?
IT'S TRUE YOU KNOW, HOW HOT GIRLS NEVER GET ASKED OUT.
THEN AGAIN, LOOK AT *CLAUDINE*. SHE'S HOT.
I *HATE* HER, BUT SHE *IS* HOT.
THE BITCH IS GOING TO GET ALL THE VOTES, I JUST KNOW IT.
I GUESS GUYS GO FOR GIRLS WITH NO PERSONALITY.
NO TITS EITHER.
MY SISTER'S DOPEY FRIEND LIED. CLEARLY THEY *DON'T* CHECK FOR BRAS.
OH, GAWD.
AS IF THIS NIGHT WASN'T BAD ENOUGH.

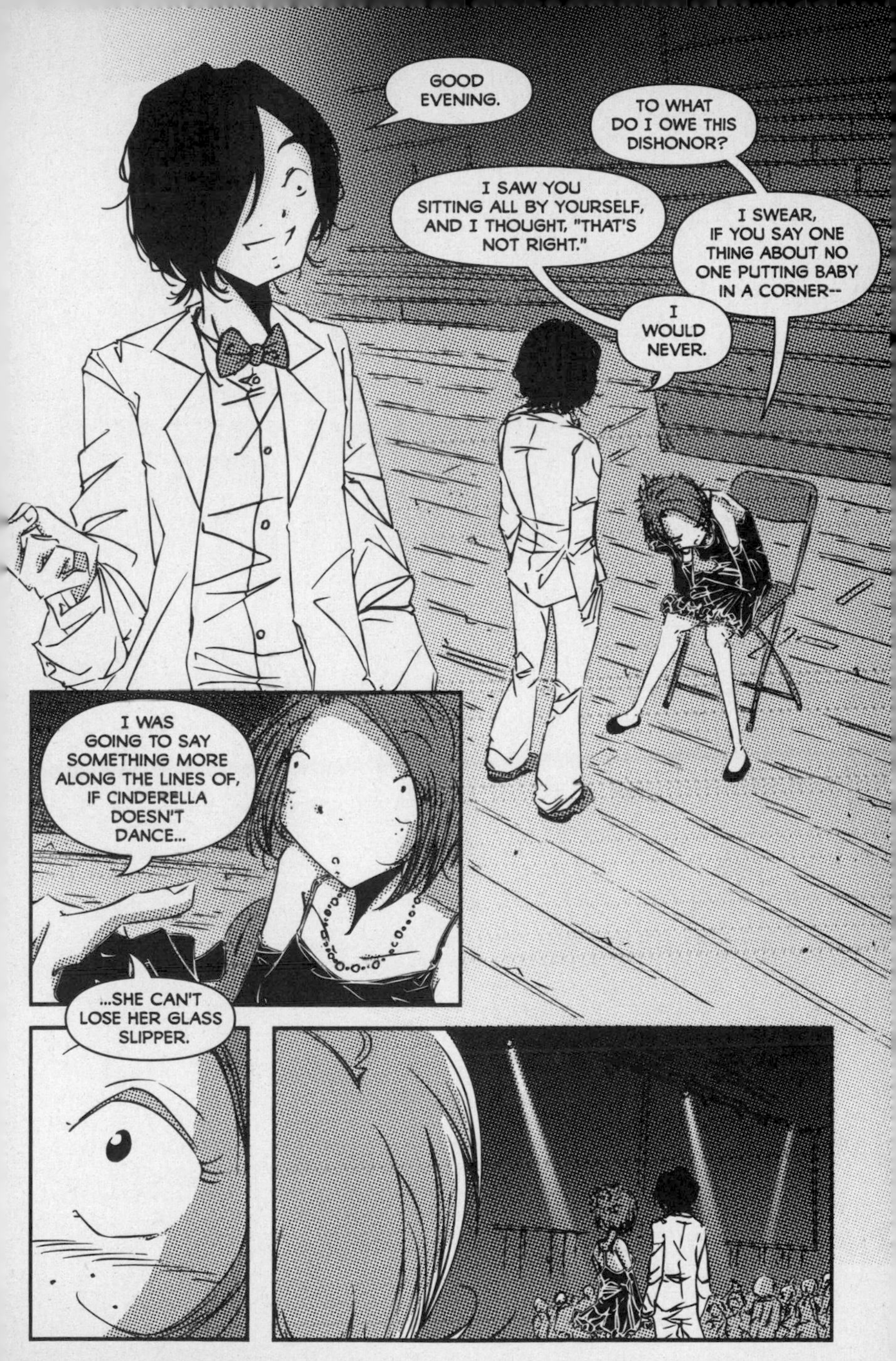
GOOD EVENING.
TO WHAT DO I OWE THIS DISHONOR?
I SAW YOU SITTING ALL BY YOURSELF, AND I THOUGHT, "THAT'S NOT RIGHT."
I SWEAR, IF YOU SAY ONE THING ABOUT NO ONE PUTTING BABY IN A CORNER--
I WOULD NEVER.
I WAS GOING TO SAY SOMETHING MORE ALONG THE LINES OF, IF CINDERELLA DOESN'T DANCE...
...SHE CAN'T LOSE HER GLASS SLIPPER.

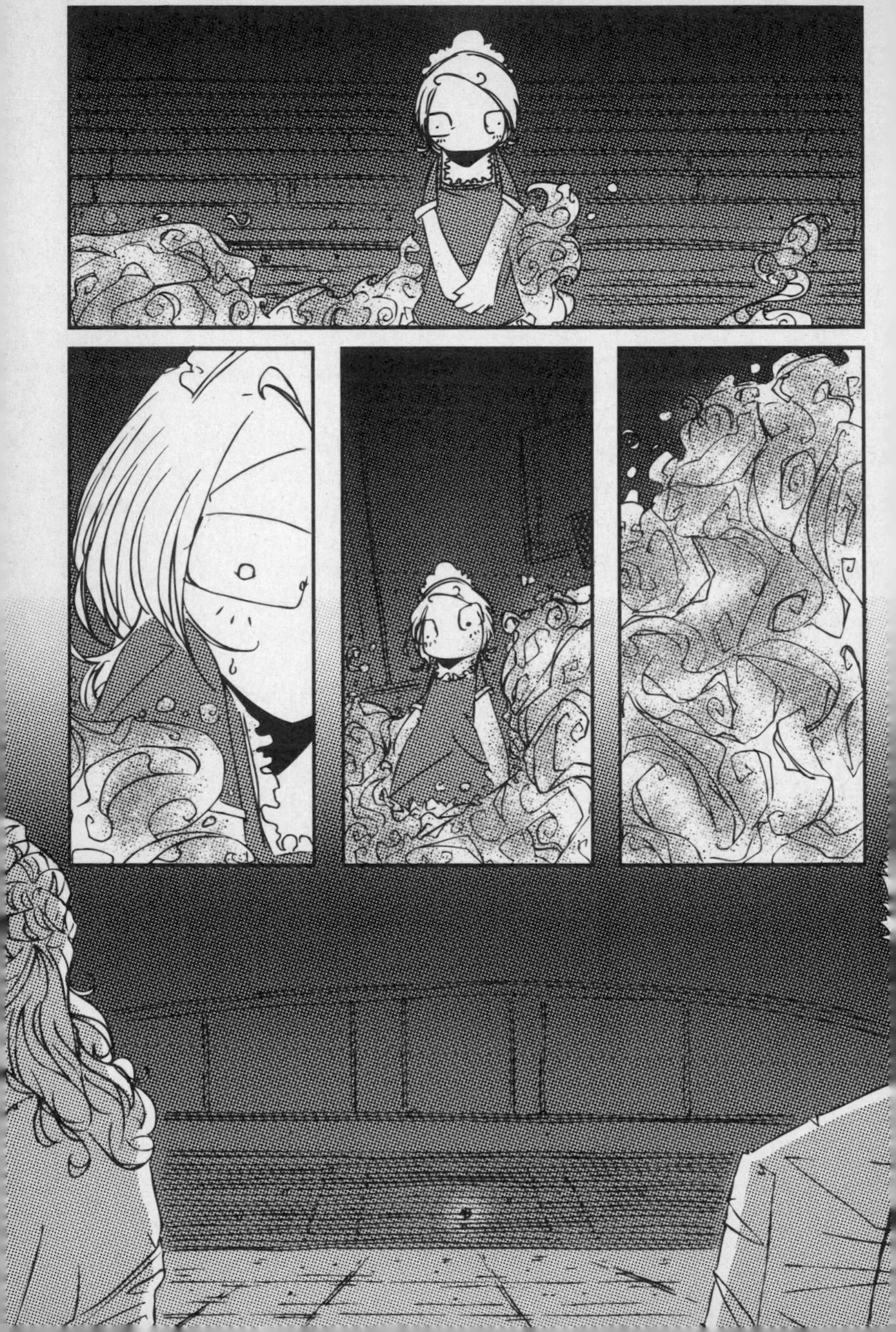

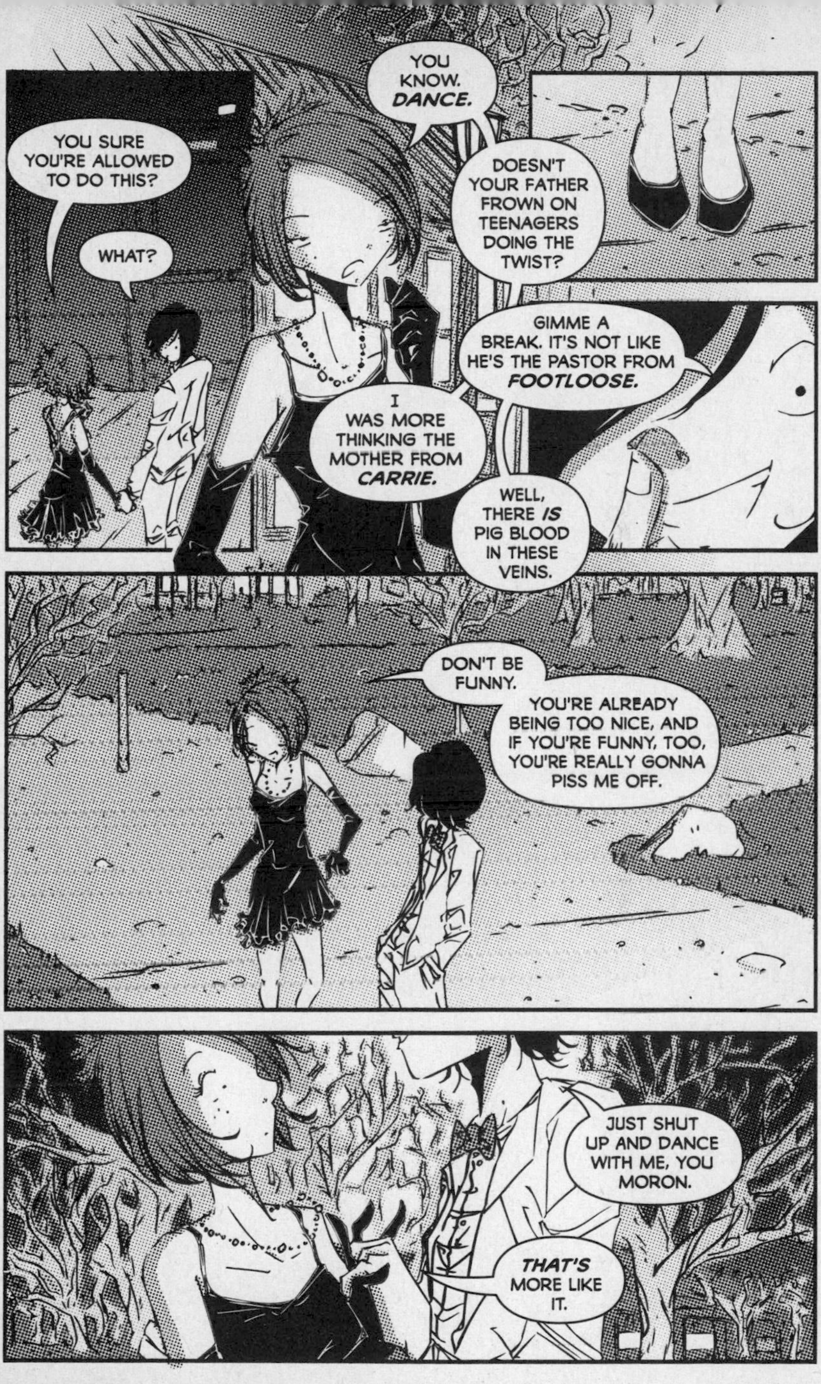
YOU SURE YOU'RE ALLOWED TO DO THIS?
WHAT?
YOU KNOW. *DANCE.*
DOESN'T YOUR FATHER FROWN ON TEENAGERS DOING THE TWIST?
GIMME A BREAK. IT'S NOT LIKE HE'S THE PASTOR FROM *FOOTLOOSE.*
I WAS MORE THINKING THE MOTHER FROM *CARRIE.*
WELL, THERE *IS* PIG BLOOD IN THESE VEINS.
DON'T BE FUNNY.
YOU'RE ALREADY BEING TOO NICE, AND IF YOU'RE FUNNY, TOO, YOU'RE REALLY GONNA PISS ME OFF.
JUST SHUT UP AND DANCE WITH ME, YOU MORON.
THAT'S MORE LIKE IT.

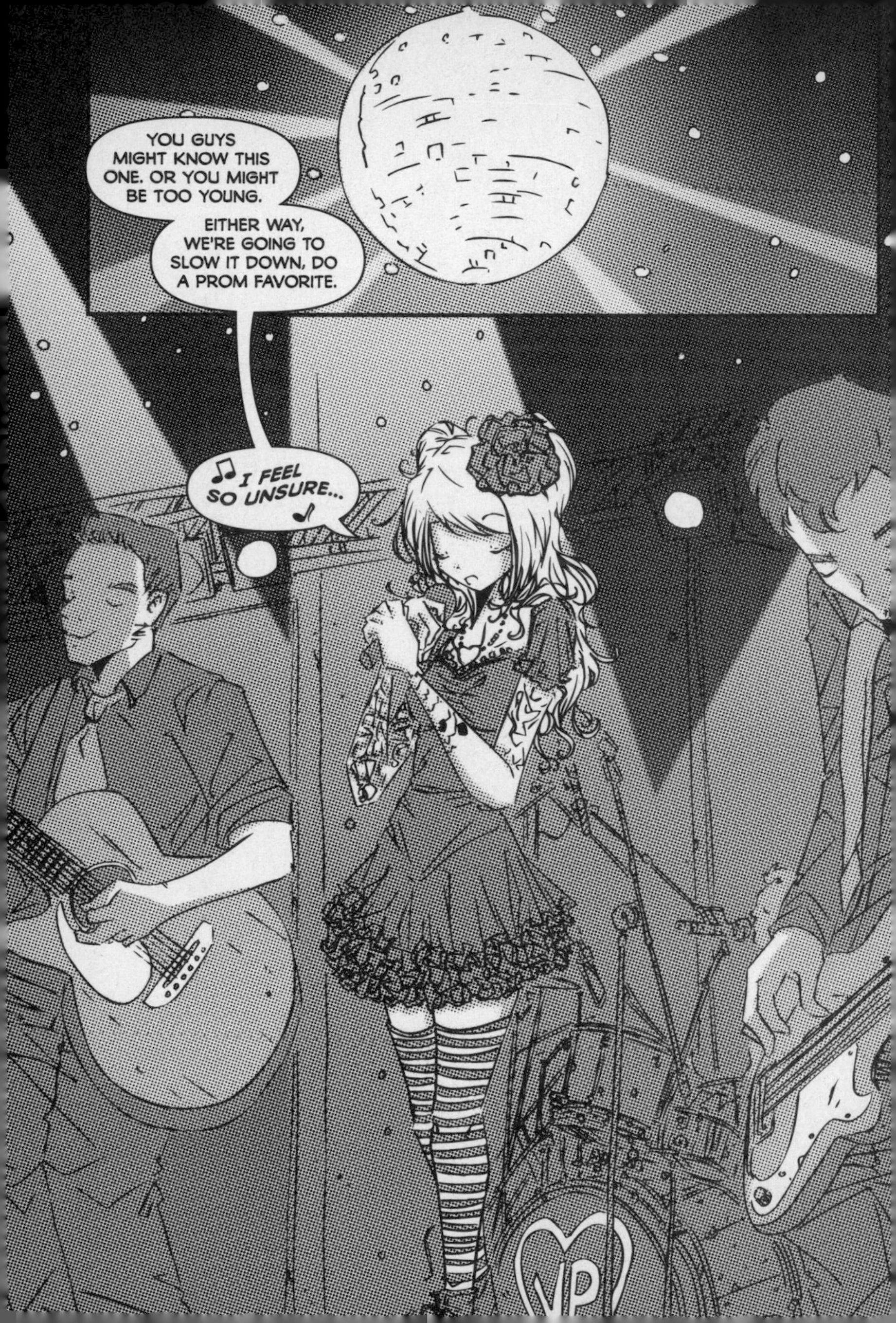
YOU GUYS MIGHT KNOW THIS ONE. OR YOU MIGHT BE TOO YOUNG.
EITHER WAY, WE'RE GOING TO SLOW IT DOWN, DO A PROM FAVORITE.
I FEEL SO UNSURE...

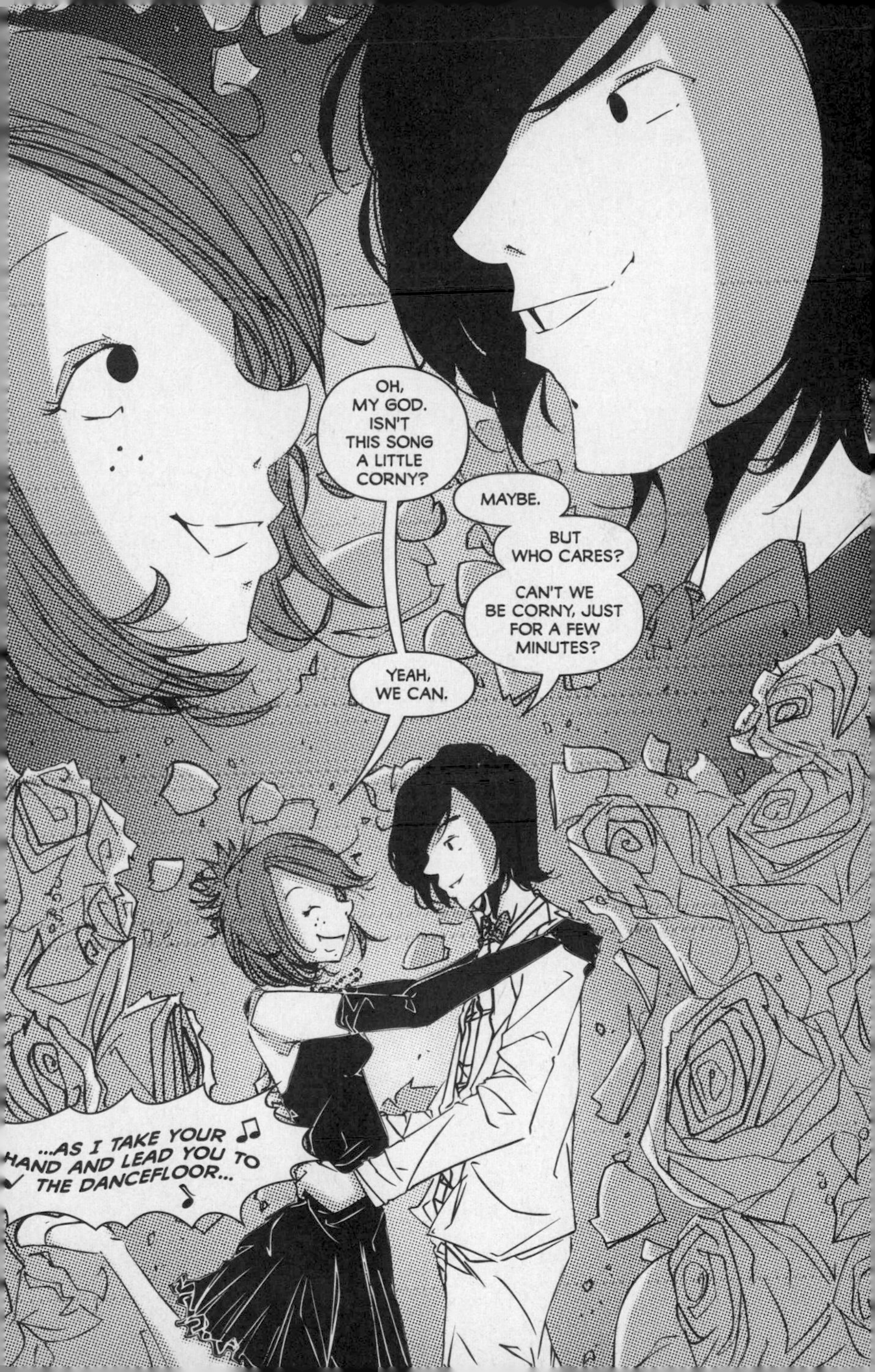
OH, MY GOD. ISN'T THIS SONG A LITTLE CORNY?
MAYBE.
BUT WHO CARES?
CAN'T WE BE CORNY, JUST FOR A FEW MINUTES?
YEAH, WE CAN.
...AS I TAKE YOUR HAND AND LEAD YOU TO THE DANCEFLOOR...

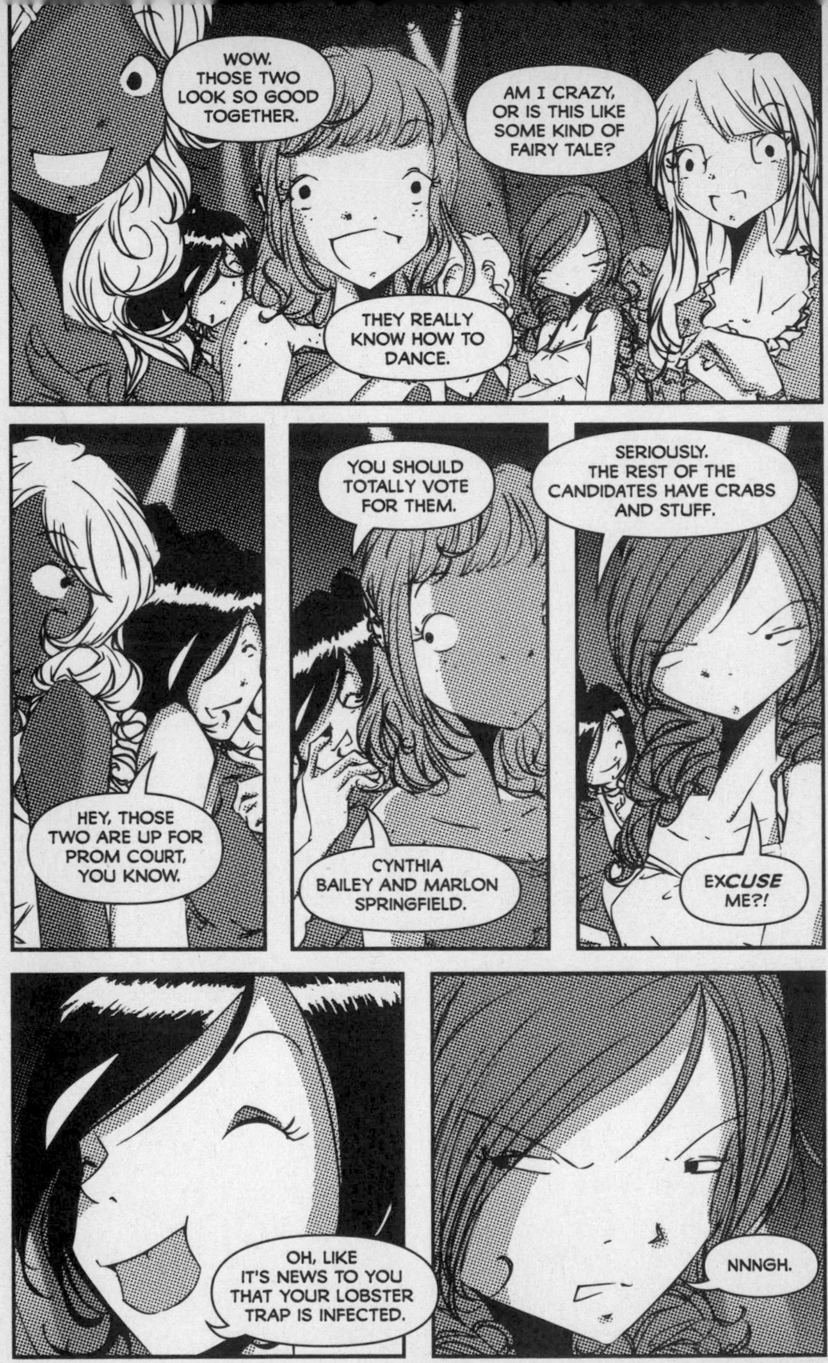
WOW. THOSE TWO LOOK SO GOOD TOGETHER.
AM I CRAZY, OR IS THIS LIKE SOME KIND OF FAIRY TALE?
THEY REALLY KNOW HOW TO DANCE.
HEY, THOSE TWO ARE UP FOR PROM COURT, YOU KNOW.
YOU SHOULD TOTALLY VOTE FOR THEM.
CYNTHIA BAILEY AND MARLON SPRINGFIELD.
SERIOUSLY. THE REST OF THE CANDIDATES HAVE CRABS AND STUFF.
EX*CUSE* ME?!
OH, LIKE IT'S NEWS TO YOU THAT YOUR LOBSTER TRAP IS INFECTED.
NNNGH.

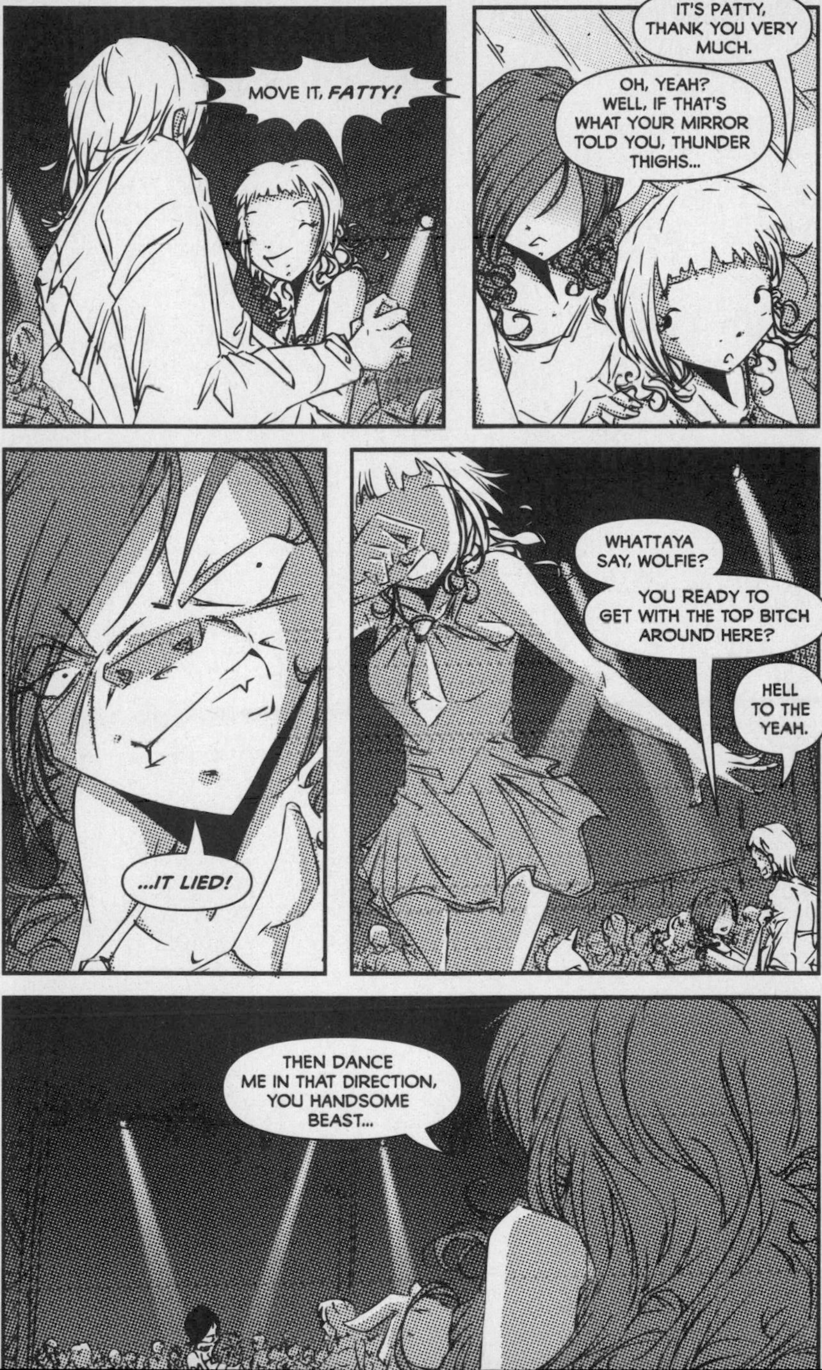
MOVE IT, *FATTY!*
IT'S PATTY, THANK YOU VERY MUCH.
OH, YEAH? WELL, IF THAT'S WHAT YOUR MIRROR TOLD YOU, THUNDER THIGHS...
...IT LIED!
WHATTAYA SAY, WOLFIE?
YOU READY TO GET WITH THE TOP BITCH AROUND HERE?
HELL TO THE YEAH.
THEN DANCE ME IN THAT DIRECTION, YOU HANDSOME BEAST...

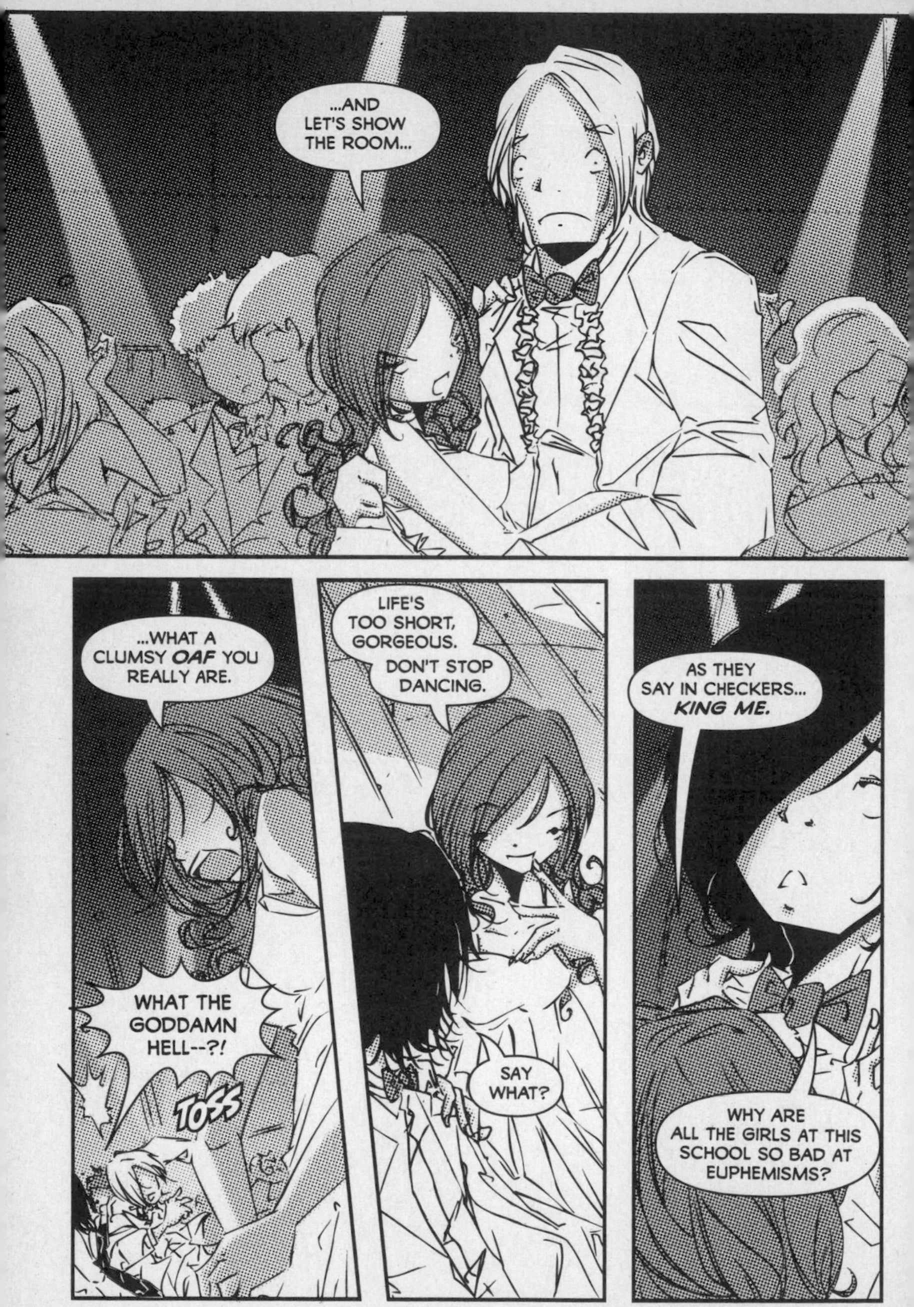
...AND LET'S SHOW THE ROOM...
...WHAT A CLUMSY *OAF* YOU REALLY ARE.
WHAT THE GODDAMN HELL--?!
TOSS
LIFE'S TOO SHORT, GORGEOUS.
DON'T STOP DANCING.
SAY WHAT?
AS THEY SAY IN CHECKERS... *KING ME.*
WHY ARE ALL THE GIRLS AT THIS SCHOOL SO BAD AT EUPHEMISMS?

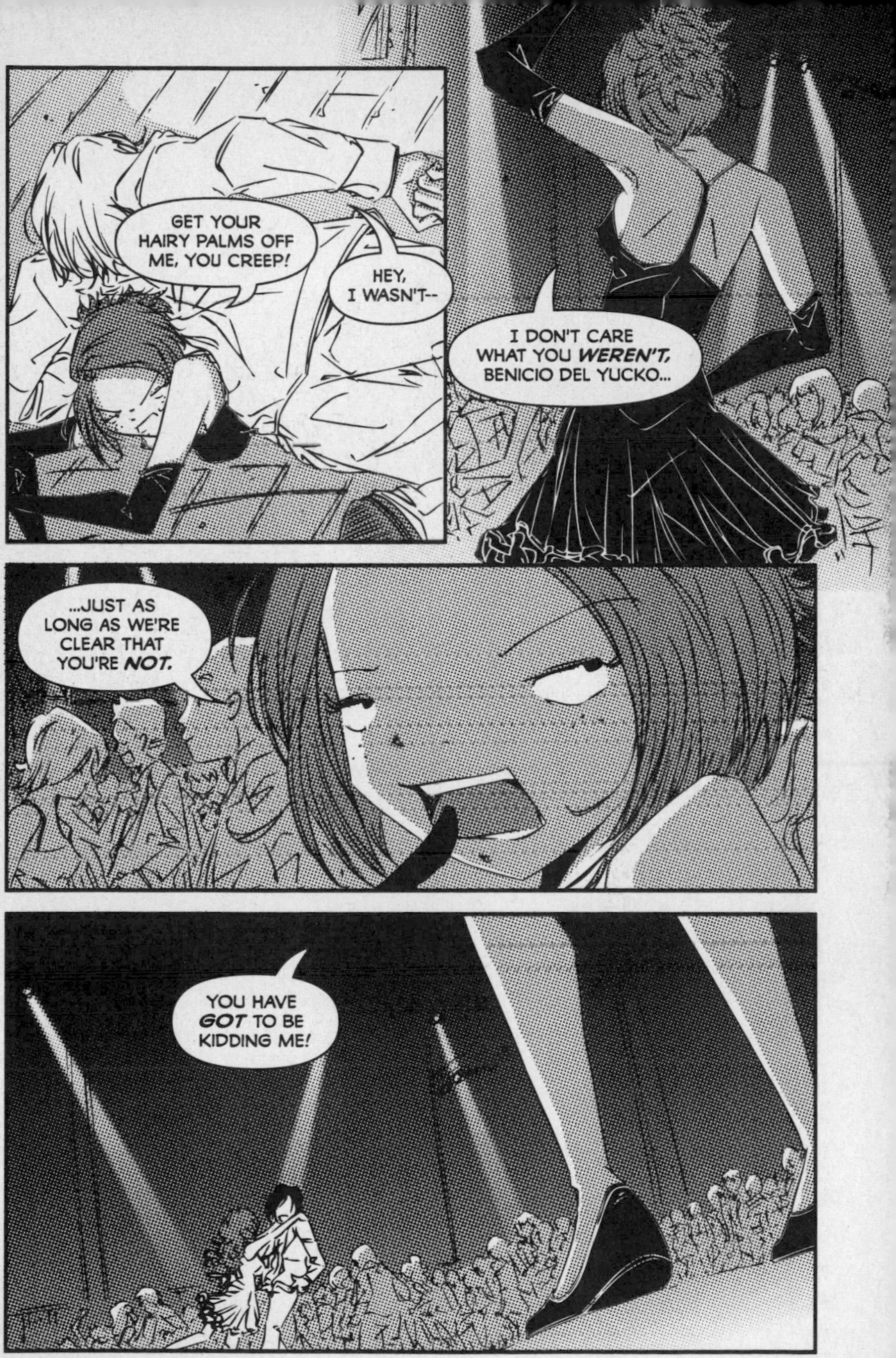
GET YOUR HAIRY PALMS OFF ME, YOU CREEP!
HEY, I WASN'T--
I DON'T CARE WHAT YOU *WEREN'T,* BENICIO DEL YUCKO...
...JUST AS LONG AS WE'RE CLEAR THAT YOU'RE *NOT.*
YOU HAVE *GOT* TO BE KIDDING ME!

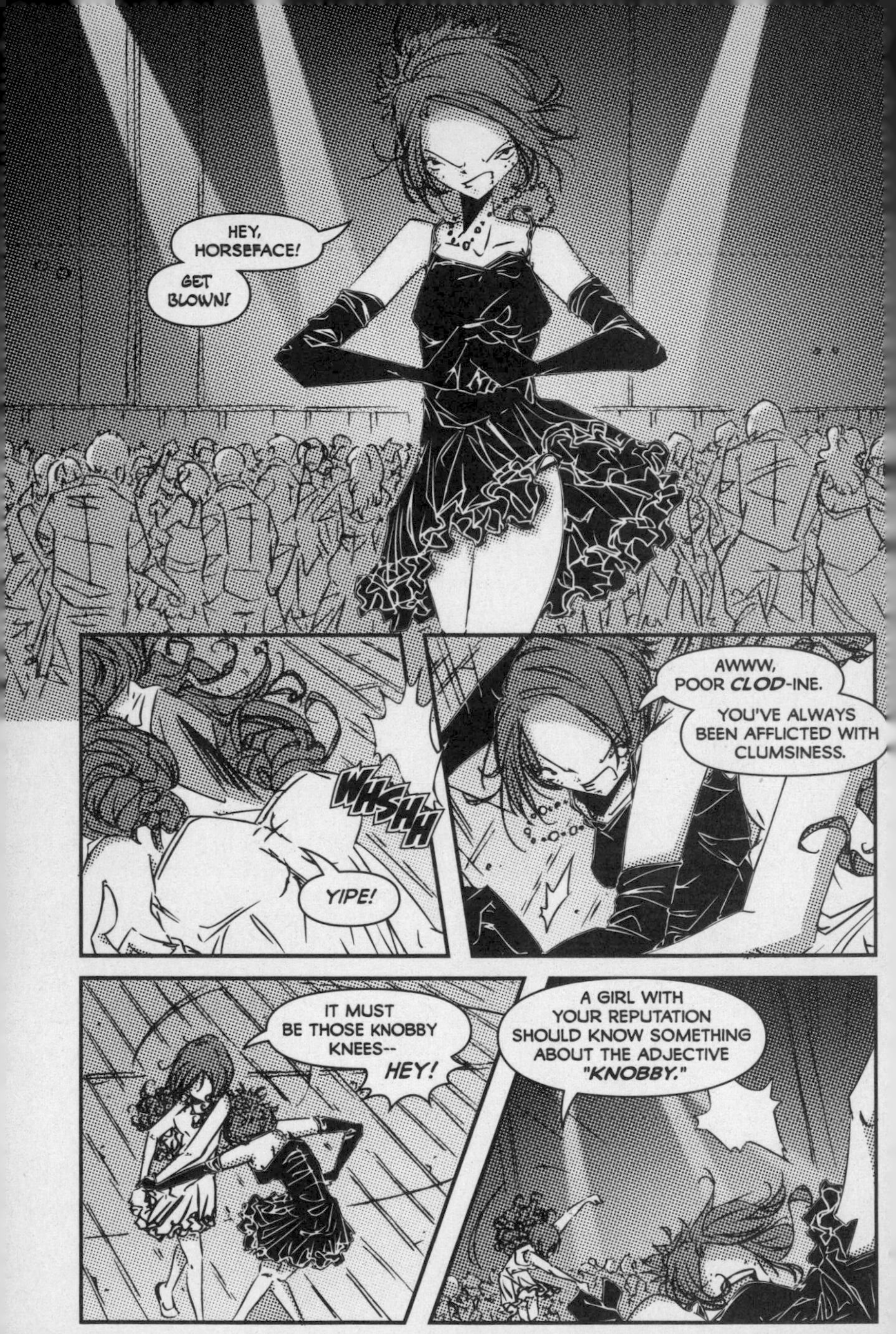
HEY, HORSEFACE!
GET BLOWN!
WHSHH
YIPE!
AWWW, POOR *CLOD*-INE.
YOU'VE ALWAYS BEEN AFFLICTED WITH CLUMSINESS.
IT MUST BE THOSE KNOBBY KNEES--
HEY!
A GIRL WITH YOUR REPUTATION SHOULD KNOW SOMETHING ABOUT THE ADJECTIVE *"KNOBBY."*

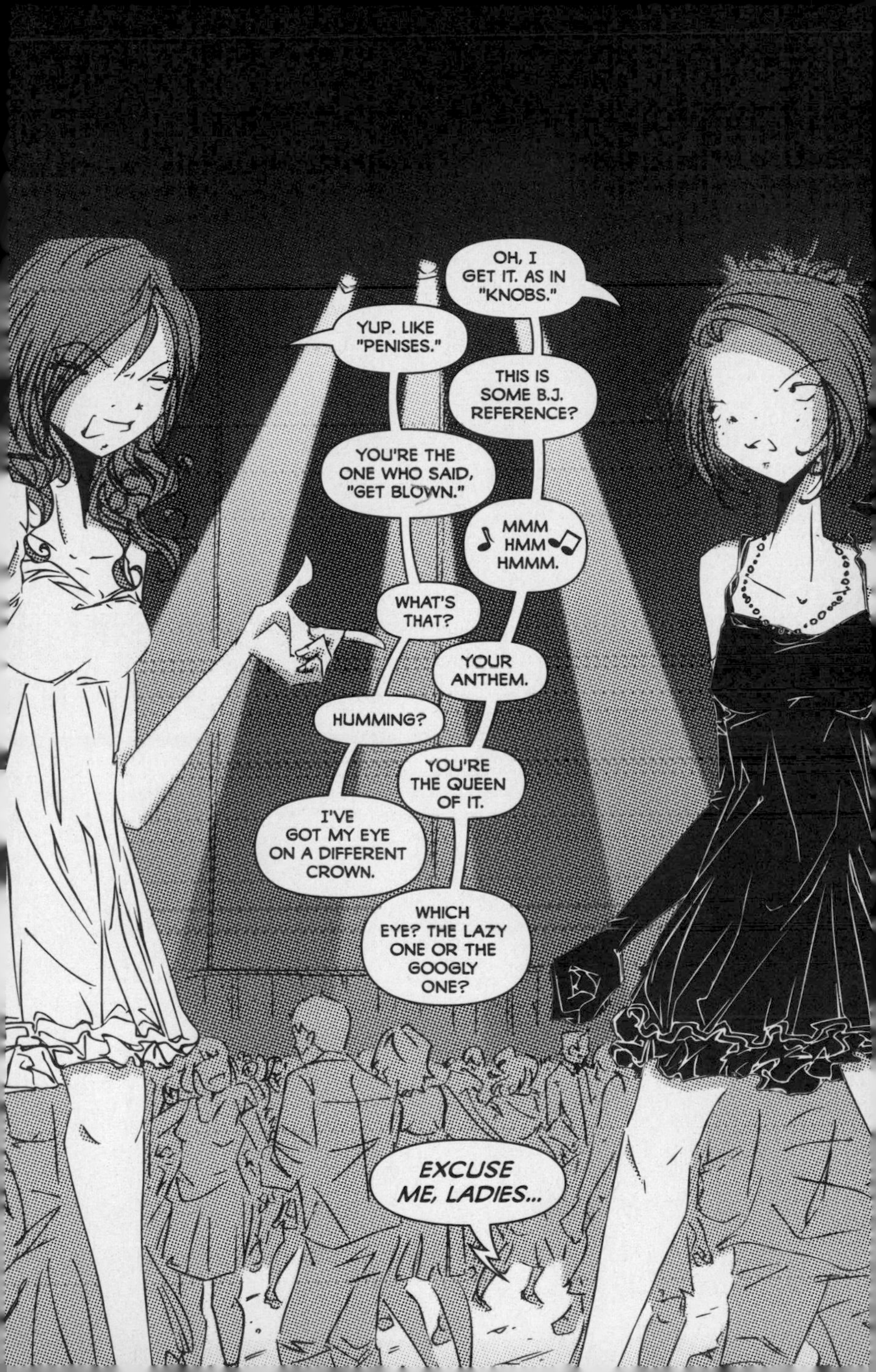
OH, I GET IT. AS IN "KNOBS."
YUP. LIKE "PENISES."
THIS IS SOME B.J. REFERENCE?
YOU'RE THE ONE WHO SAID, "GET BLOWN."
MMM HMM HMMM.
WHAT'S THAT?
YOUR ANTHEM.
HUMMING?
YOU'RE THE QUEEN OF IT.
I'VE GOT MY EYE ON A DIFFERENT CROWN.
WHICH EYE? THE LAZY ONE OR THE GOOGLY ONE?
EXCUSE ME, LADIES...

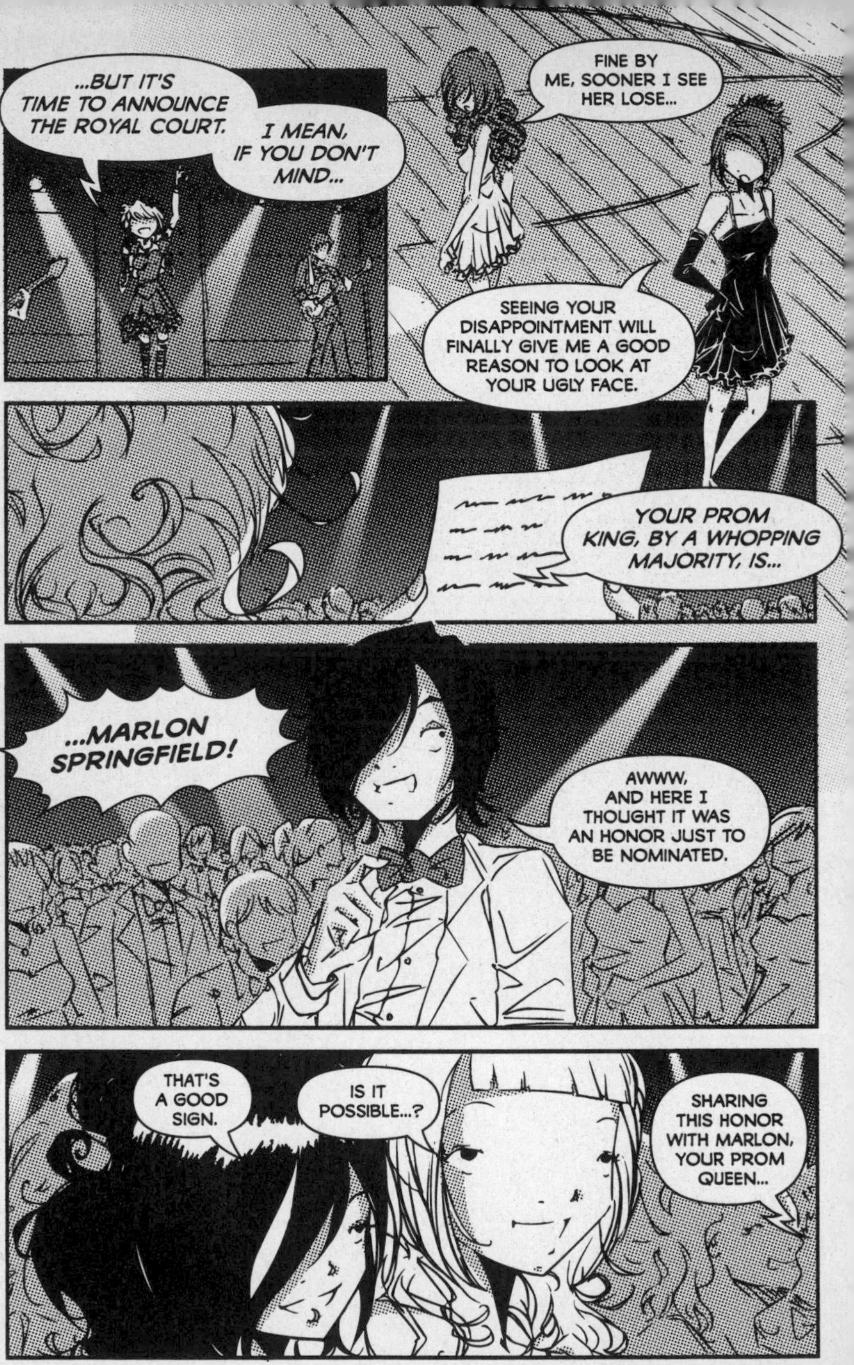
...BUT IT'S TIME TO ANNOUNCE THE ROYAL COURT.
I MEAN, IF YOU DON'T MIND...
FINE BY ME, SOONER I SEE HER LOSE...
SEEING YOUR DISAPPOINTMENT WILL FINALLY GIVE ME A GOOD REASON TO LOOK AT YOUR UGLY FACE.
YOUR PROM KING, BY A WHOPPING MAJORITY, IS...
...MARLON SPRINGFIELD!
AWWW, AND HERE I THOUGHT IT WAS AN HONOR JUST TO BE NOMINATED.
THAT'S A GOOD SIGN.
IS IT POSSIBLE...?
SHARING THIS HONOR WITH MARLON, YOUR PROM QUEEN...

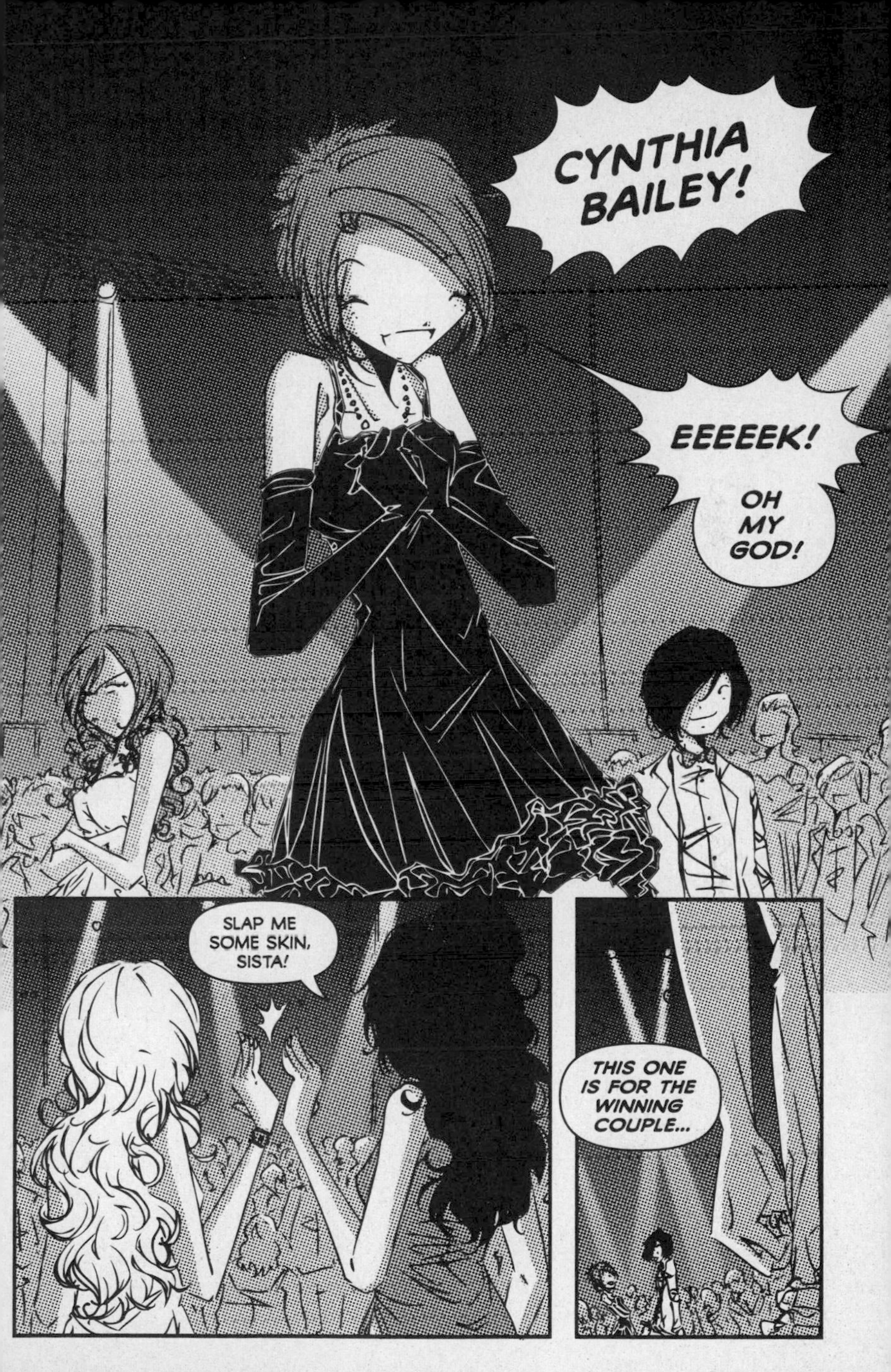
CYNTHIA BAILEY!
EEEEEK!
OH MY GOD!
SLAP ME SOME SKIN, SISTA!
THIS ONE IS FOR THE WINNING COUPLE...

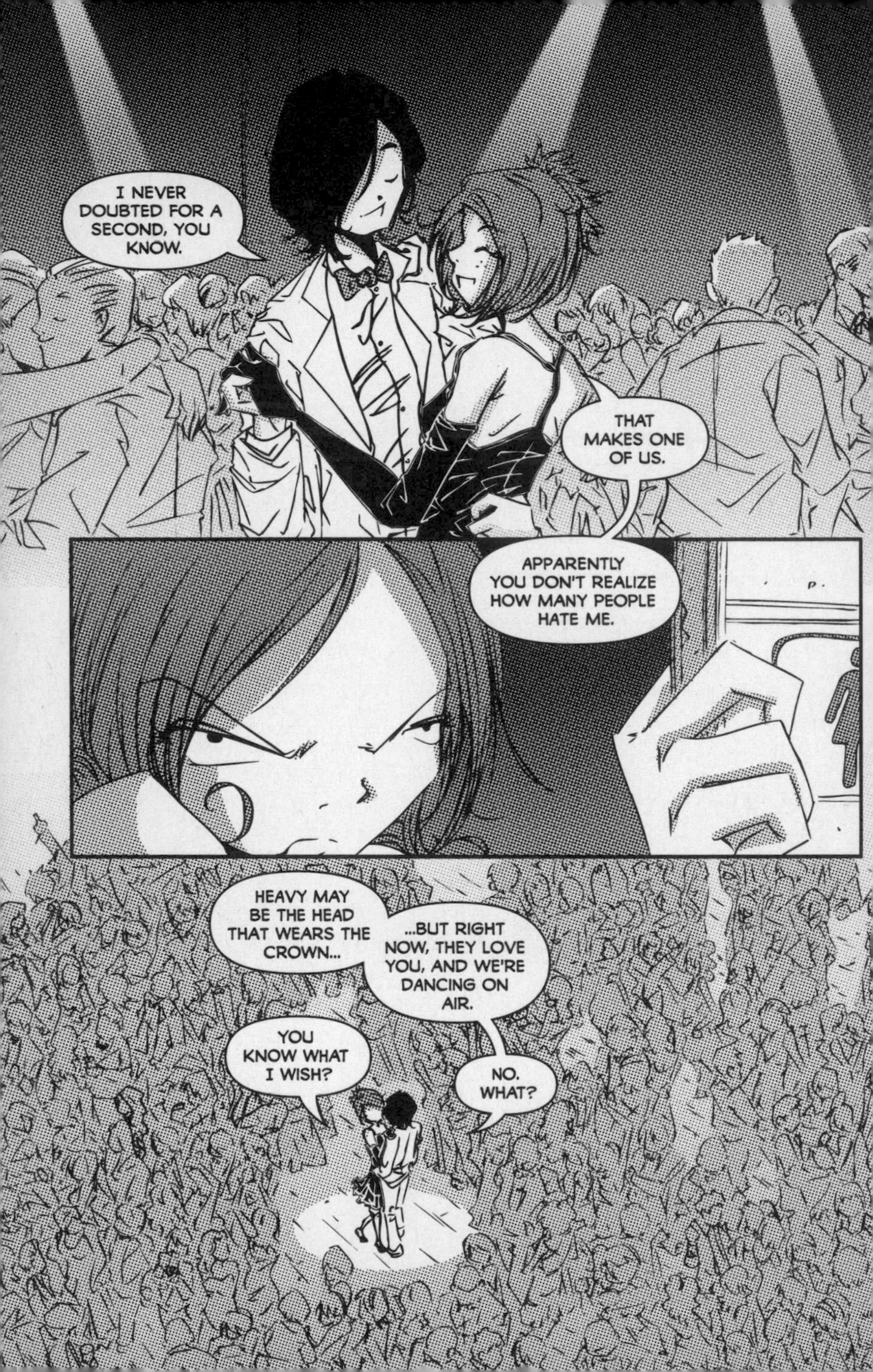
I NEVER DOUBTED FOR A SECOND, YOU KNOW.
THAT MAKES ONE OF US.
APPARENTLY YOU DON'T REALIZE HOW MANY PEOPLE HATE ME.
HEAVY MAY BE THE HEAD THAT WEARS THE CROWN...
...BUT RIGHT NOW, THEY LOVE YOU, AND WE'RE DANCING ON AIR.
YOU KNOW WHAT I WISH?
NO. WHAT?

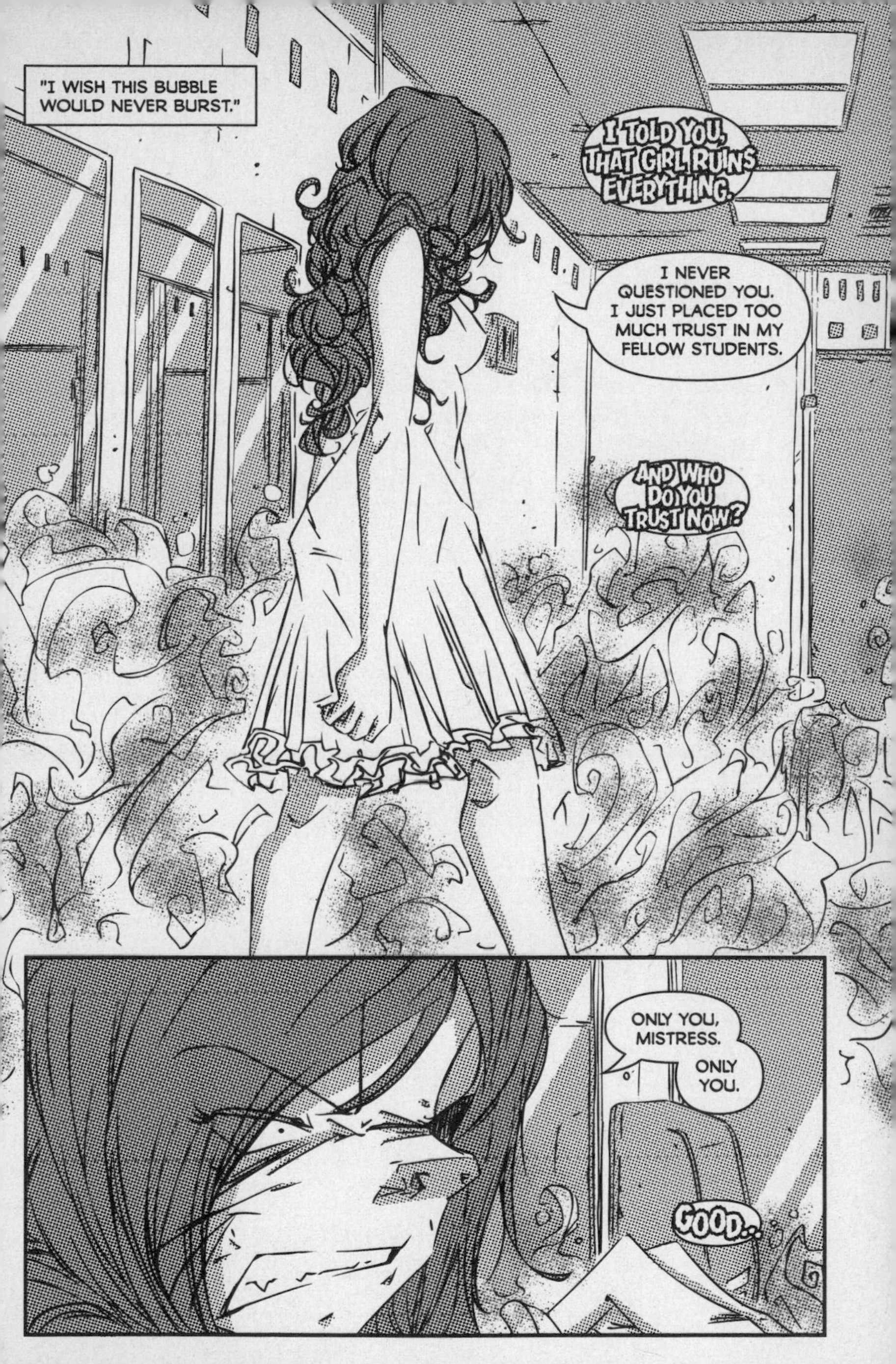
"I WISH THIS BUBBLE WOULD NEVER BURST."
I TOLD YOU, THAT GIRL RUINS EVERYTHING.
I NEVER QUESTIONED YOU. I JUST PLACED TOO MUCH TRUST IN MY FELLOW STUDENTS.
AND WHO DO YOU TRUST NOW?
ONLY YOU, MISTRESS.
ONLY YOU.
GOOD...

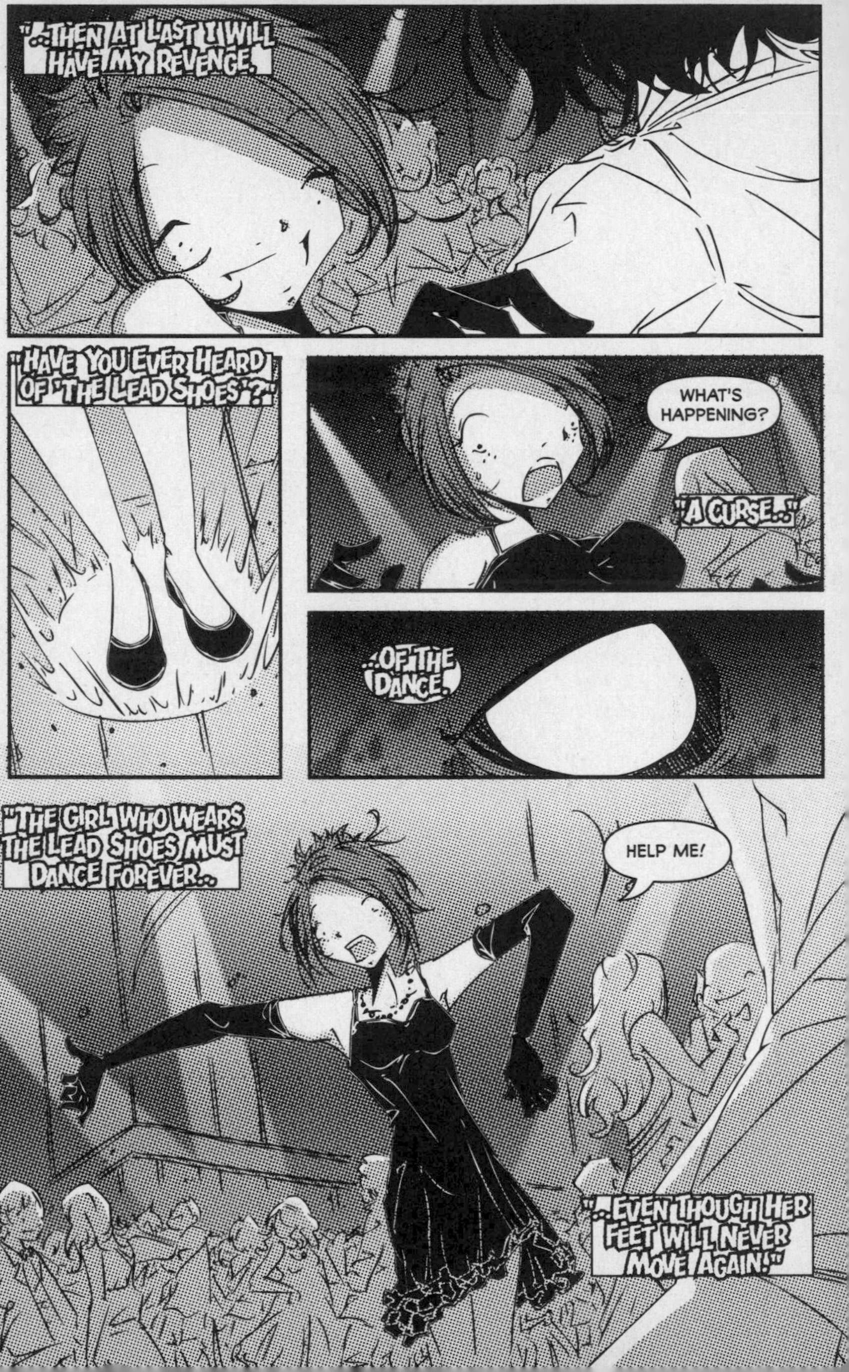
"...THEN AT LAST I WILL HAVE MY REVENGE.
"HAVE YOU EVER HEARD OF 'THE LEAD SHOES'?"
WHAT'S HAPPENING?
"A CURSE...
...OF THE DANCE.
"THE GIRL WHO WEARS THE LEAD SHOES MUST DANCE FOREVER...
HELP ME!
"...EVEN THOUGH HER FEET WILL NEVER MOVE AGAIN."

Chapter 4
"Oh, What's A Matter, Kim?"

4

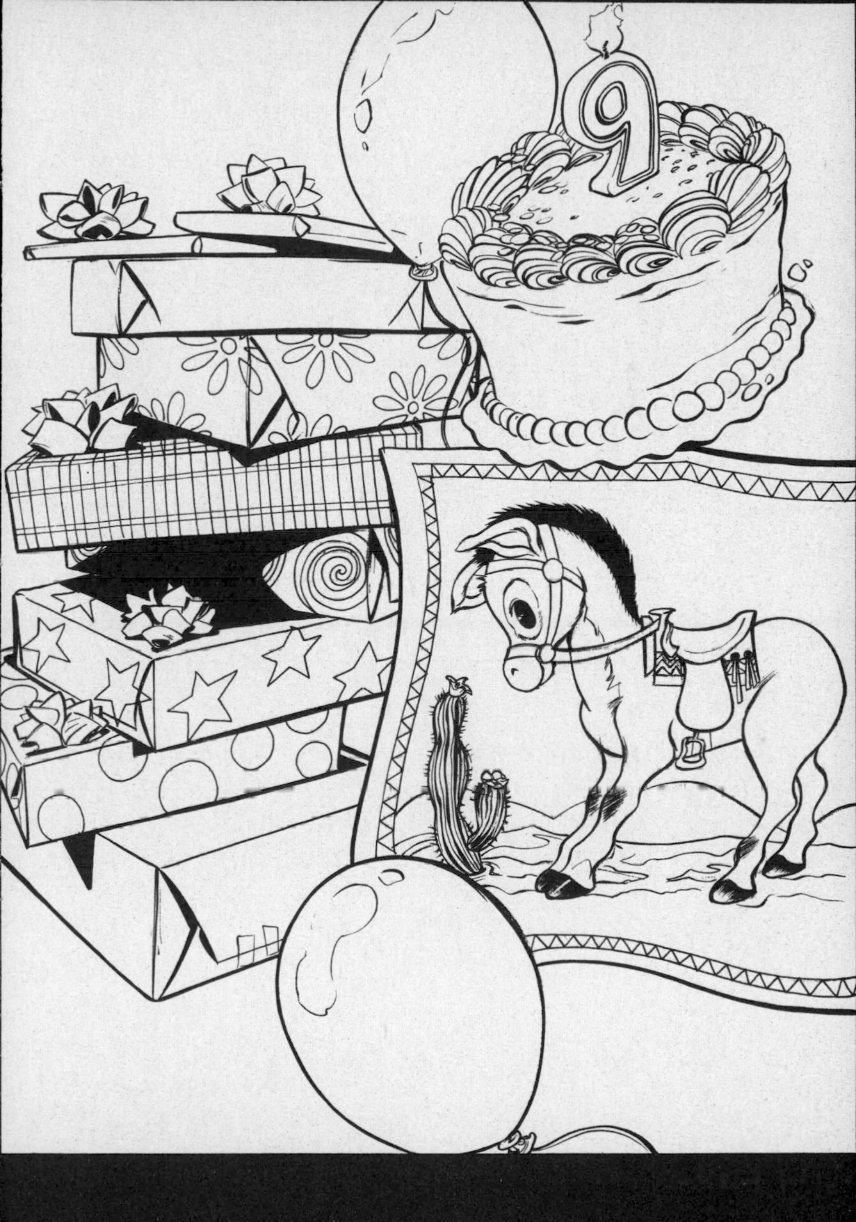
9

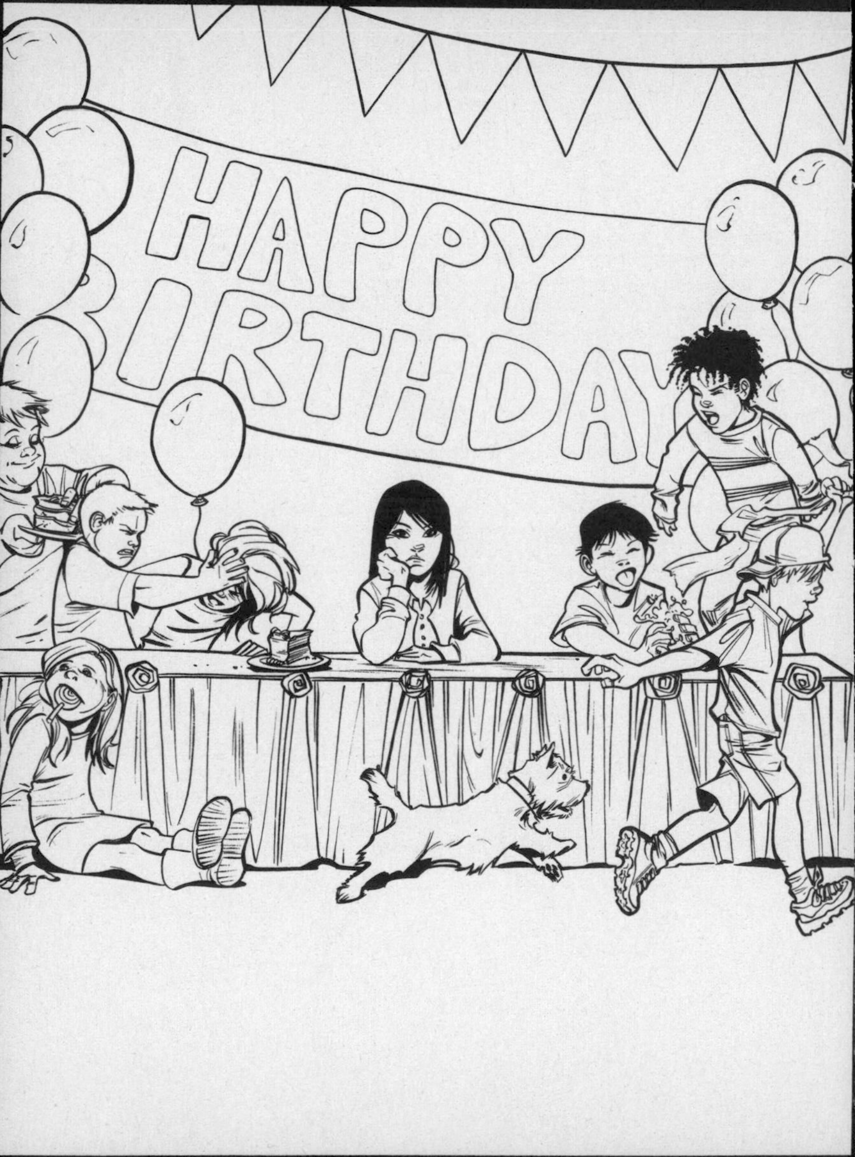
HAPPY
IRTHDAY

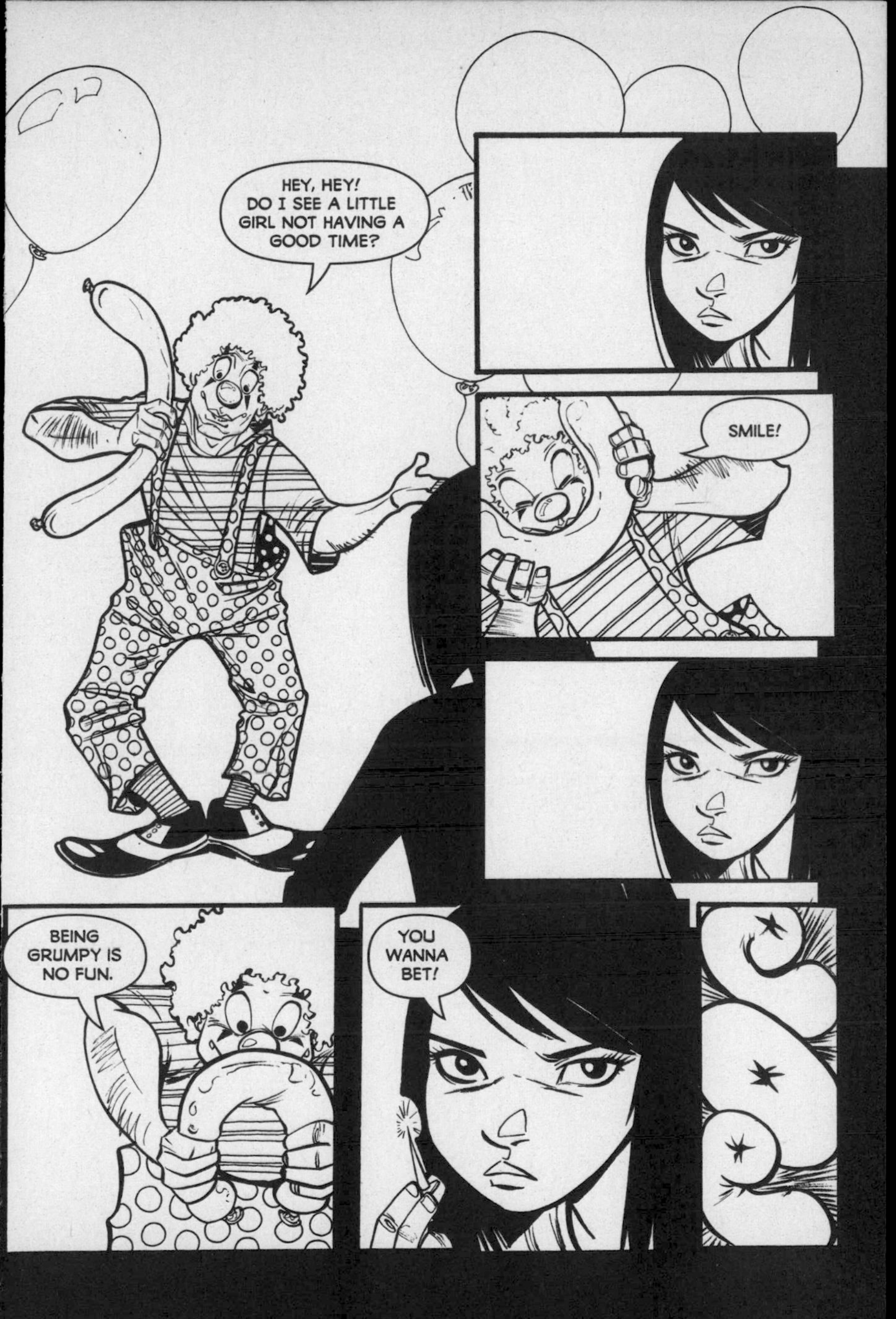
HEY, HEY! DO I SEE A LITTLE GIRL NOT HAVING A GOOD TIME?
SMILE!
BEING GRUMPY IS NO FUN.
YOU WANNA BET!

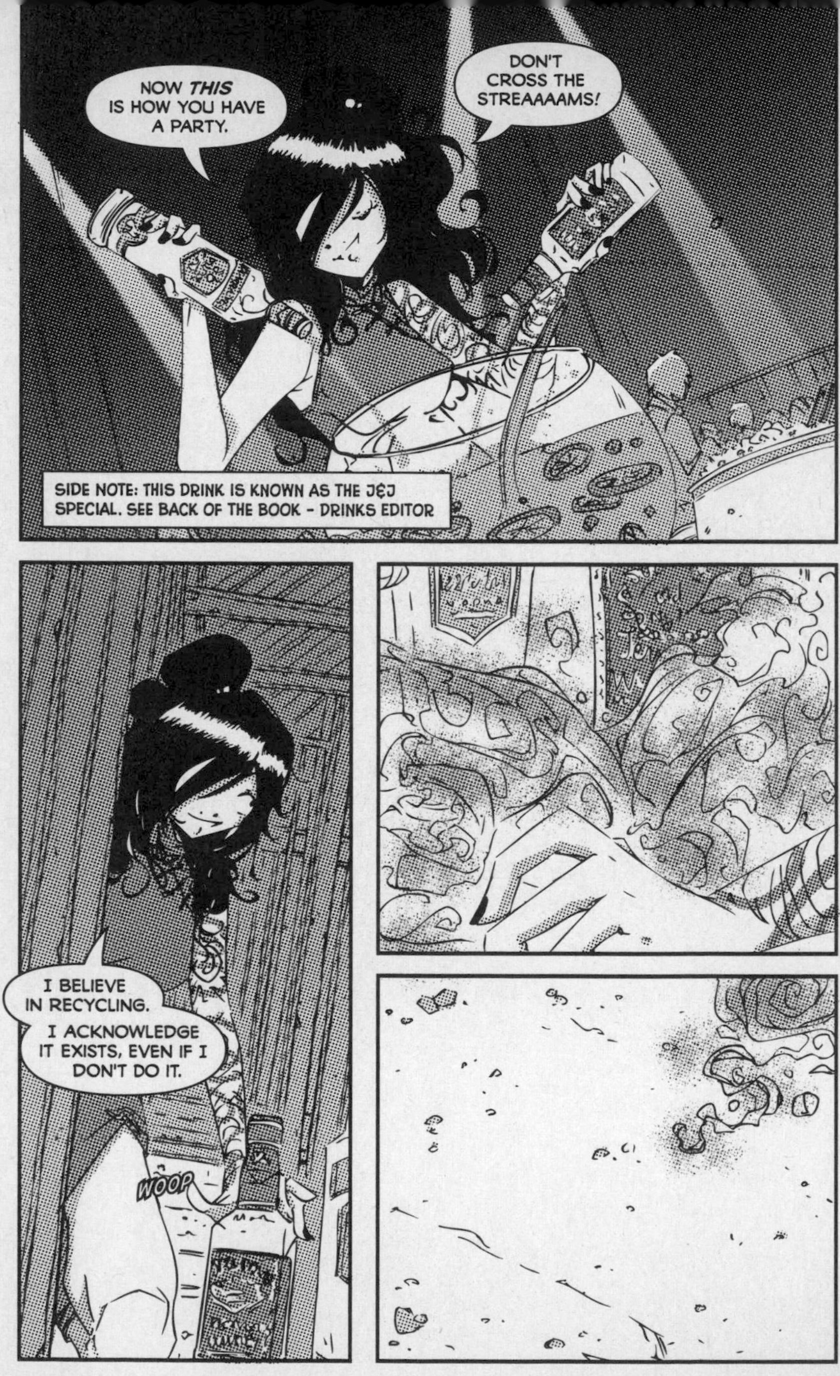
NOW *THIS* IS HOW YOU HAVE A PARTY.
DON'T CROSS THE STREAAAAMS!
SIDE NOTE: THIS DRINK IS KNOWN AS THE J&J SPECIAL. SEE BACK OF THE BOOK - DRINKS EDITOR
I BELIEVE IN RECYCLING.
I ACKNOWLEDGE IT EXISTS, EVEN IF I DON'T DO IT.
WOOP

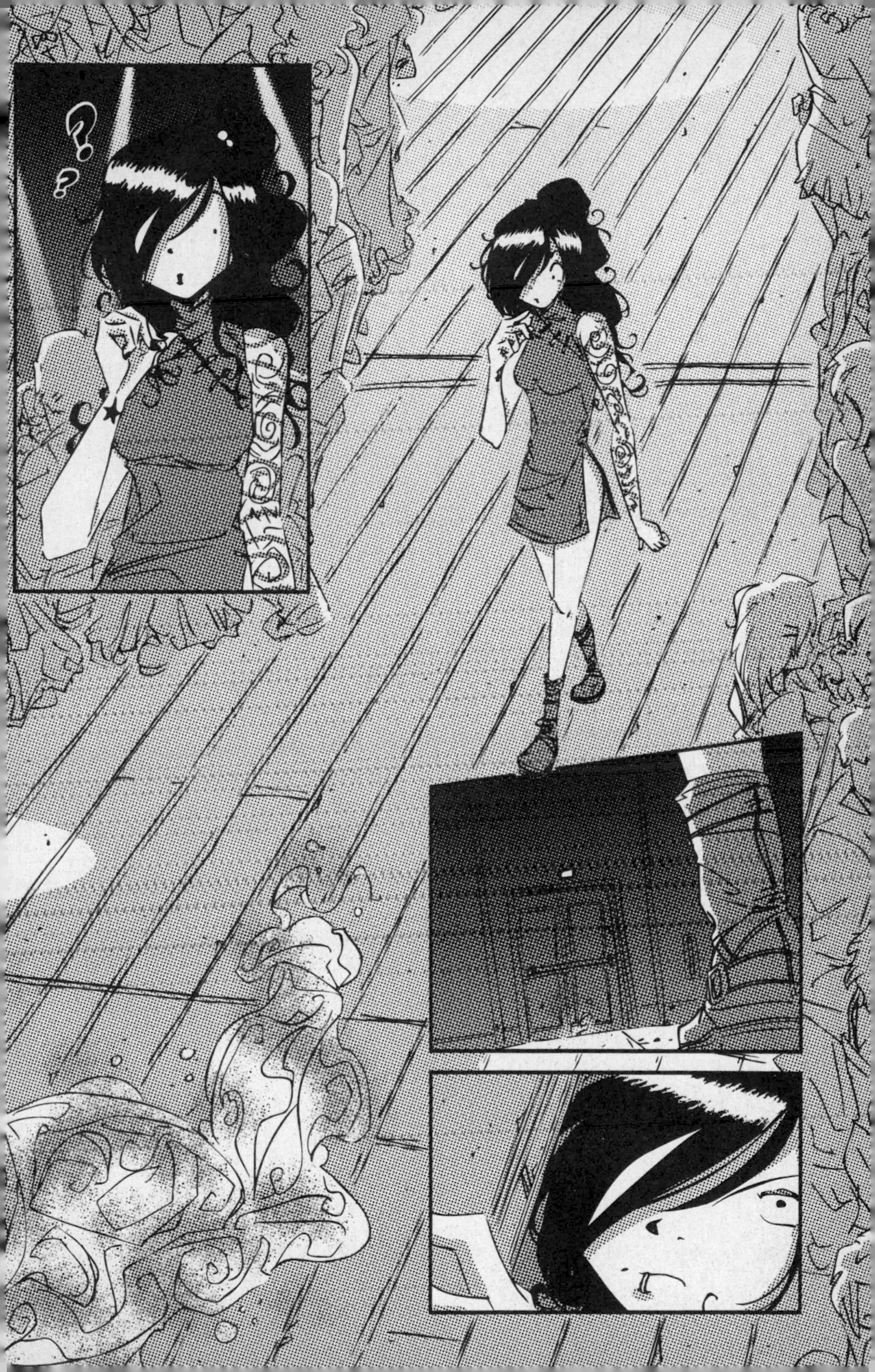
?
?

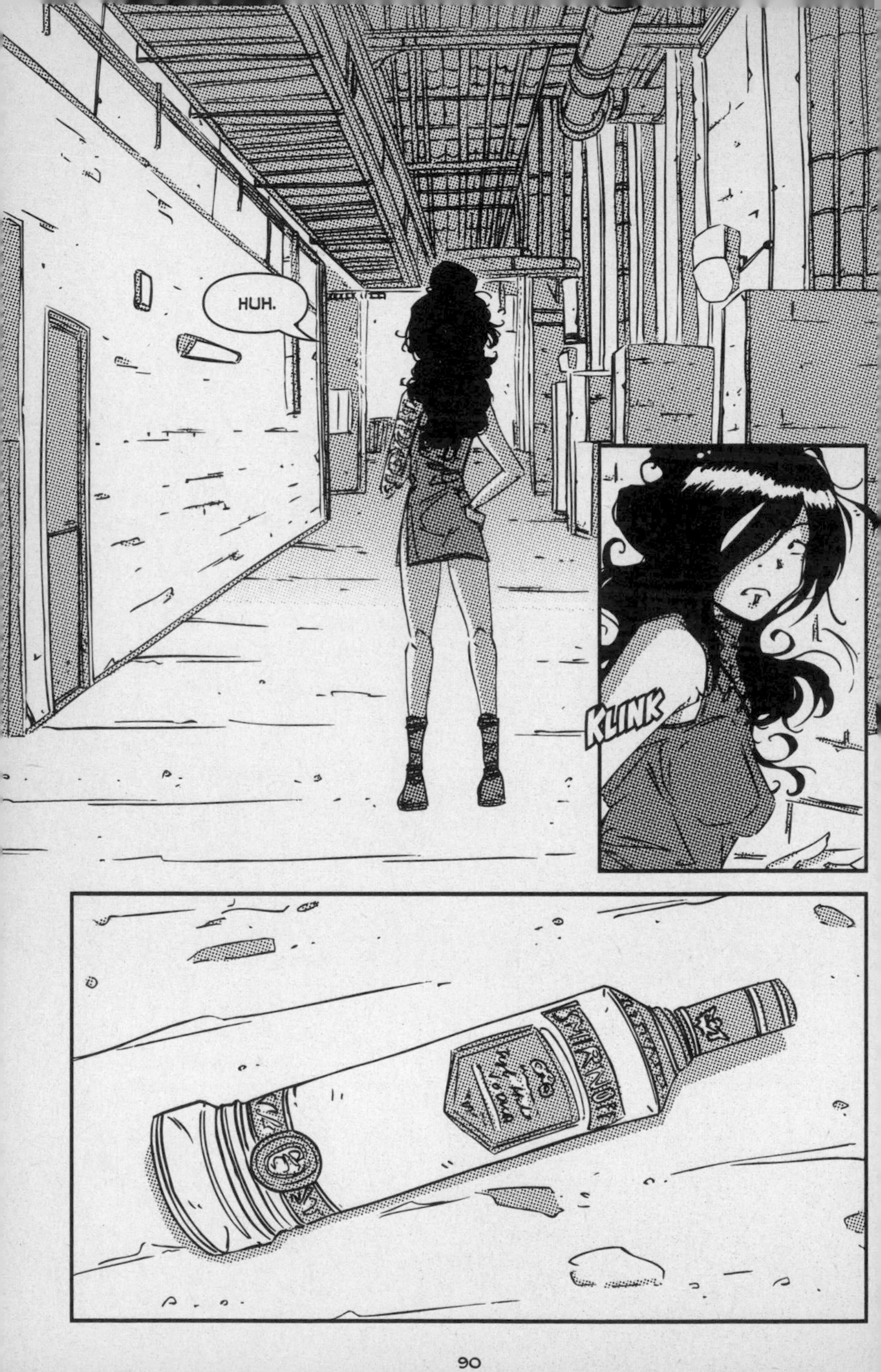
HUH.
KLINK
SMIRNOFF

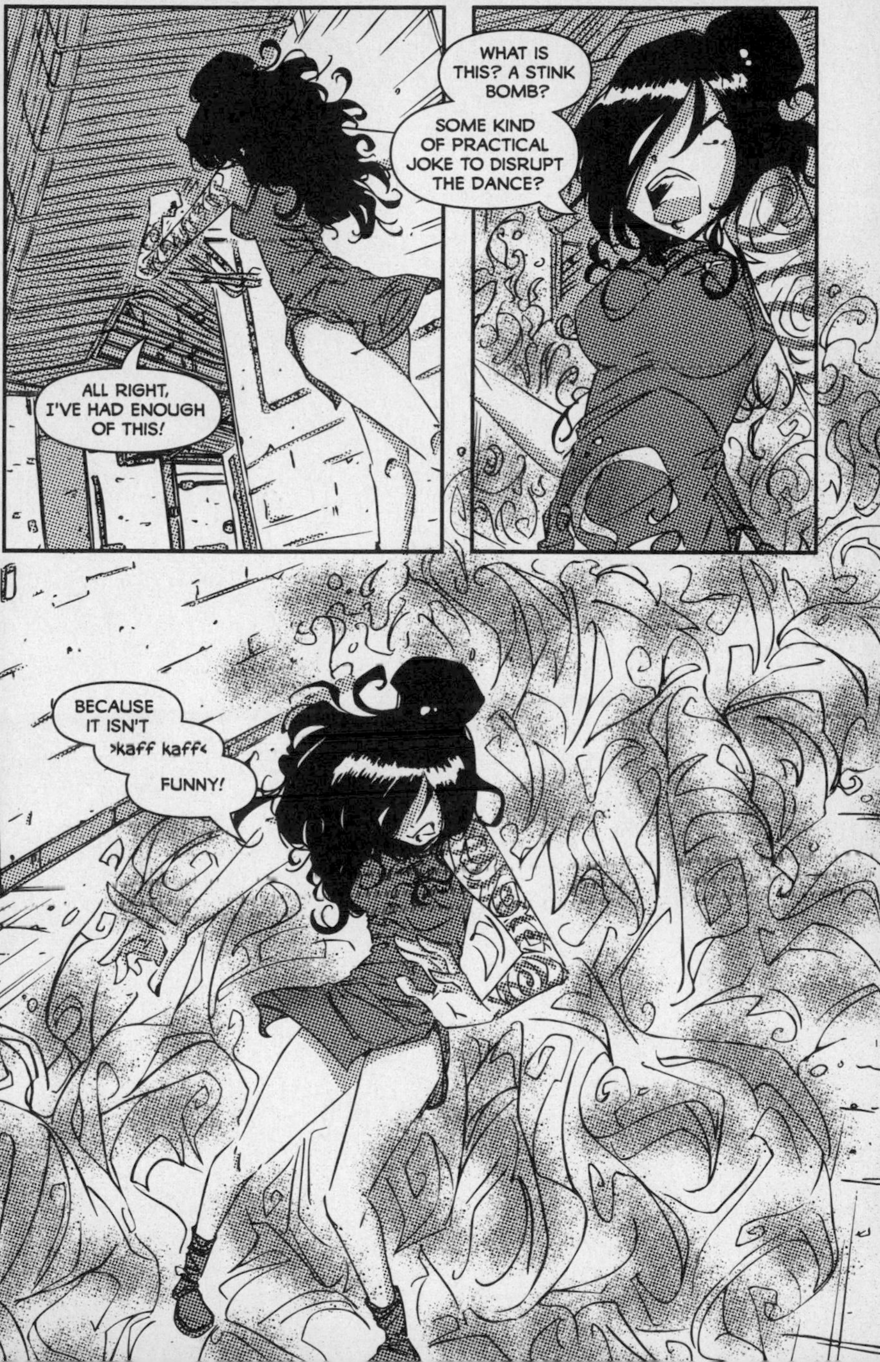
ALL RIGHT, I'VE HAD ENOUGH OF THIS!
WHAT IS THIS? A STINK BOMB?
SOME KIND OF PRACTICAL JOKE TO DISRUPT THE DANCE?
BECAUSE IT ISN'T
>kaff kaff<
FUNNY!

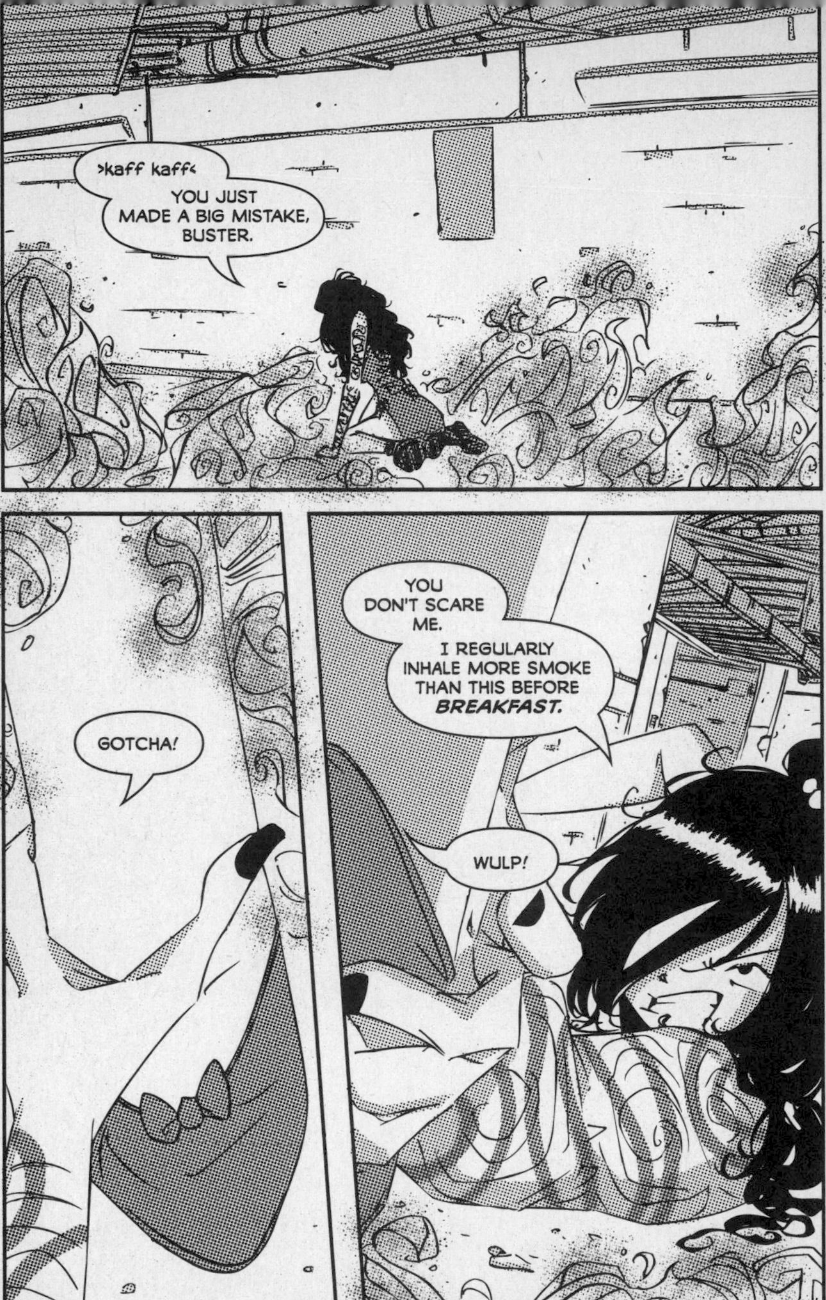
>kaff kaff<
YOU JUST MADE A BIG MISTAKE, BUSTER.
YOU DON'T SCARE ME.
I REGULARLY INHALE MORE SMOKE THAN THIS BEFORE *BREAKFAST.*
GOTCHA!
WULP!

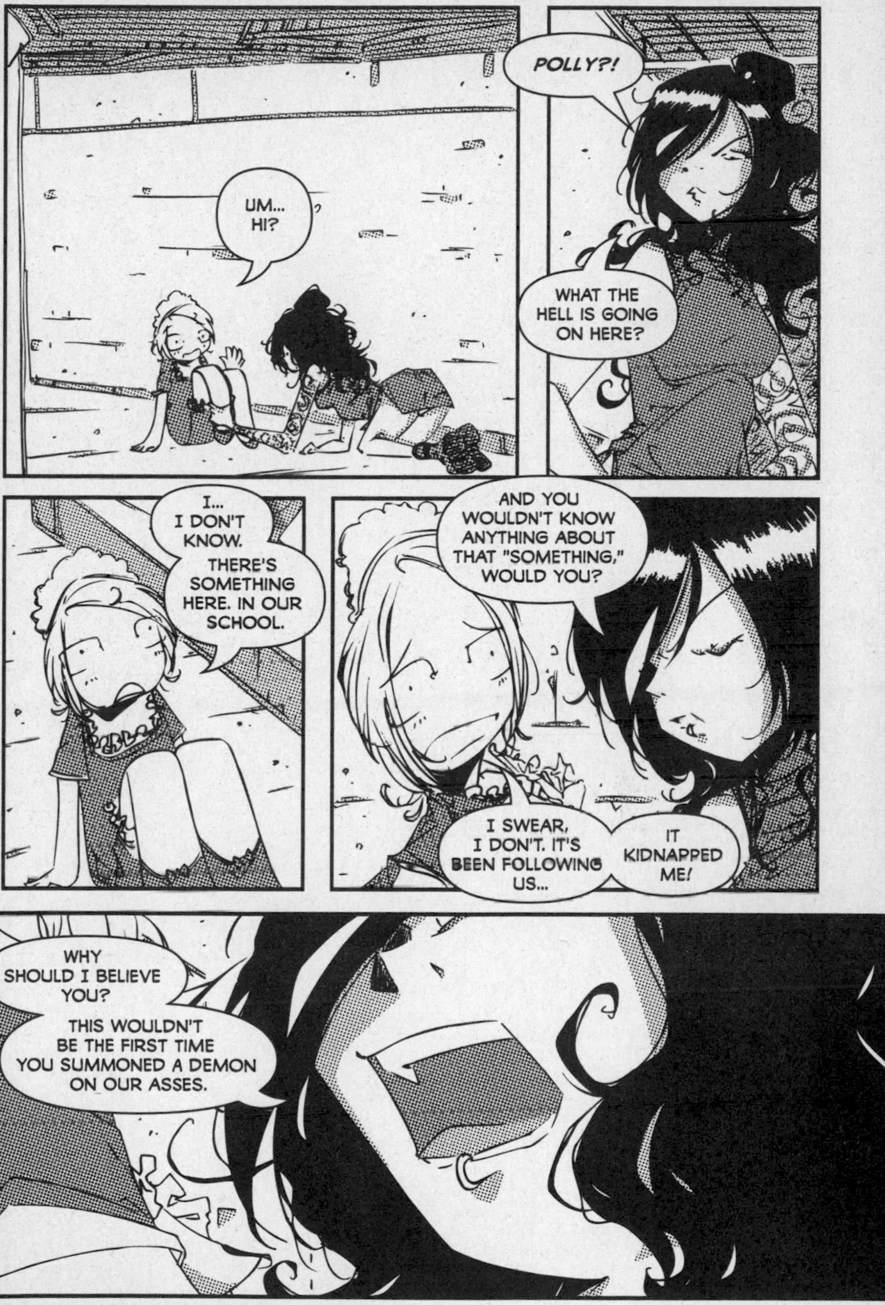
UM... HI?
POLLY?!
WHAT THE HELL IS GOING ON HERE?
I... I DON'T KNOW.
THERE'S SOMETHING HERE. IN OUR SCHOOL.
AND YOU WOULDN'T KNOW ANYTHING ABOUT THAT "SOMETHING," WOULD YOU?
I SWEAR, I DON'T. IT'S BEEN FOLLOWING US...
IT KIDNAPPED ME!
WHY SHOULD I BELIEVE YOU?
THIS WOULDN'T BE THE FIRST TIME YOU SUMMONED A DEMON ON OUR ASSES.

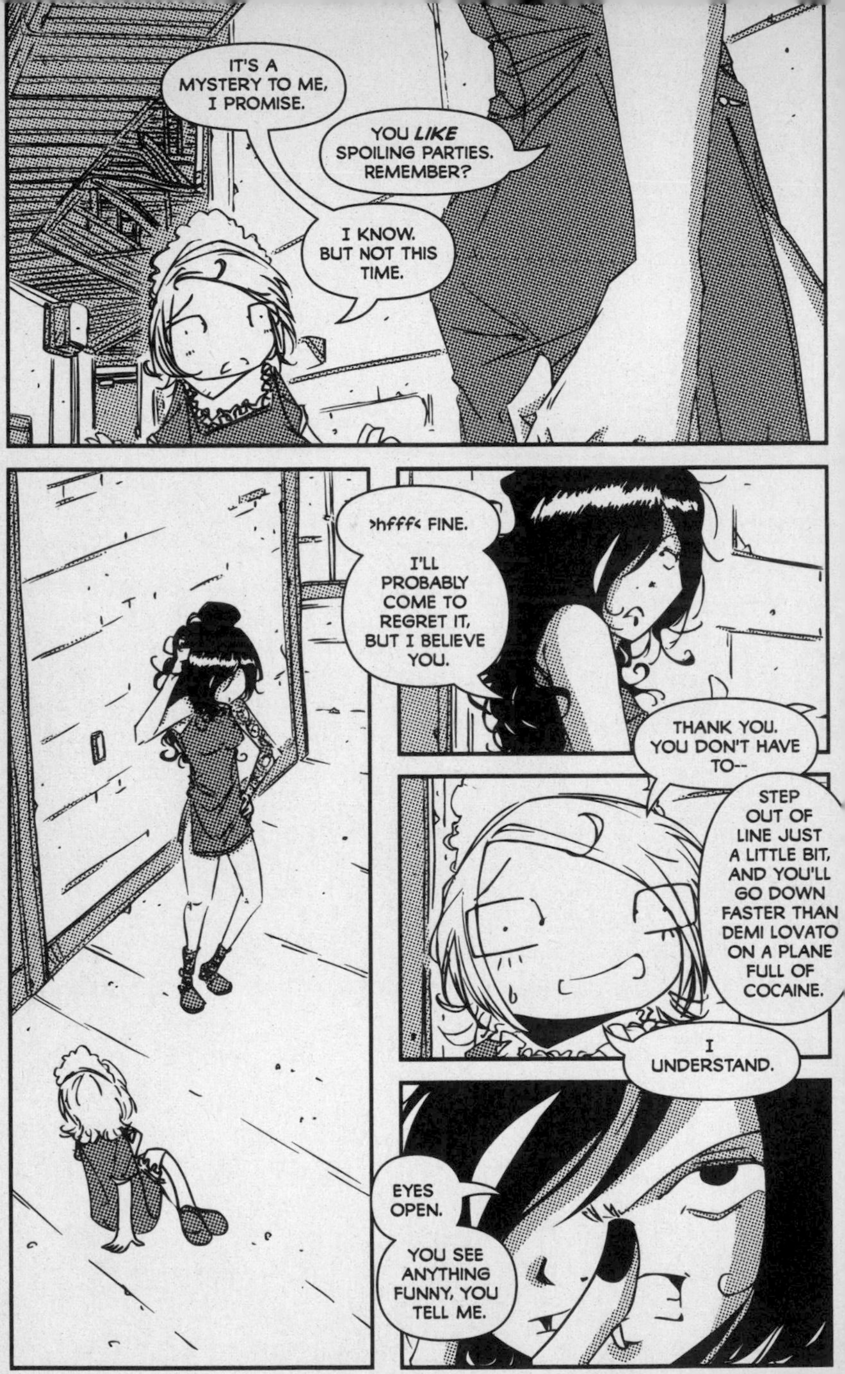
IT'S A MYSTERY TO ME, I PROMISE.
YOU *LIKE* SPOILING PARTIES. REMEMBER?
I KNOW. BUT NOT THIS TIME.
>hfff< FINE.
I'LL PROBABLY COME TO REGRET IT, BUT I BELIEVE YOU.
THANK YOU. YOU DON'T HAVE TO--
STEP OUT OF LINE JUST A LITTLE BIT, AND YOU'LL GO DOWN FASTER THAN DEMI LOVATO ON A PLANE FULL OF COCAINE.
I UNDERSTAND.
EYES OPEN.
YOU SEE ANYTHING FUNNY, YOU TELL ME.

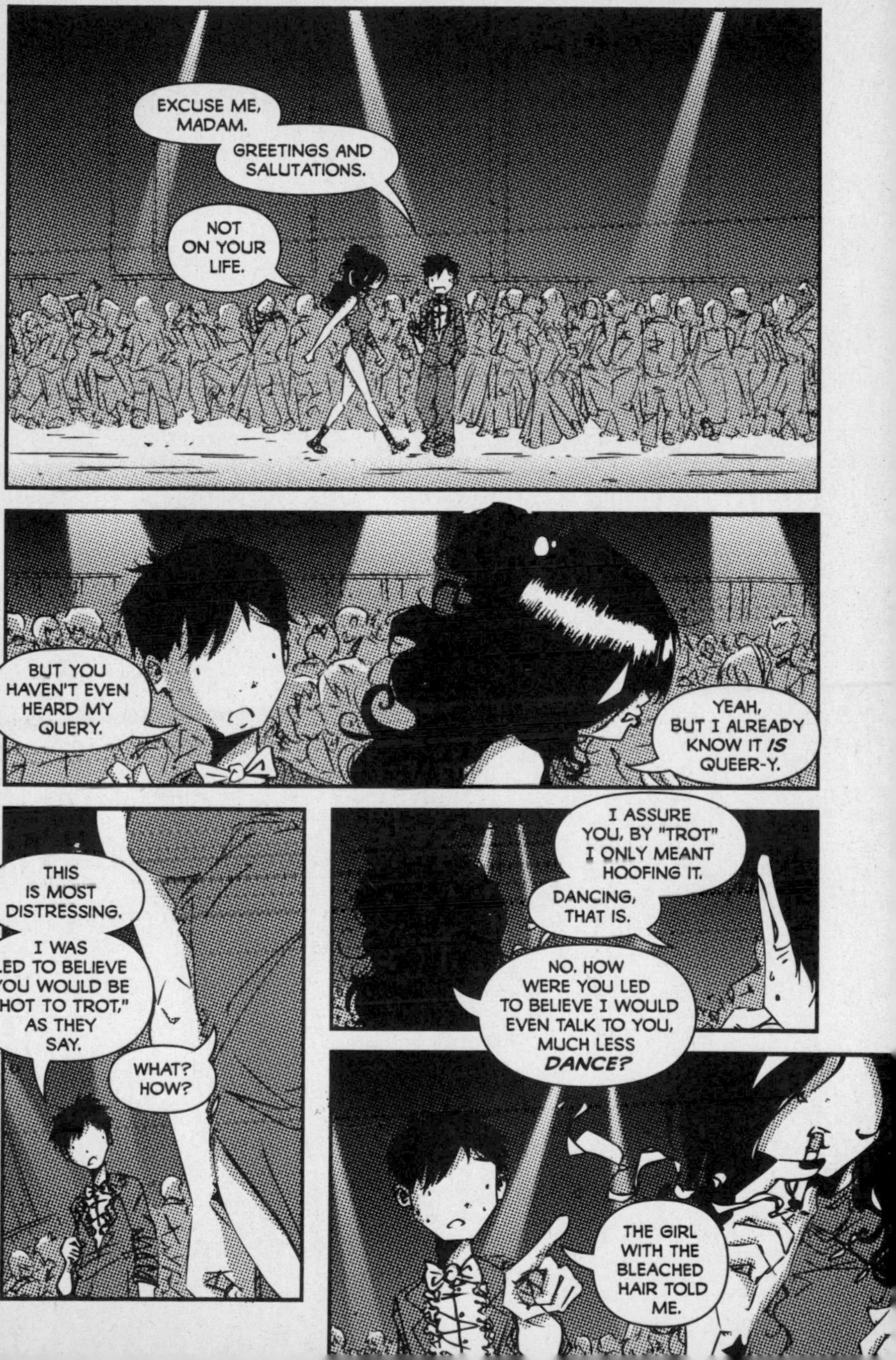
EXCUSE ME, MADAM.
GREETINGS AND SALUTATIONS.
NOT ON YOUR LIFE.
BUT YOU HAVEN'T EVEN HEARD MY QUERY.
YEAH, BUT I ALREADY KNOW IT *IS* QUEER-Y.
THIS IS MOST DISTRESSING.
I WAS LED TO BELIEVE YOU WOULD BE "HOT TO TROT," AS THEY SAY.
WHAT? HOW?
I ASSURE YOU, BY "TROT" I ONLY MEANT HOOFING IT.
DANCING, THAT IS.
NO. HOW WERE YOU LED TO BELIEVE I WOULD EVEN TALK TO YOU, MUCH LESS *DANCE?*
THE GIRL WITH THE BLEACHED HAIR TOLD ME.

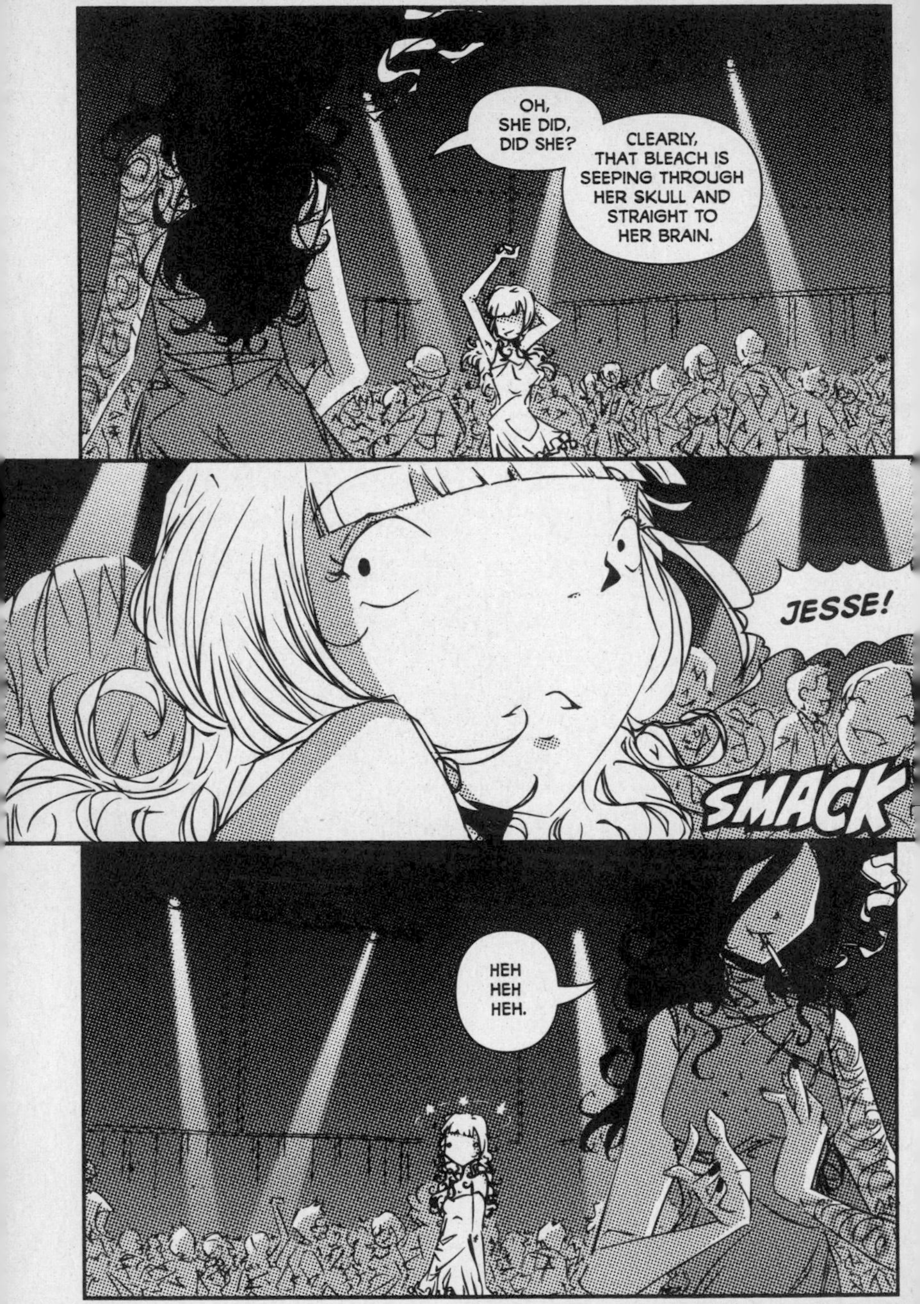
OH, SHE DID, DID SHE?
CLEARLY, THAT BLEACH IS SEEPING THROUGH HER SKULL AND STRAIGHT TO HER BRAIN.
JESSE!
SMACK
HEH HEH HEH.

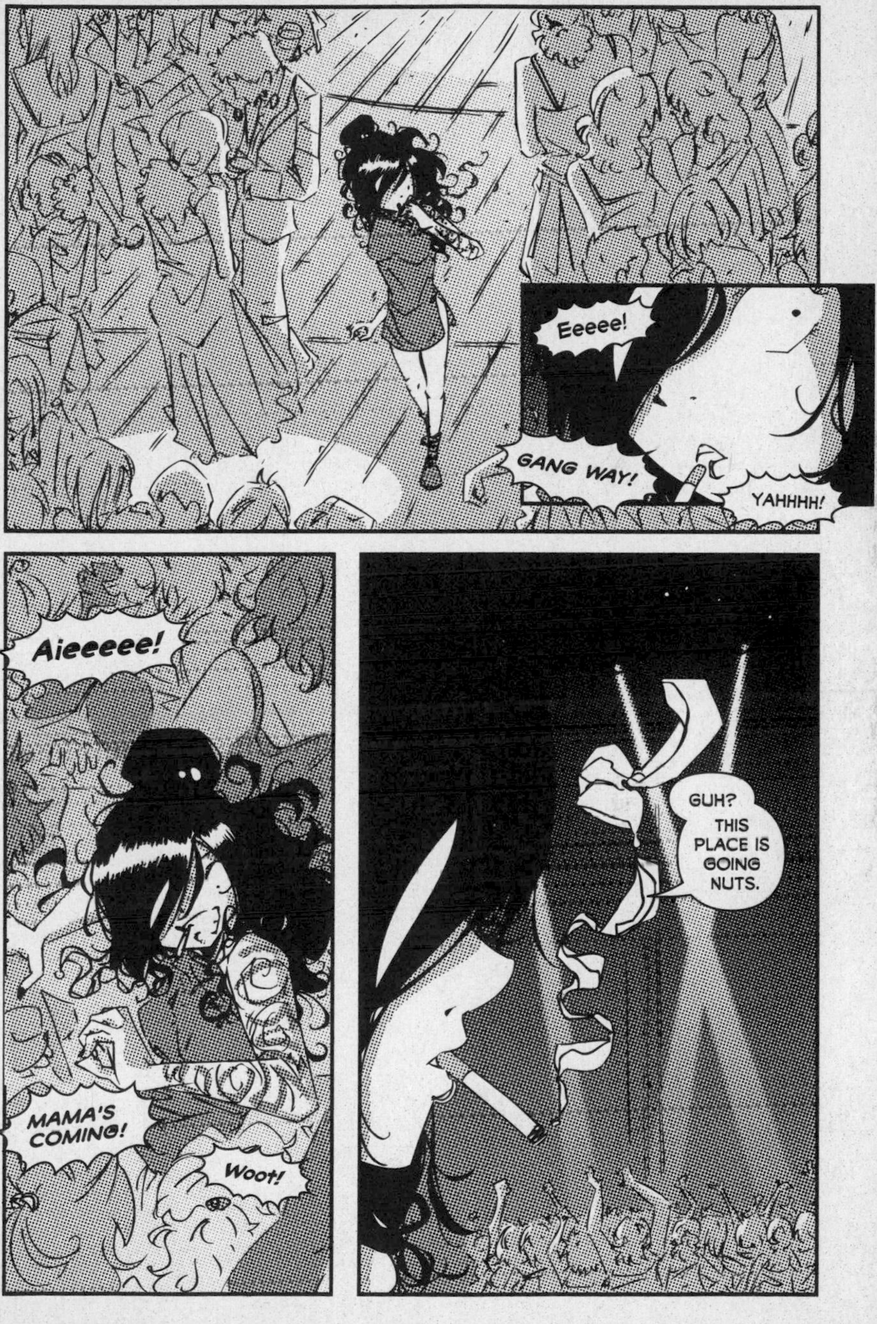

Eeeee!
GANG WAY!
YAHHHH!
Aieeeee!
MAMA'S COMING!
Woot!
GUH? THIS PLACE IS GOING NUTS.

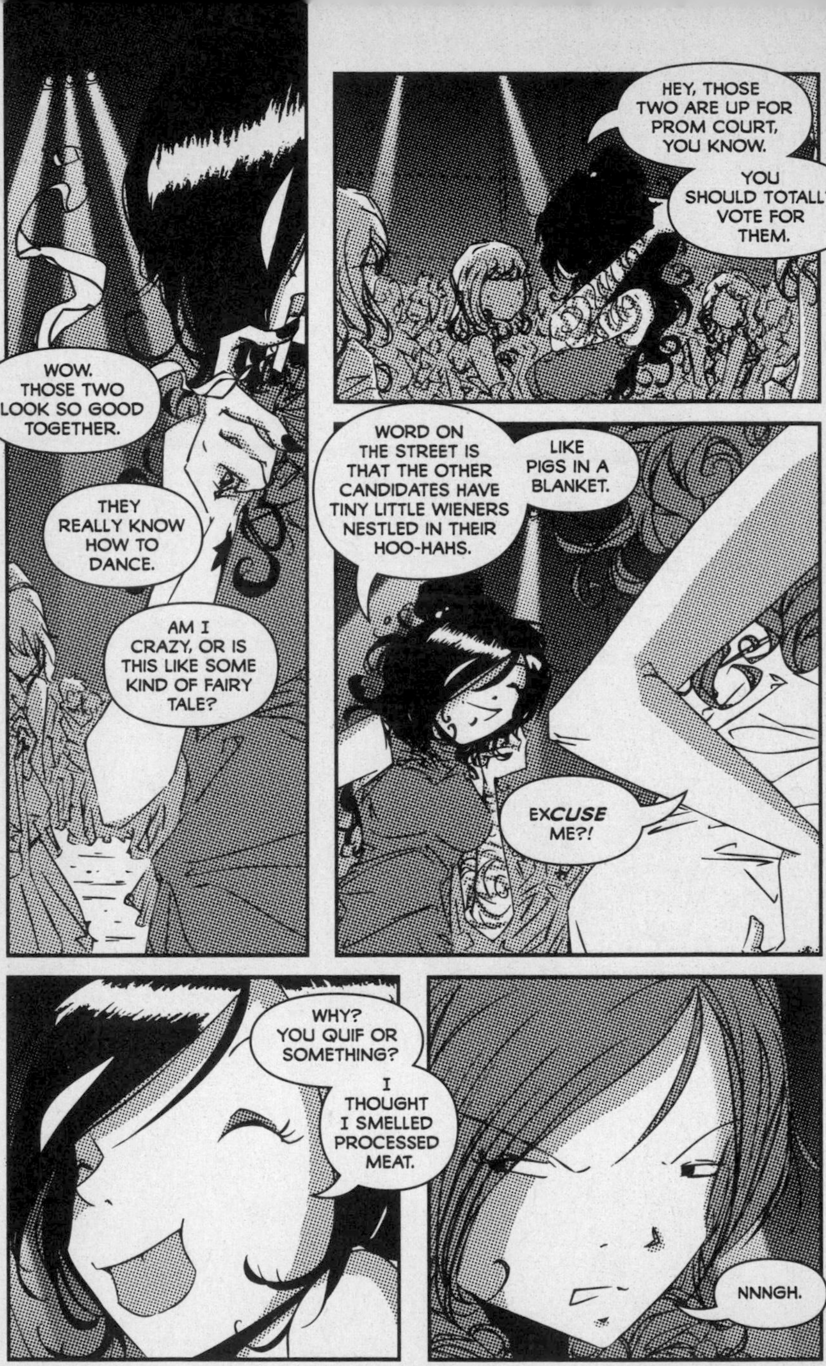

WOW. THOSE TWO LOOK SO GOOD TOGETHER.
THEY REALLY KNOW HOW TO DANCE.
AM I CRAZY, OR IS THIS LIKE SOME KIND OF FAIRY TALE?
HEY, THOSE TWO ARE UP FOR PROM COURT, YOU KNOW.
YOU SHOULD TOTALLY VOTE FOR THEM.
WORD ON THE STREET IS THAT THE OTHER CANDIDATES HAVE TINY LITTLE WIENERS NESTLED IN THEIR HOO-HAHS.
LIKE PIGS IN A BLANKET.
EX*CUSE* ME?!
WHY? YOU QUIF OR SOMETHING?
I THOUGHT I SMELLED PROCESSED MEAT.
NNNGH.

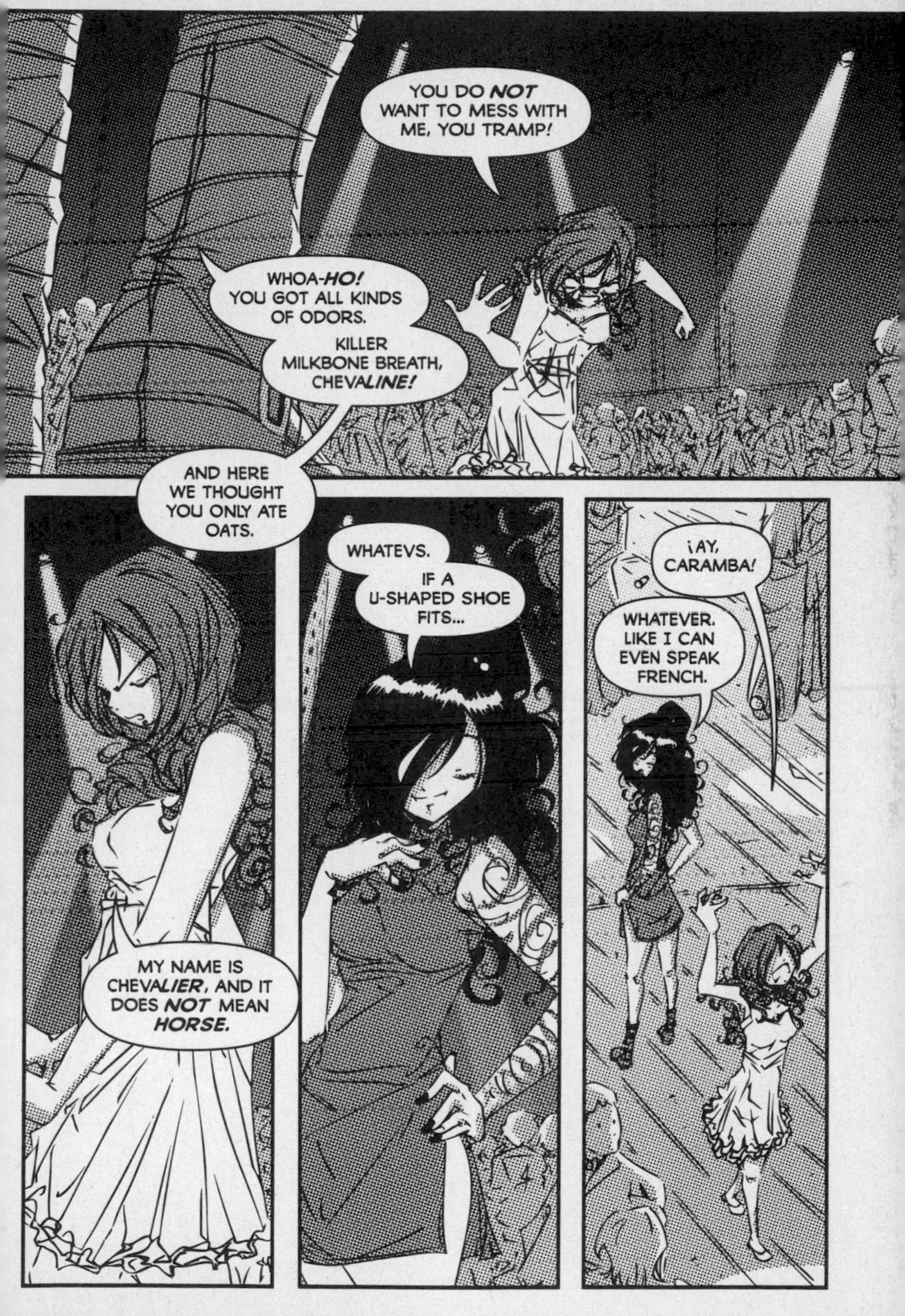
YOU DO NOT WANT TO MESS WITH ME, YOU TRAMP!
WHOA-HO! YOU GOT ALL KINDS OF ODORS.
KILLER MILKBONE BREATH, CHEVALINE!
AND HERE WE THOUGHT YOU ONLY ATE OATS.
MY NAME IS CHEVALIER, AND IT DOES NOT MEAN HORSE.
WHATEVS.
IF A U-SHAPED SHOE FITS...
¡AY, CARAMBA!
WHATEVER. LIKE I CAN EVEN SPEAK FRENCH.

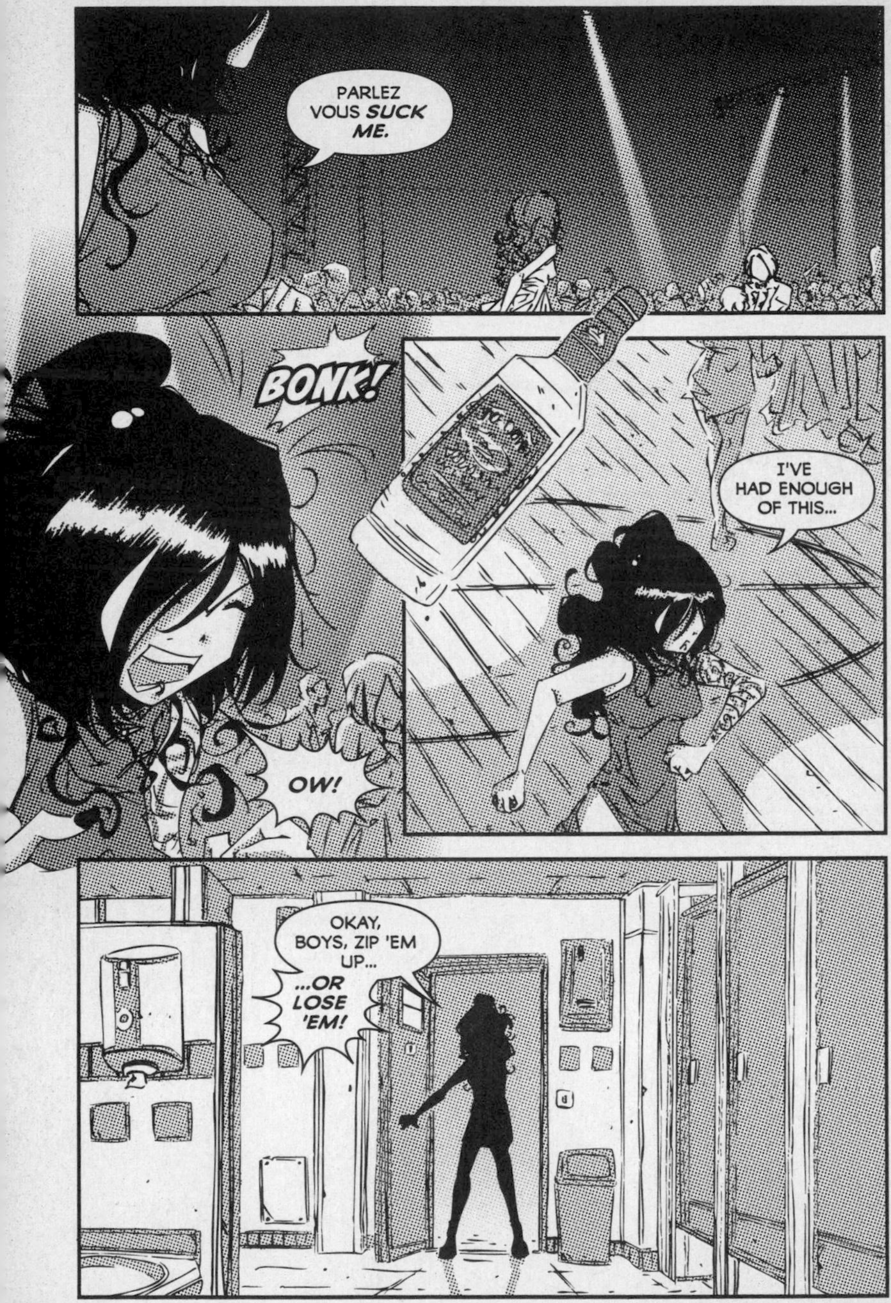
PARLEZ VOUS SUCK ME.
BONK!
OW!
I'VE HAD ENOUGH OF THIS...
OKAY, BOYS, ZIP 'EM UP...
...OR LOSE 'EM!

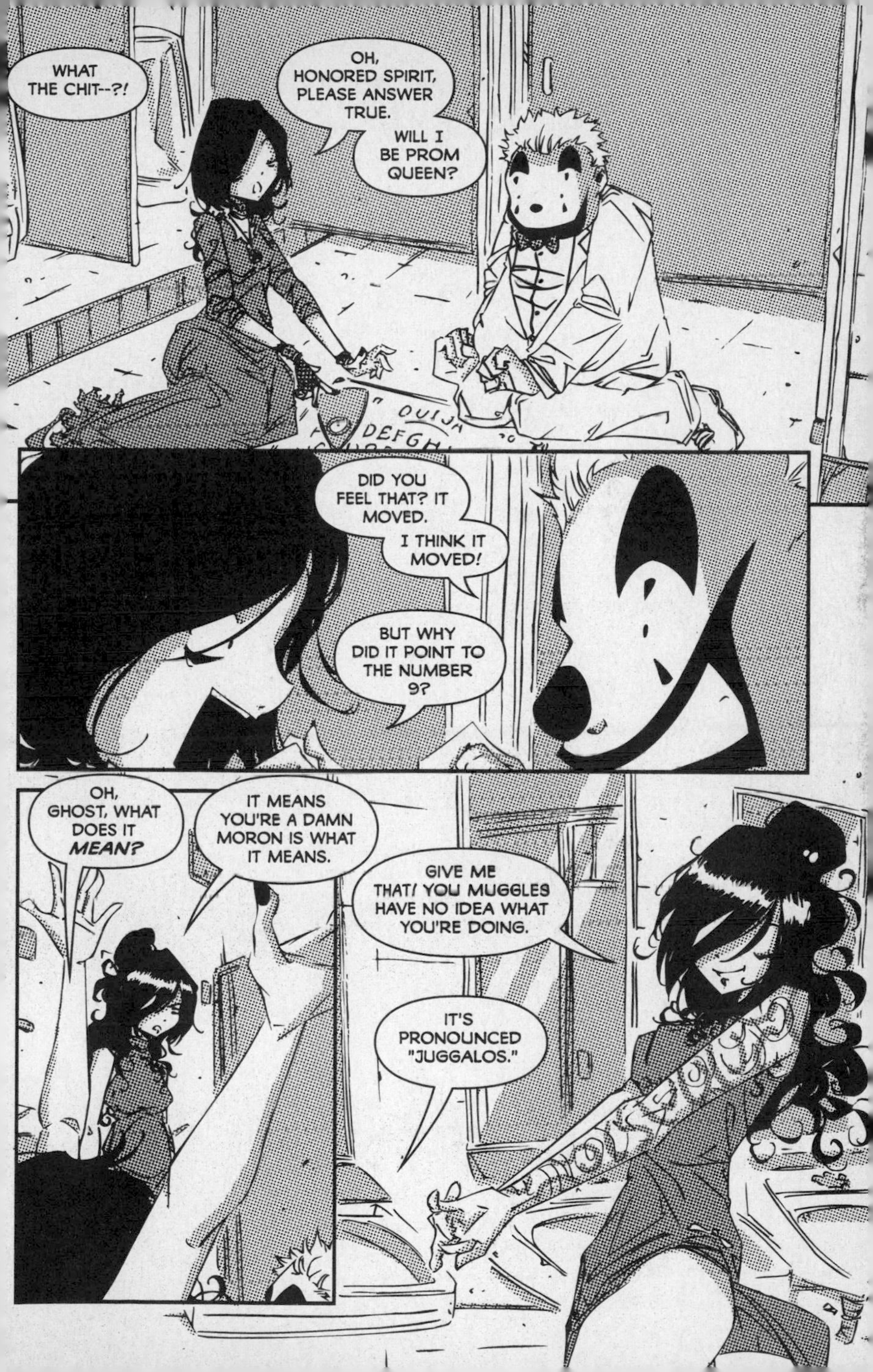
WHAT THE CHIT--?!
OH, HONORED SPIRIT, PLEASE ANSWER TRUE.
WILL I BE PROM QUEEN?
OUIJA
DEFGH
DID YOU FEEL THAT? IT MOVED.
I THINK IT MOVED!
BUT WHY DID IT POINT TO THE NUMBER 9?
OH, GHOST, WHAT DOES IT *MEAN?*
IT MEANS YOU'RE A DAMN MORON IS WHAT IT MEANS.
GIVE ME THAT! YOU MUGGLES HAVE NO IDEA WHAT YOU'RE DOING.
IT'S PRONOUNCED "JUGGALOS."

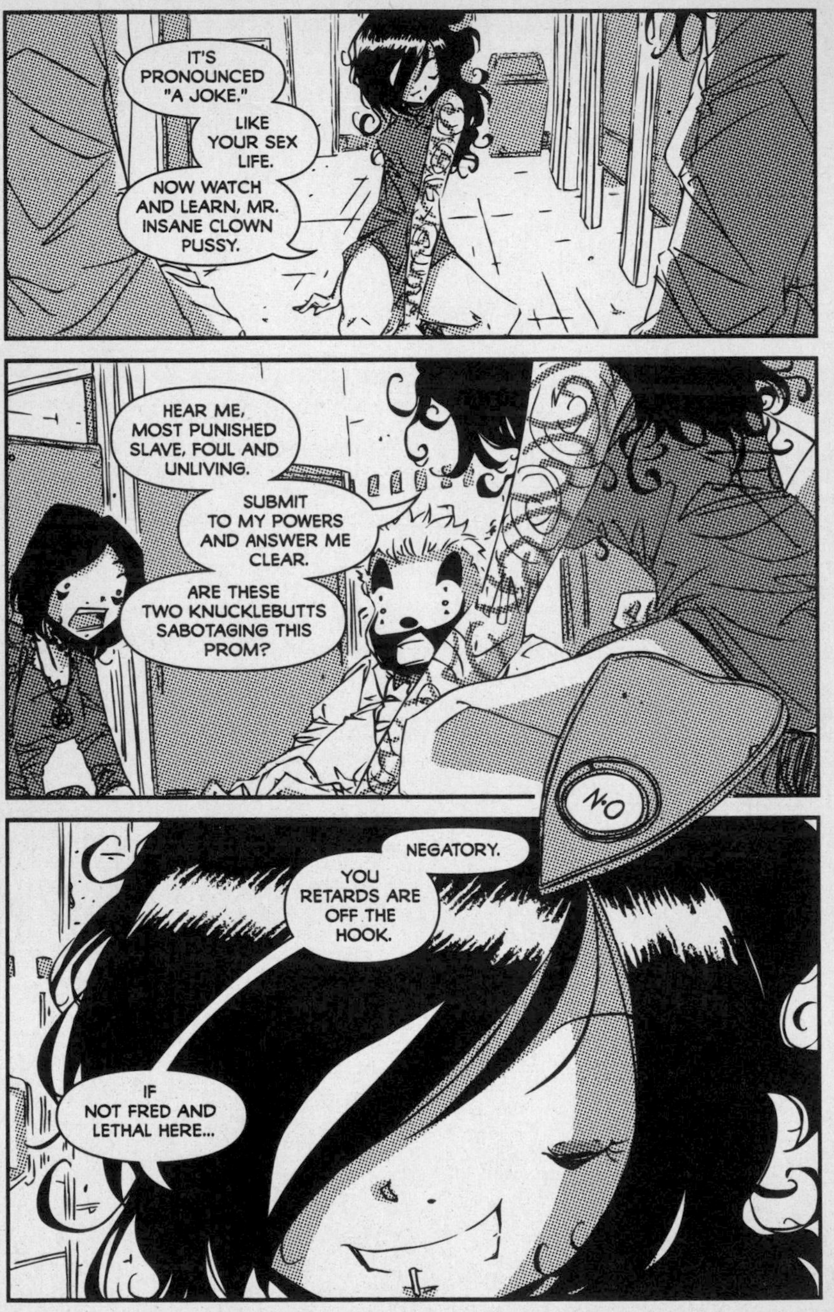
IT'S PRONOUNCED "A JOKE."
LIKE YOUR SEX LIFE.
NOW WATCH AND LEARN, MR. INSANE CLOWN PUSSY.
HEAR ME, MOST PUNISHED SLAVE, FOUL AND UNLIVING.
SUBMIT TO MY POWERS AND ANSWER ME CLEAR.
ARE THESE TWO KNUCKLEBUTTS SABOTAGING THIS PROM?
NO
NEGATORY.
YOU RETARDS ARE OFF THE HOOK.
IF NOT FRED AND LETHAL HERE...

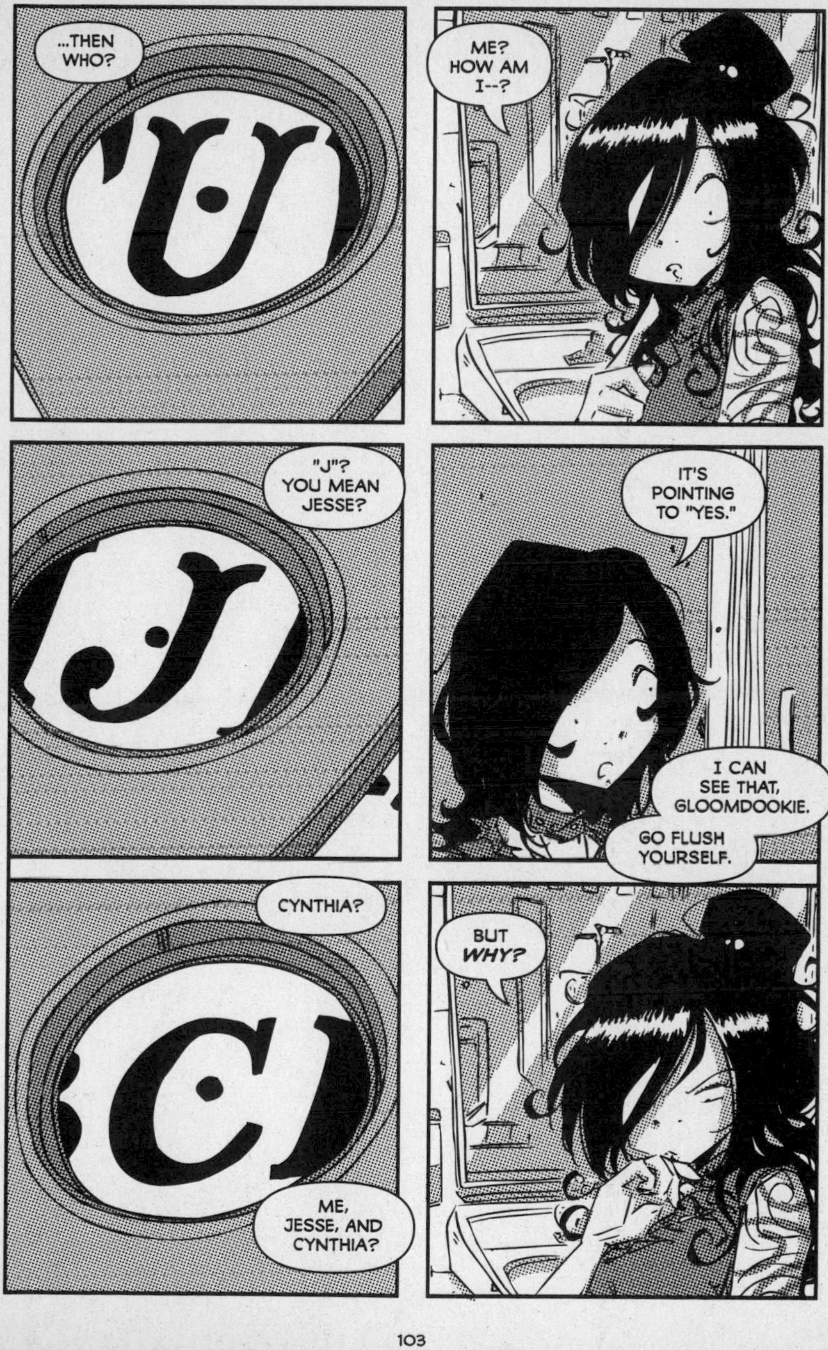
...THEN WHO?
ME? HOW AM I--?
"J"? YOU MEAN JESSE?
IT'S POINTING TO "YES."
I CAN SEE THAT, GLOOMDOOKIE.
GO FLUSH YOURSELF.
CYNTHIA?
BUT WHY?
ME, JESSE, AND CYNTHIA?

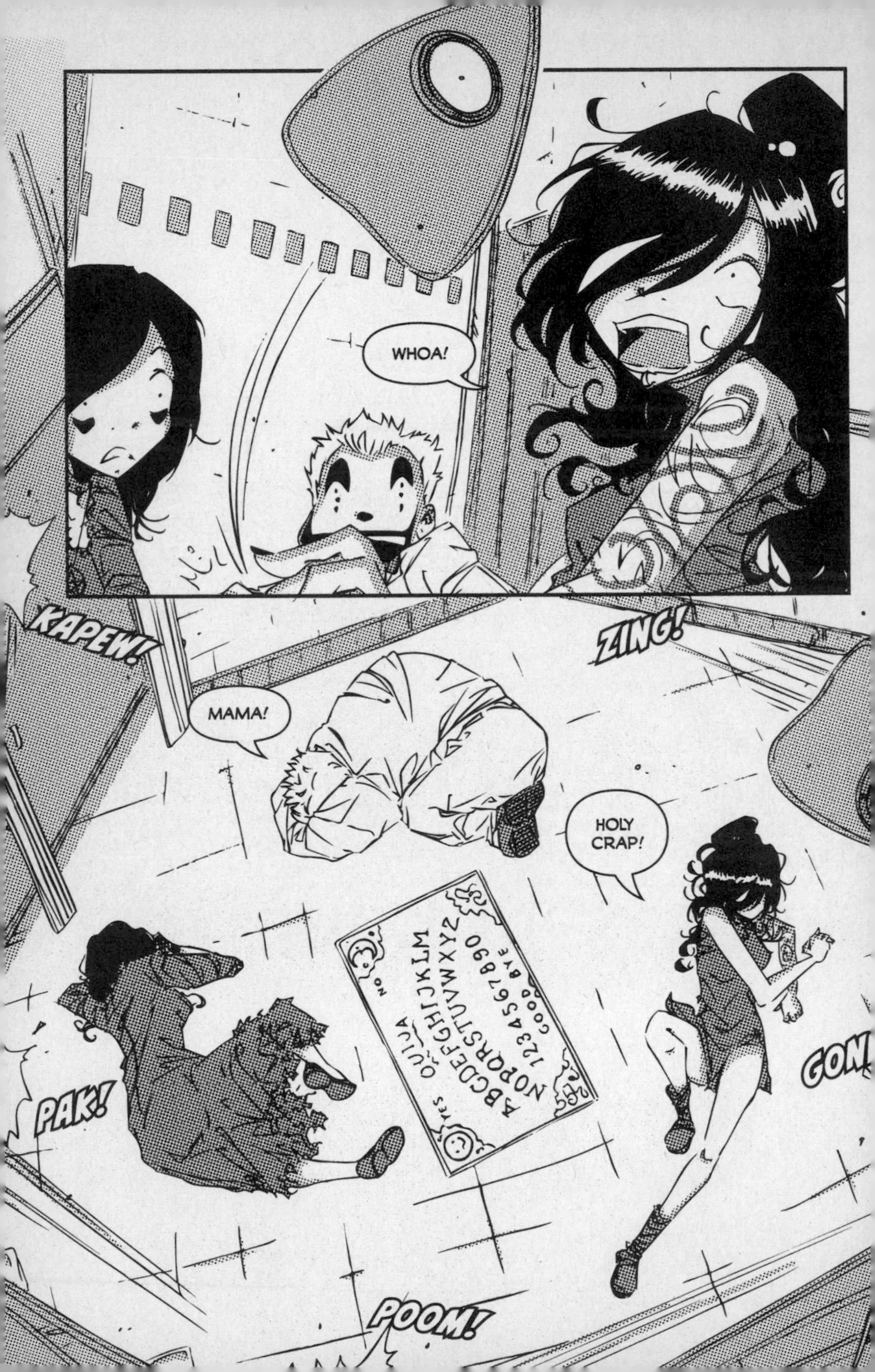
WHOA!
KAPEW!
ZING!
MAMA!
HOLY CRAP!
OUIJA
YES
NO
ABCDEFGHIJKLM
NOPQRSTUVWXYZ
1234567890
GOOD BYE
GON
PAK!
POOM!

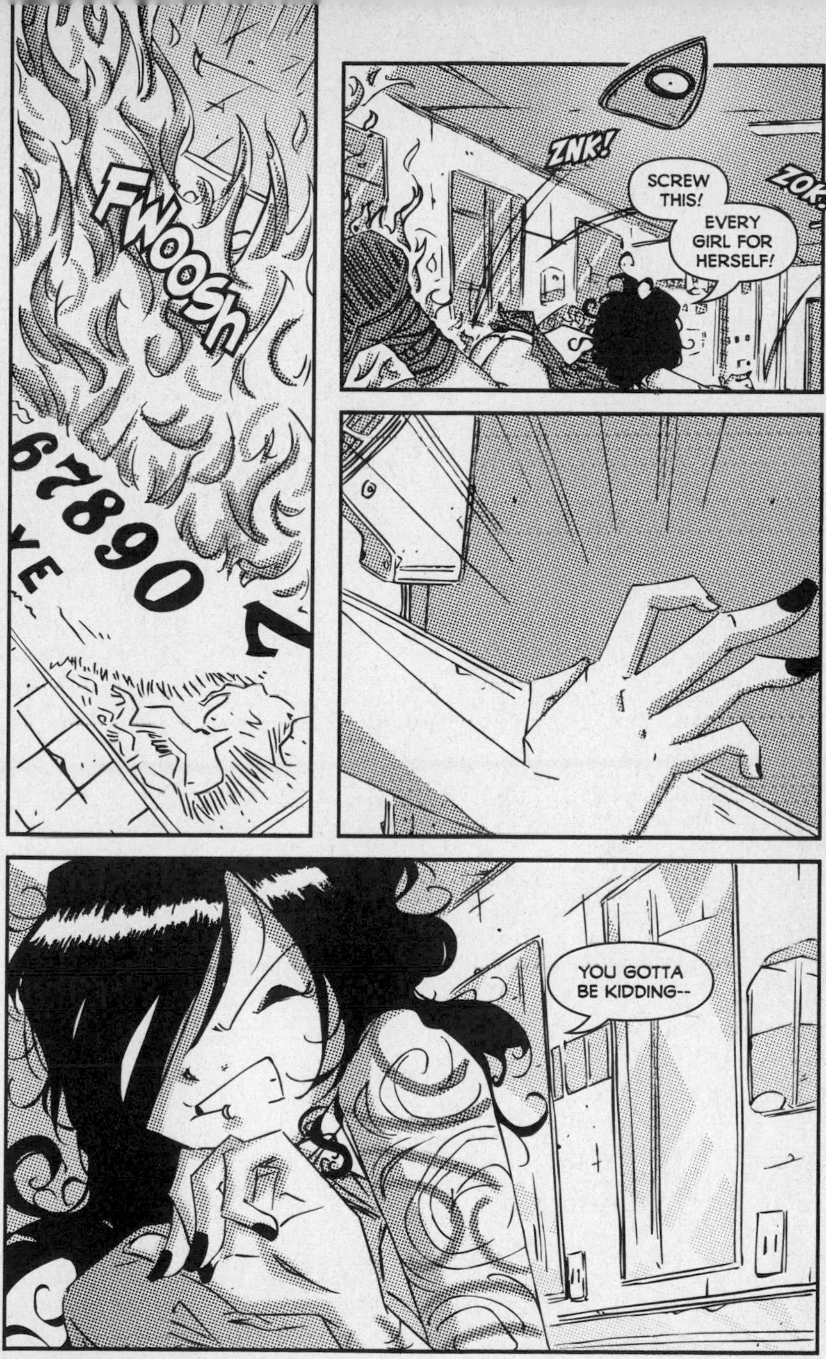
FWOOSh
67890
ZNK!
SCREW THIS!
EVERY GIRL FOR HERSELF!
ZOK!
YOU GOTTA BE KIDDING--

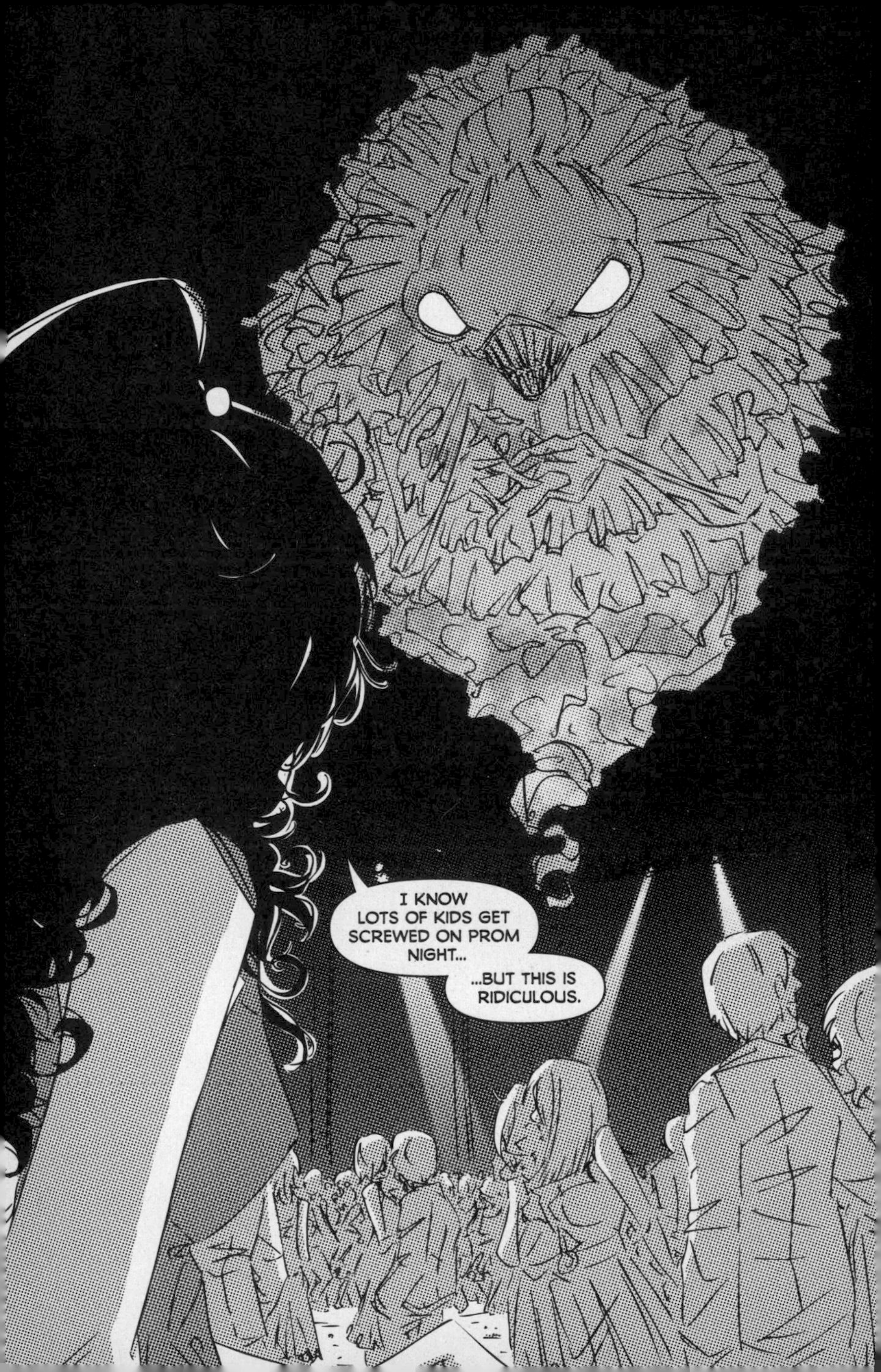
I KNOW LOTS OF KIDS GET SCREWED ON PROM NIGHT...
...BUT THIS IS RIDICULOUS.

Chapter 5
"Dance or Die"

5

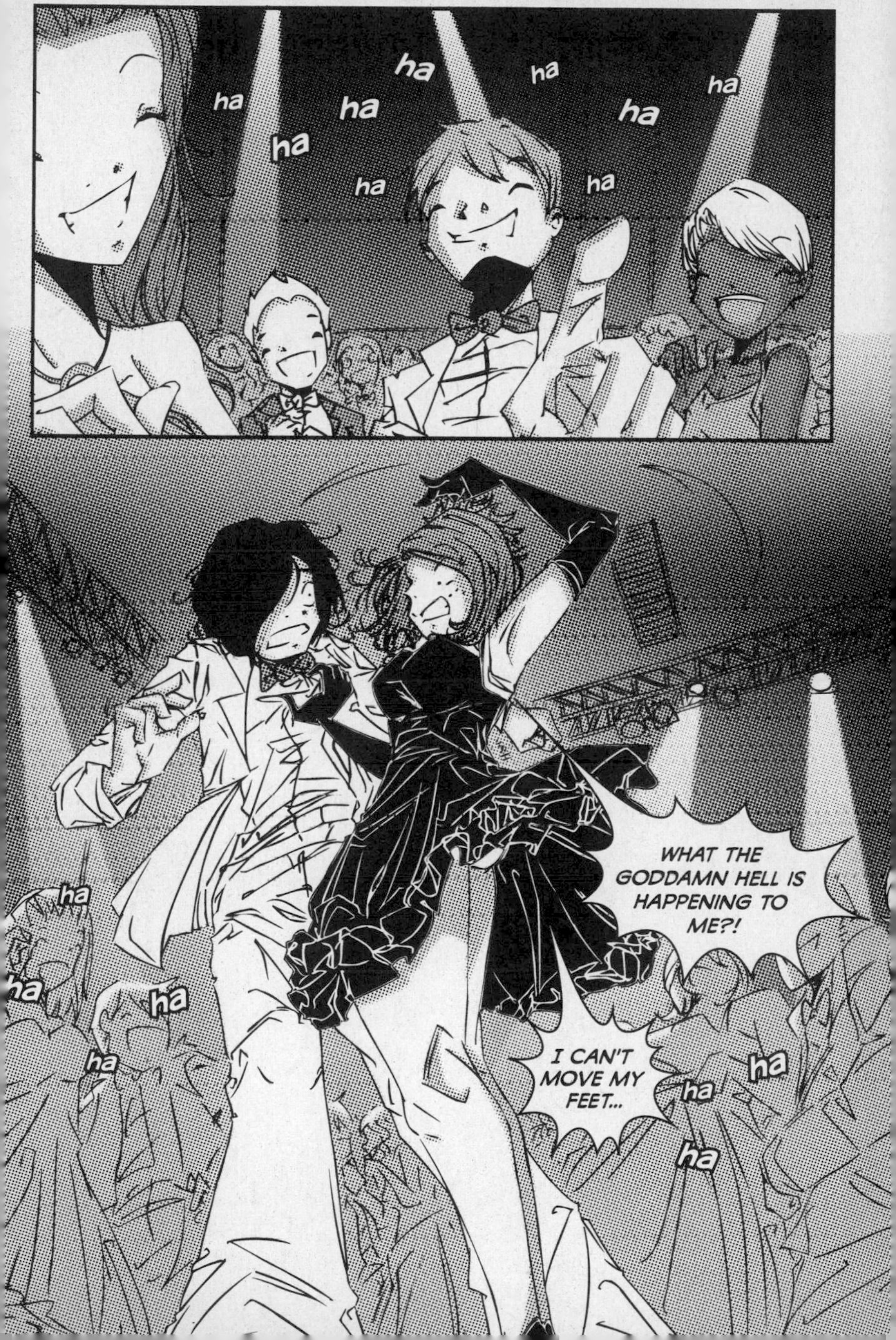
ha
ha
ha
ha
ha
ha
ha
ha
ha
WHAT THE GODDAMN HELL IS HAPPENING TO ME?!
I CAN'T MOVE MY FEET...
ha
ha
ha
ha
ha
ha
ha

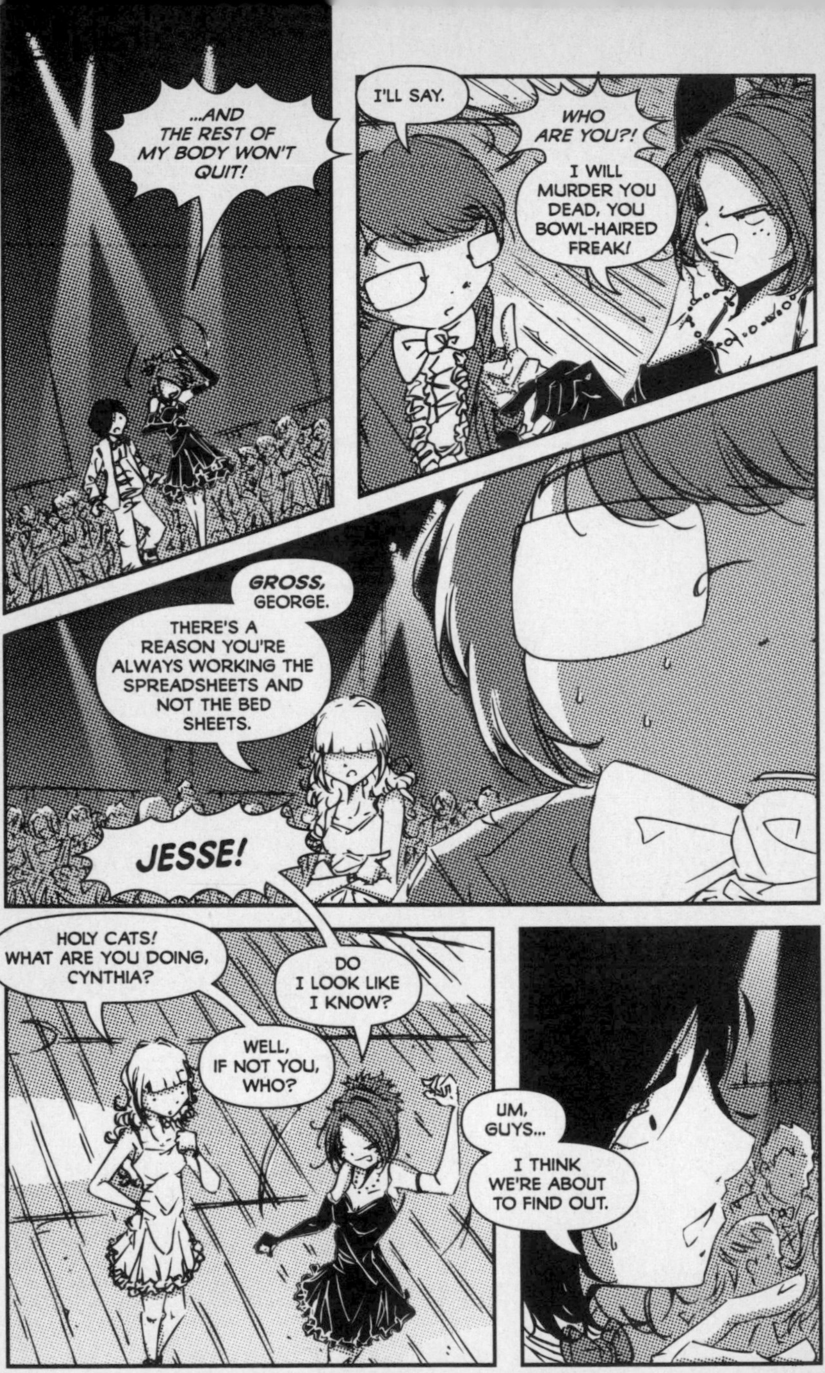
...AND THE REST OF MY BODY WON'T QUIT!
I'LL SAY.
WHO ARE YOU?!
I WILL MURDER YOU DEAD, YOU BOWL-HAIRED FREAK!
GROSS, GEORGE.
THERE'S A REASON YOU'RE ALWAYS WORKING THE SPREADSHEETS AND NOT THE BED SHEETS.
JESSE!
HOLY CATS! WHAT ARE YOU DOING, CYNTHIA?
DO I LOOK LIKE I KNOW?
WELL, IF NOT YOU, WHO?
UM, GUYS...
I THINK WE'RE ABOUT TO FIND OUT.

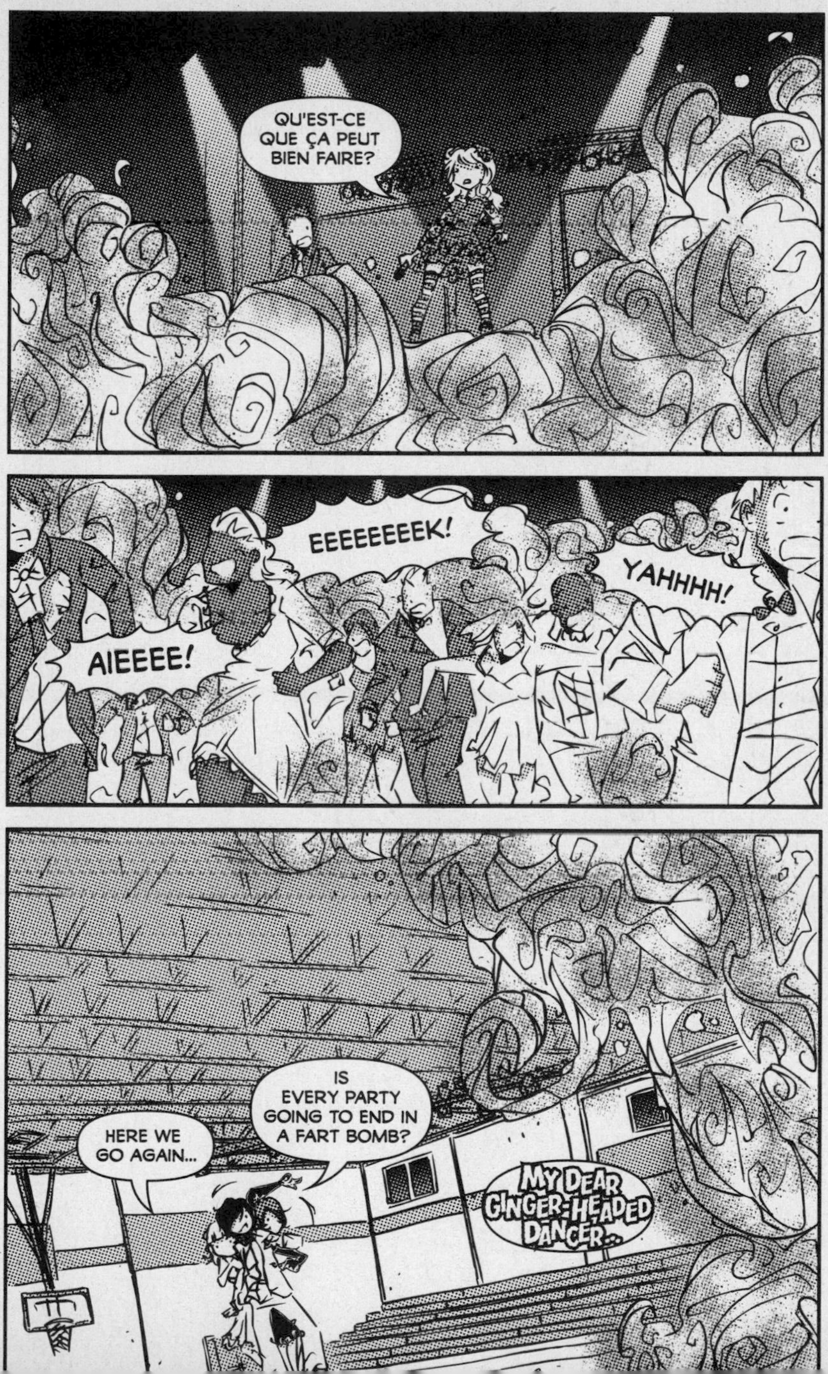
QU'EST-CE QUE ÇA PEUT BIEN FAIRE?
EEEEEEEEK!
YAHHHH!
AIEEEE!
IS EVERY PARTY GOING TO END IN A FART BOMB?
HERE WE GO AGAIN...
MY DEAR GINGER-HEADED DANCER...

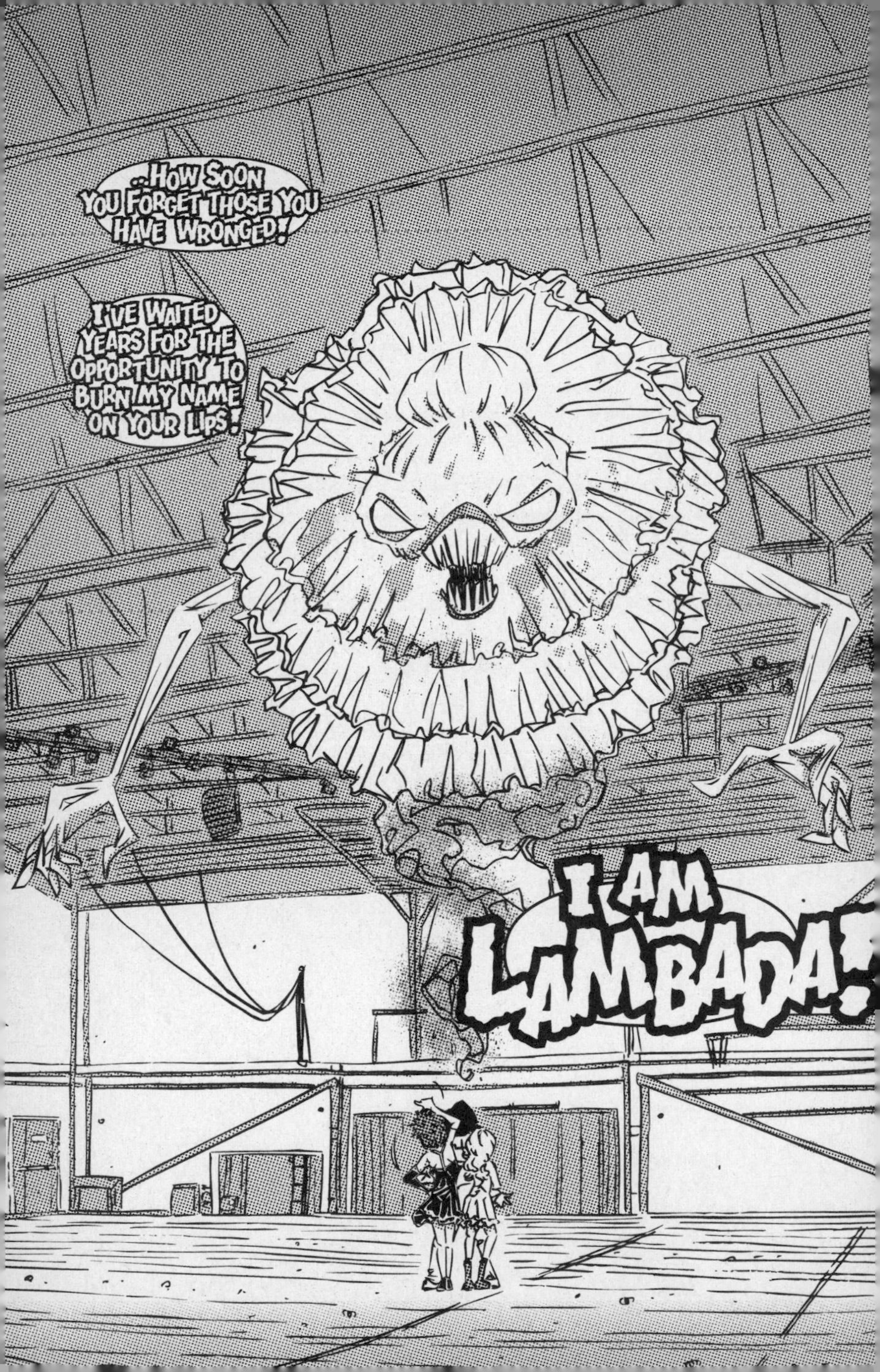
..HOW SOON YOU FORGET THOSE YOU HAVE WRONGED!
I'VE WAITED YEARS FOR THE OPPORTUNITY TO BURN MY NAME ON YOUR LIPS!
I AM LAMBADA!

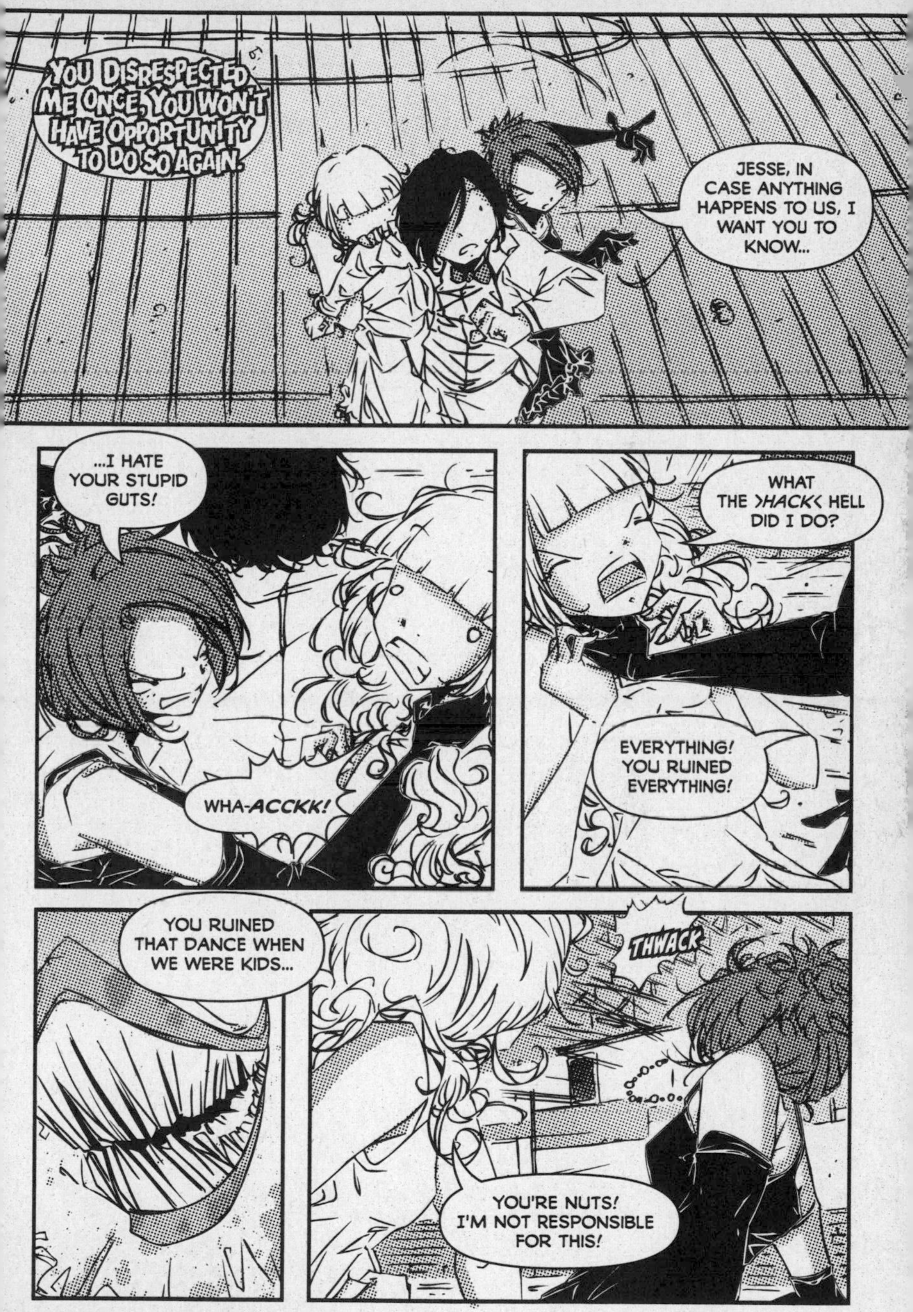
YOU DISRESPECTED ME ONCE, YOU WON'T HAVE OPPORTUNITY TO DO SO AGAIN.
JESSE, IN CASE ANYTHING HAPPENS TO US, I WANT YOU TO KNOW...
...I HATE YOUR STUPID GUTS!
WHA-ACCKK!
WHAT THE >HACK< HELL DID I DO?
EVERYTHING! YOU RUINED EVERYTHING!
YOU RUINED THAT DANCE WHEN WE WERE KIDS...
THWACK
YOU'RE NUTS! I'M NOT RESPONSIBLE FOR THIS!

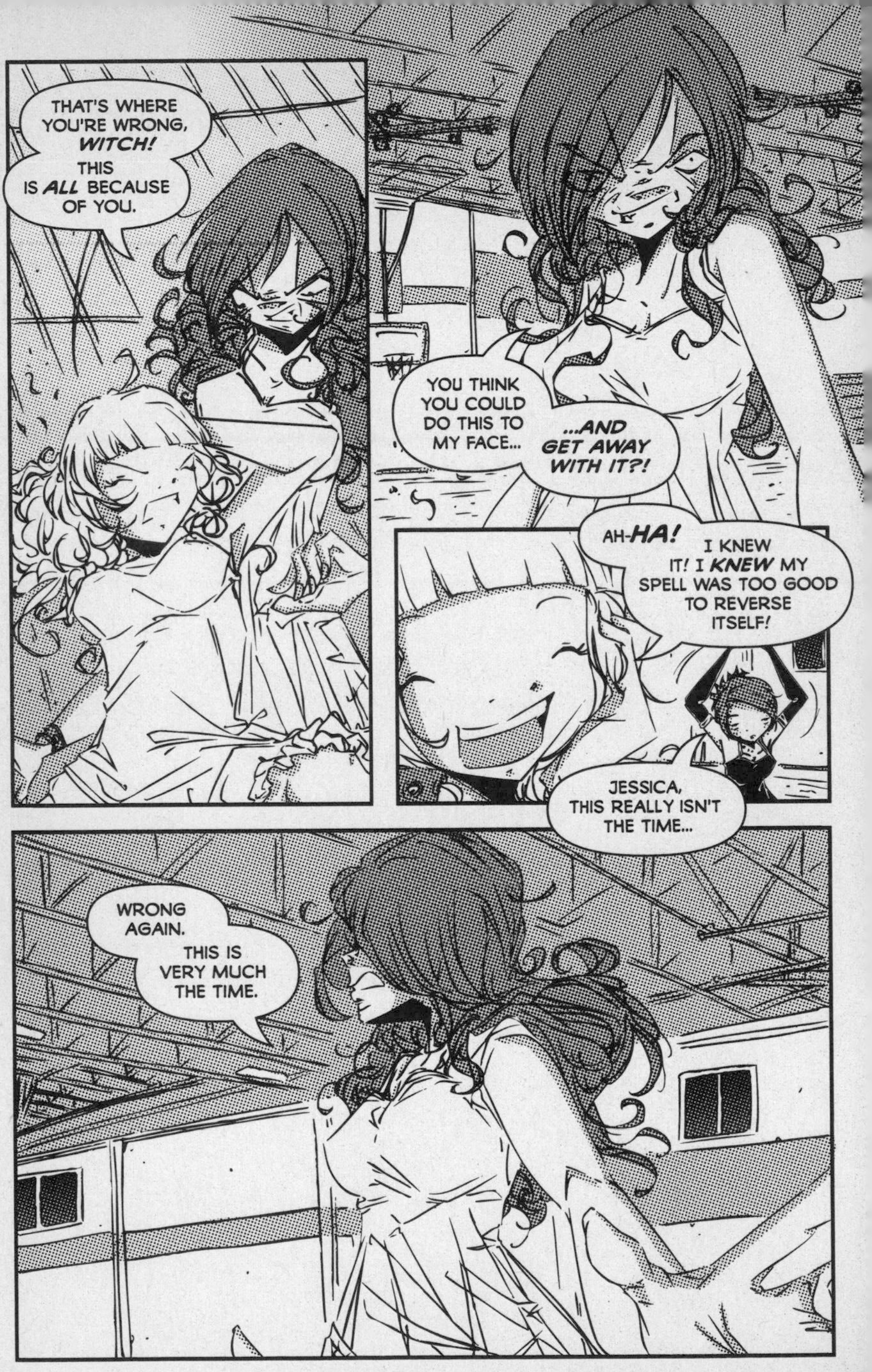
THAT'S WHERE YOU'RE WRONG, *WITCH!*
THIS IS *ALL* BECAUSE OF YOU.
YOU THINK YOU COULD DO THIS TO MY FACE...
...AND GET AWAY WITH IT?!
AH-*HA!*
I KNEW IT! I *KNEW* MY SPELL WAS TOO GOOD TO REVERSE ITSELF!
JESSICA, THIS REALLY ISN'T THE TIME...
WRONG AGAIN.
THIS IS VERY MUCH THE TIME.

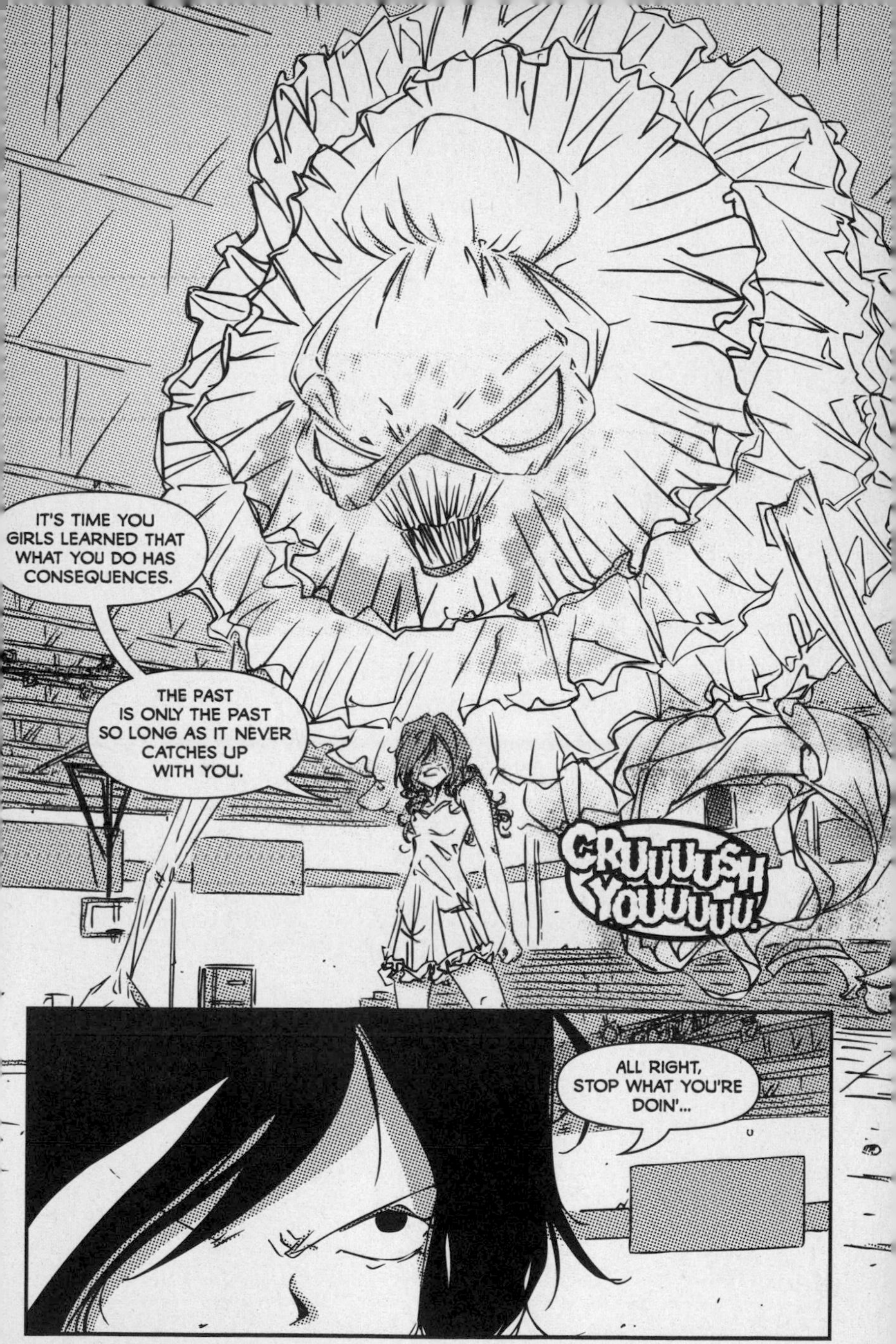
IT'S TIME YOU GIRLS LEARNED THAT WHAT YOU DO HAS CONSEQUENCES.
THE PAST IS ONLY THE PAST SO LONG AS IT NEVER CATCHES UP WITH YOU.
CRUUUUSH YOUUUUU!
ALL RIGHT, STOP WHAT YOU'RE DOIN'...

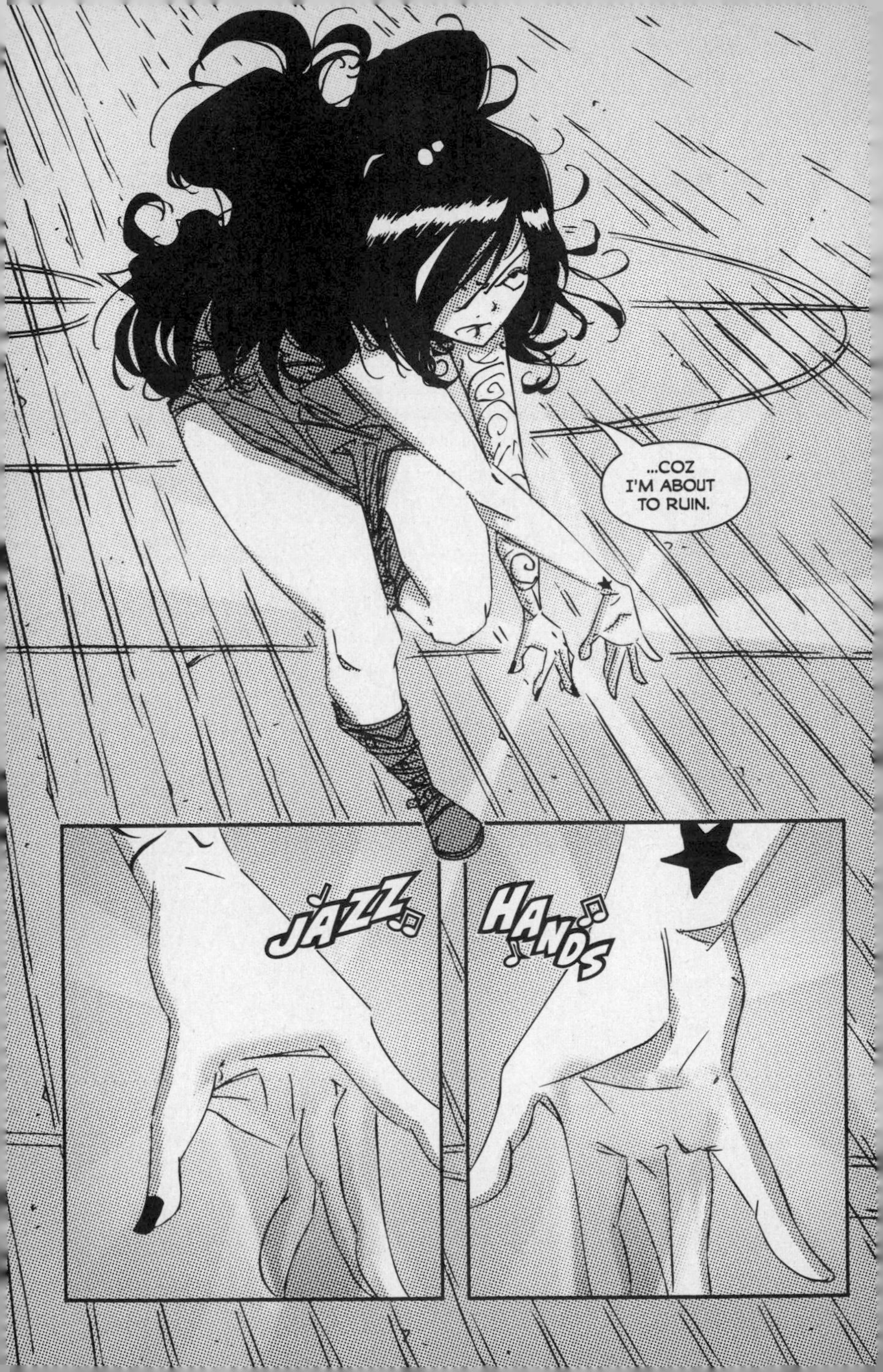
...COZ I'M ABOUT TO RUIN.
JAZZ
HANDS

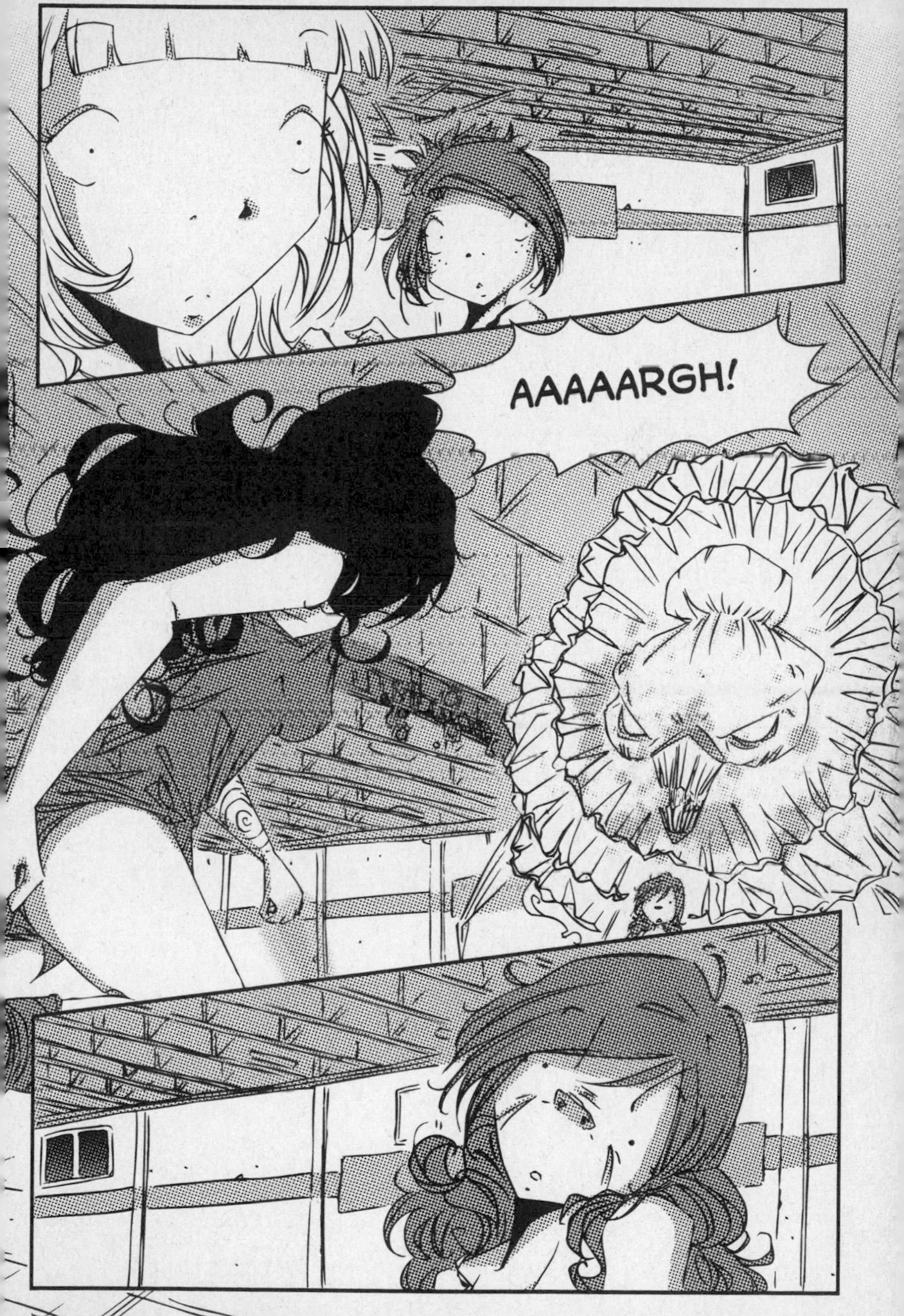
AAAAARGH!

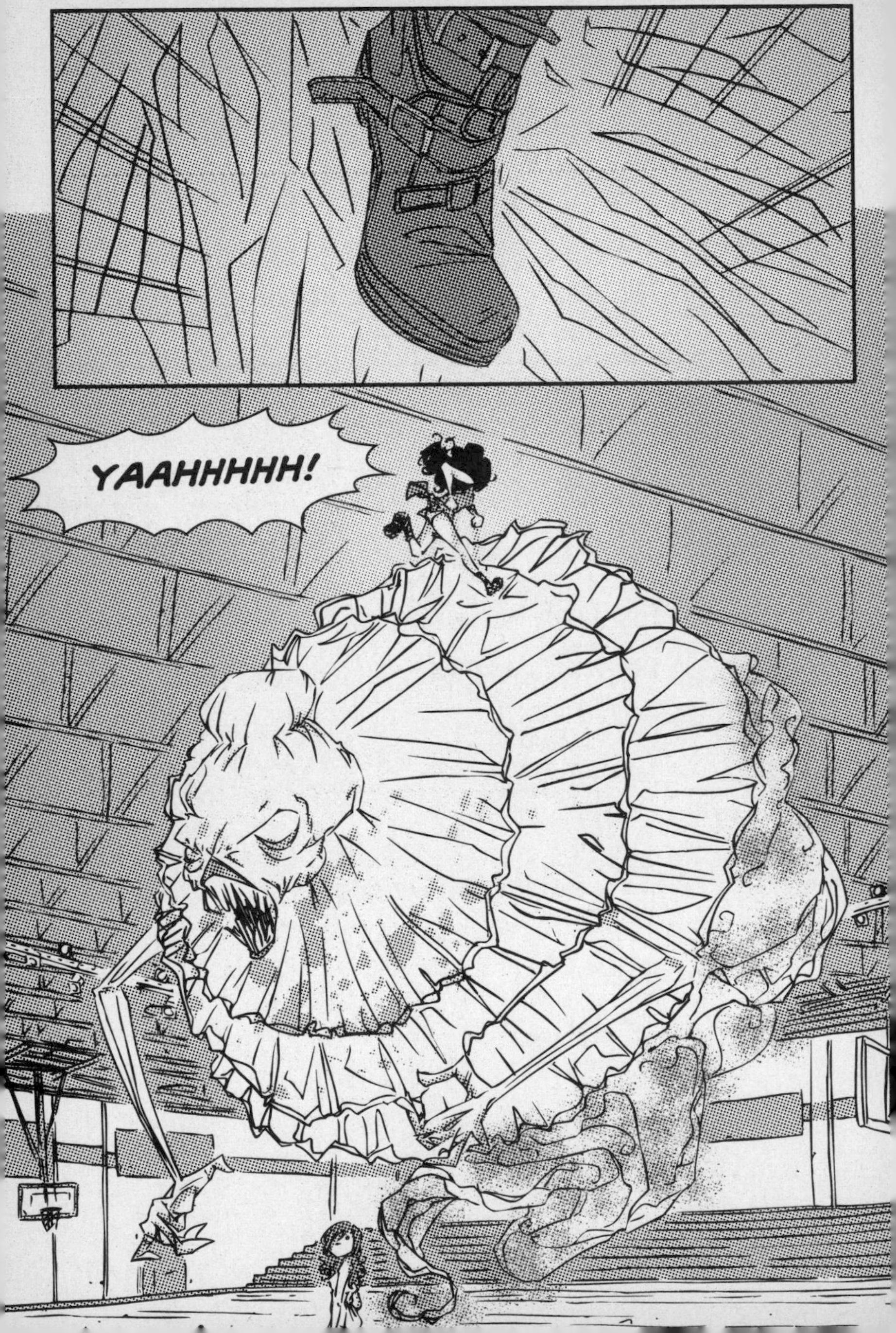
YAAHHHHH!

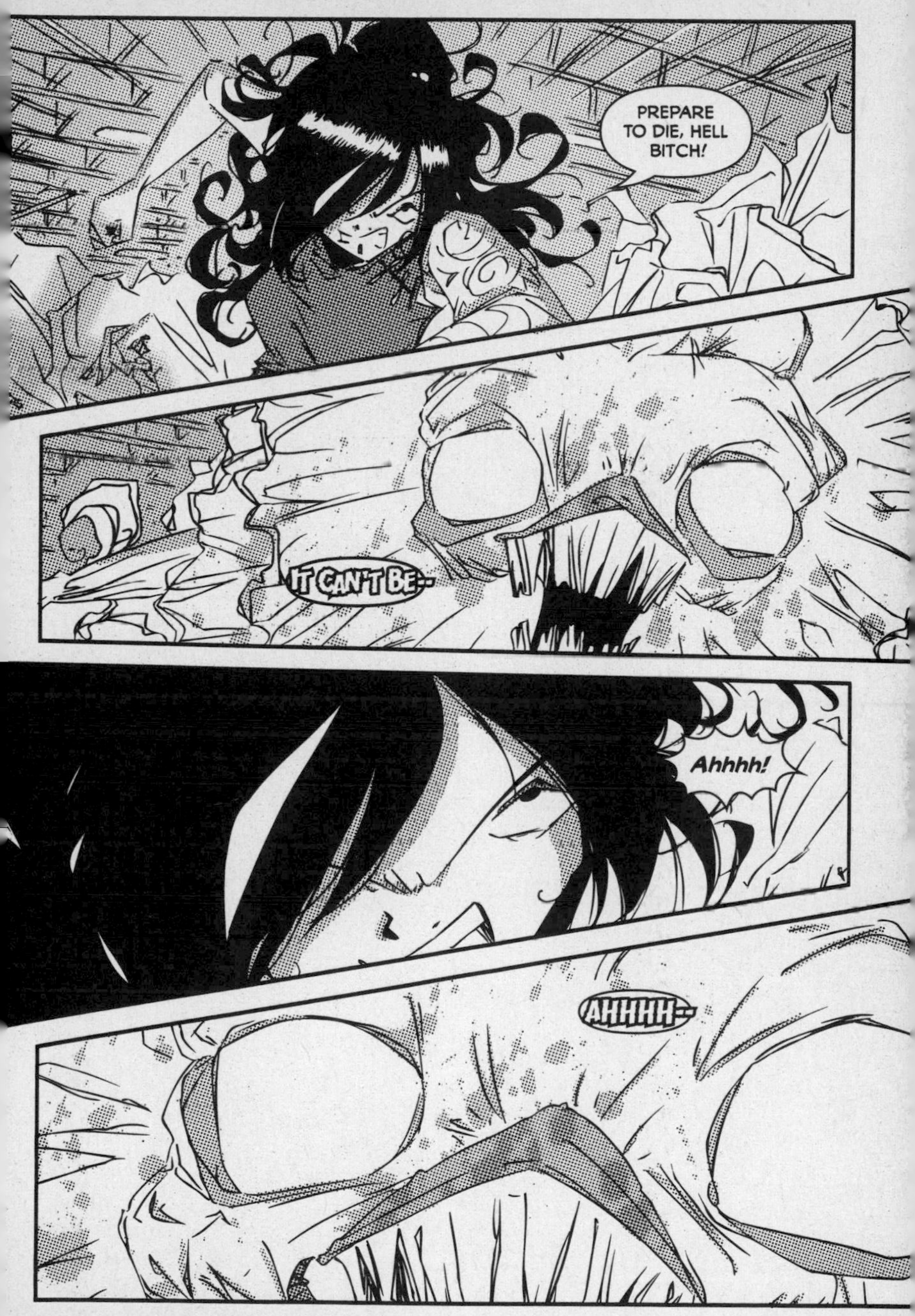
PREPARE TO DIE, HELL BITCH!
IT CAN'T BE--
Ahhhh!
AHHHH--

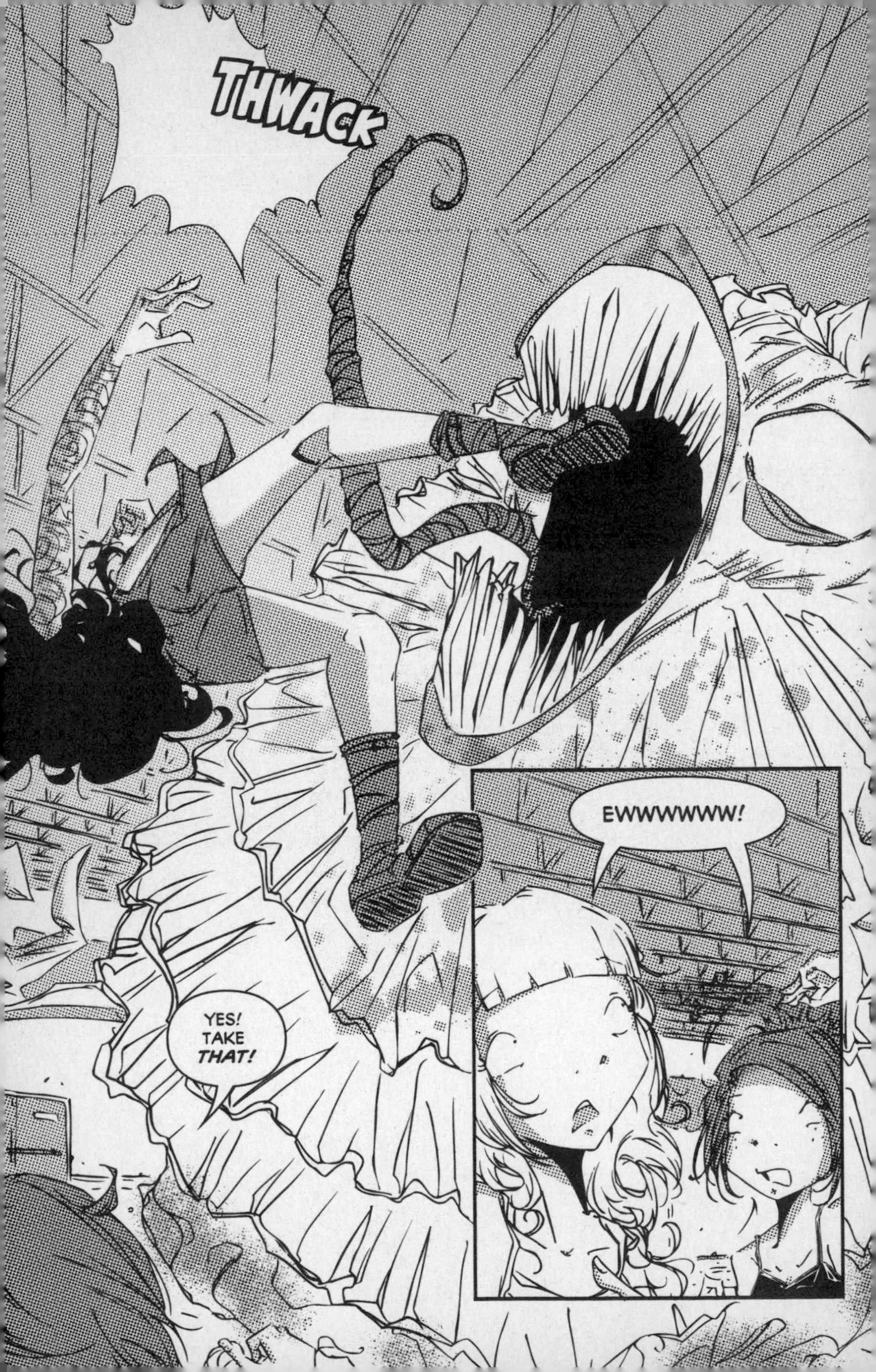
THWACK
EWWWWWW!
YES! TAKE *THAT!*

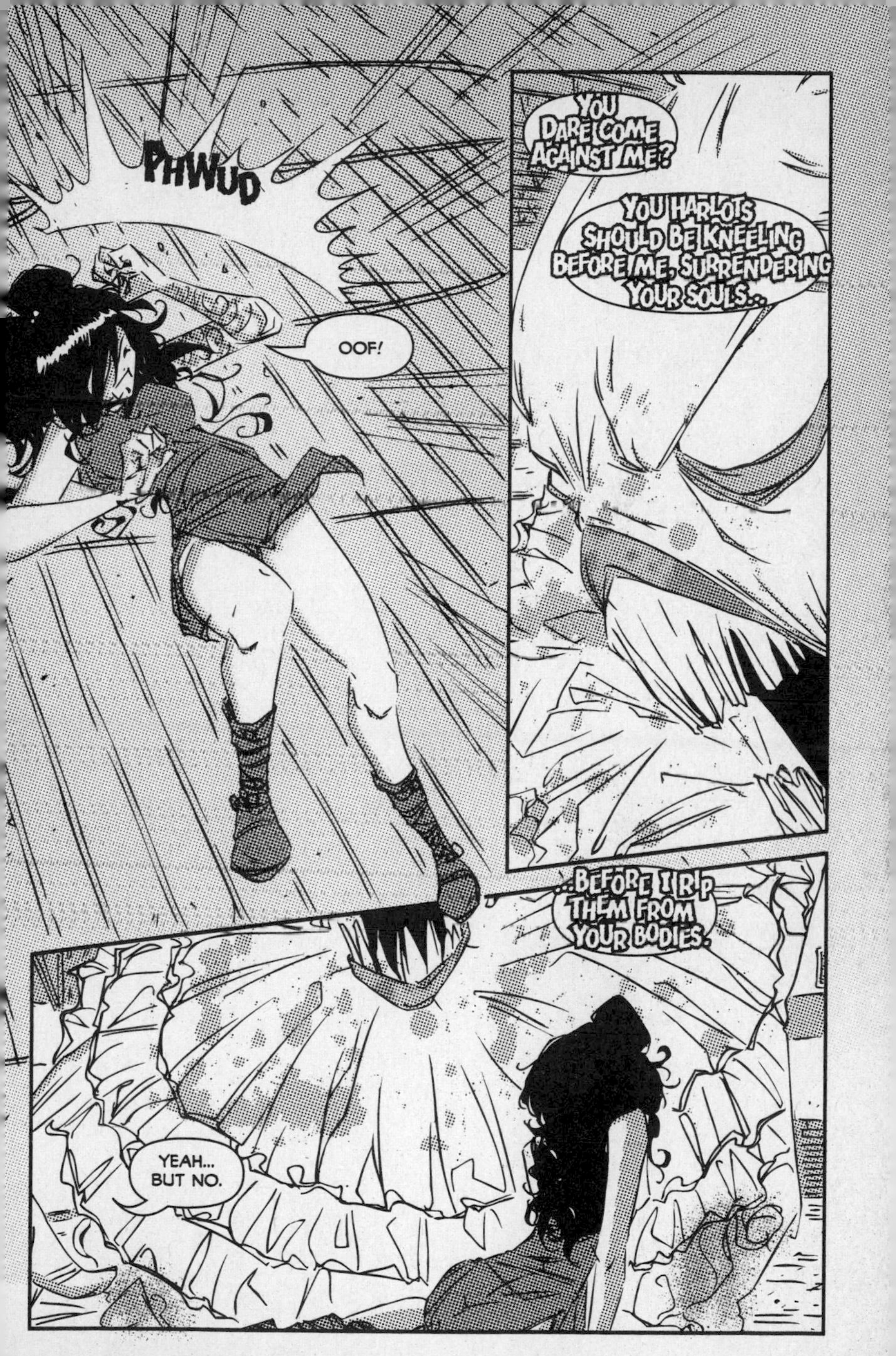
PHWUD
OOF!
YOU DARE COME AGAINST ME?
YOU HARLOTS SHOULD BE KNEELING BEFORE ME, SURRENDERING YOUR SOULS...
...BEFORE I RIP THEM FROM YOUR BODIES.
YEAH... BUT NO.

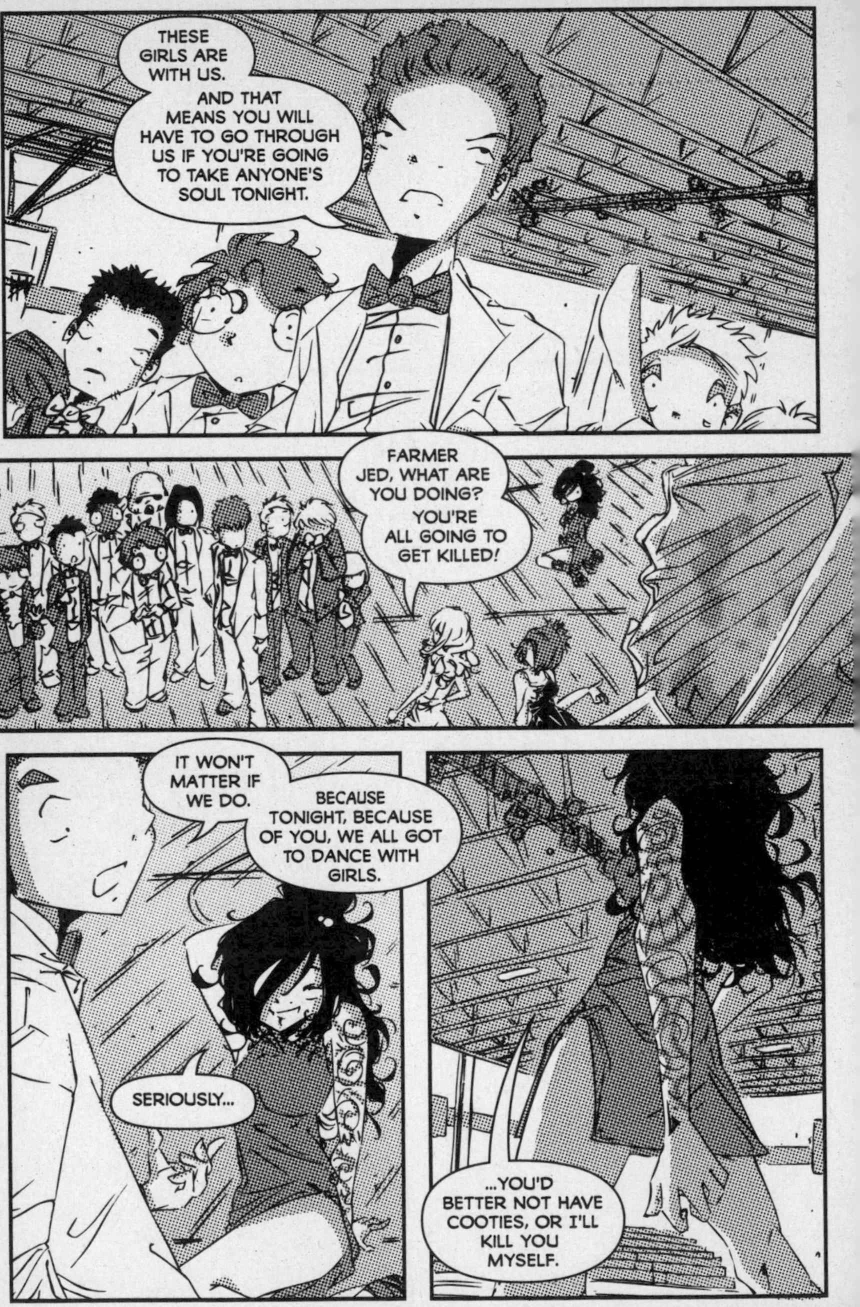
THESE GIRLS ARE WITH US.
AND THAT MEANS YOU WILL HAVE TO GO THROUGH US IF YOU'RE GOING TO TAKE ANYONE'S SOUL TONIGHT.
FARMER JED, WHAT ARE YOU DOING?
YOU'RE ALL GOING TO GET KILLED!
IT WON'T MATTER IF WE DO.
BECAUSE TONIGHT, BECAUSE OF YOU, WE ALL GOT TO DANCE WITH GIRLS.
SERIOUSLY...
...YOU'D BETTER NOT HAVE COOTIES, OR I'LL KILL YOU MYSELF.

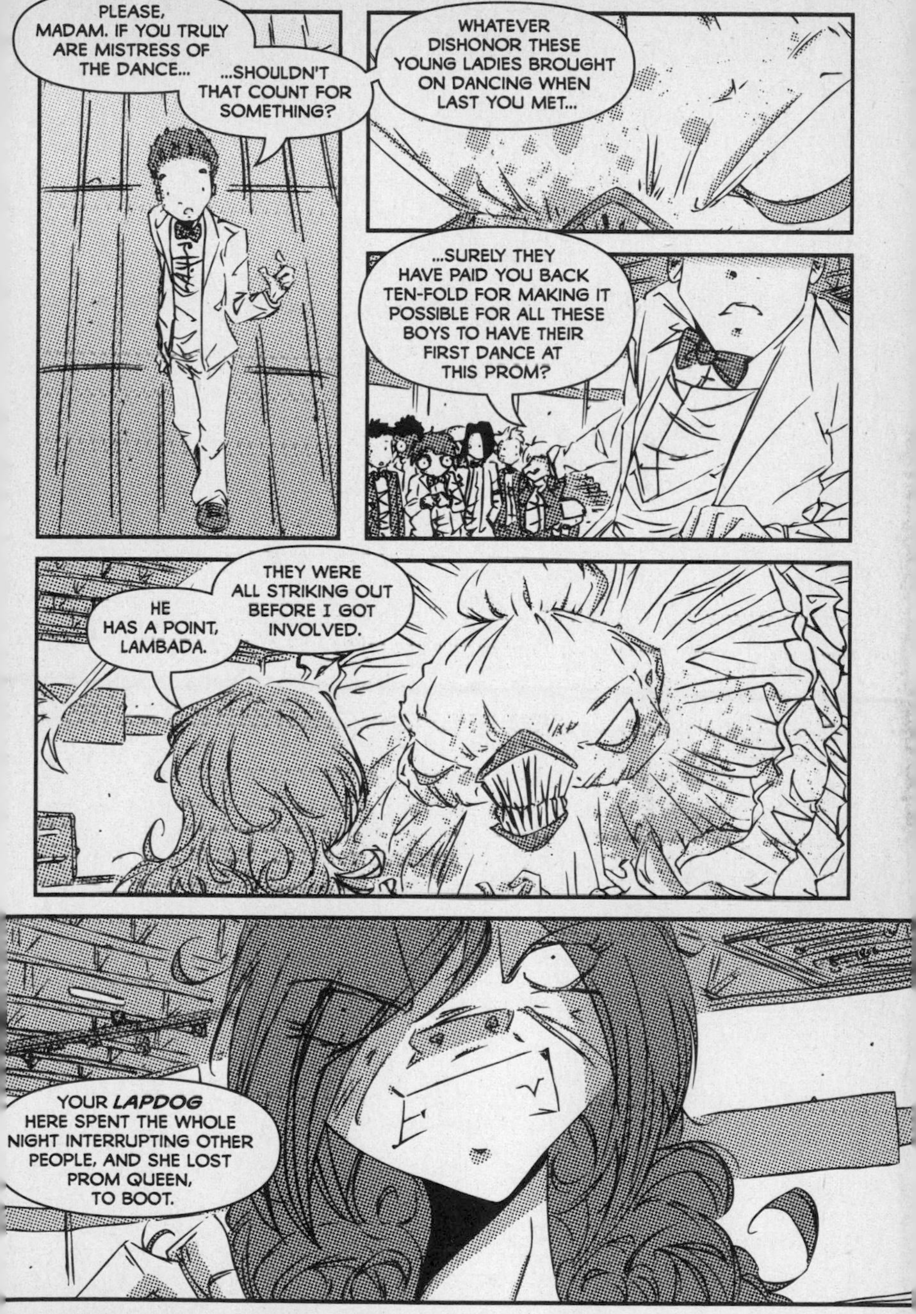
PLEASE, MADAM. IF YOU TRULY ARE MISTRESS OF THE DANCE...
...SHOULDN'T THAT COUNT FOR SOMETHING?
WHATEVER DISHONOR THESE YOUNG LADIES BROUGHT ON DANCING WHEN LAST YOU MET...
...SURELY THEY HAVE PAID YOU BACK TEN-FOLD FOR MAKING IT POSSIBLE FOR ALL THESE BOYS TO HAVE THEIR FIRST DANCE AT THIS PROM?
HE HAS A POINT, LAMBADA.
THEY WERE ALL STRIKING OUT BEFORE I GOT INVOLVED.
YOUR *LAPDOG* HERE SPENT THE WHOLE NIGHT INTERRUPTING OTHER PEOPLE, AND SHE LOST PROM QUEEN, TO BOOT.

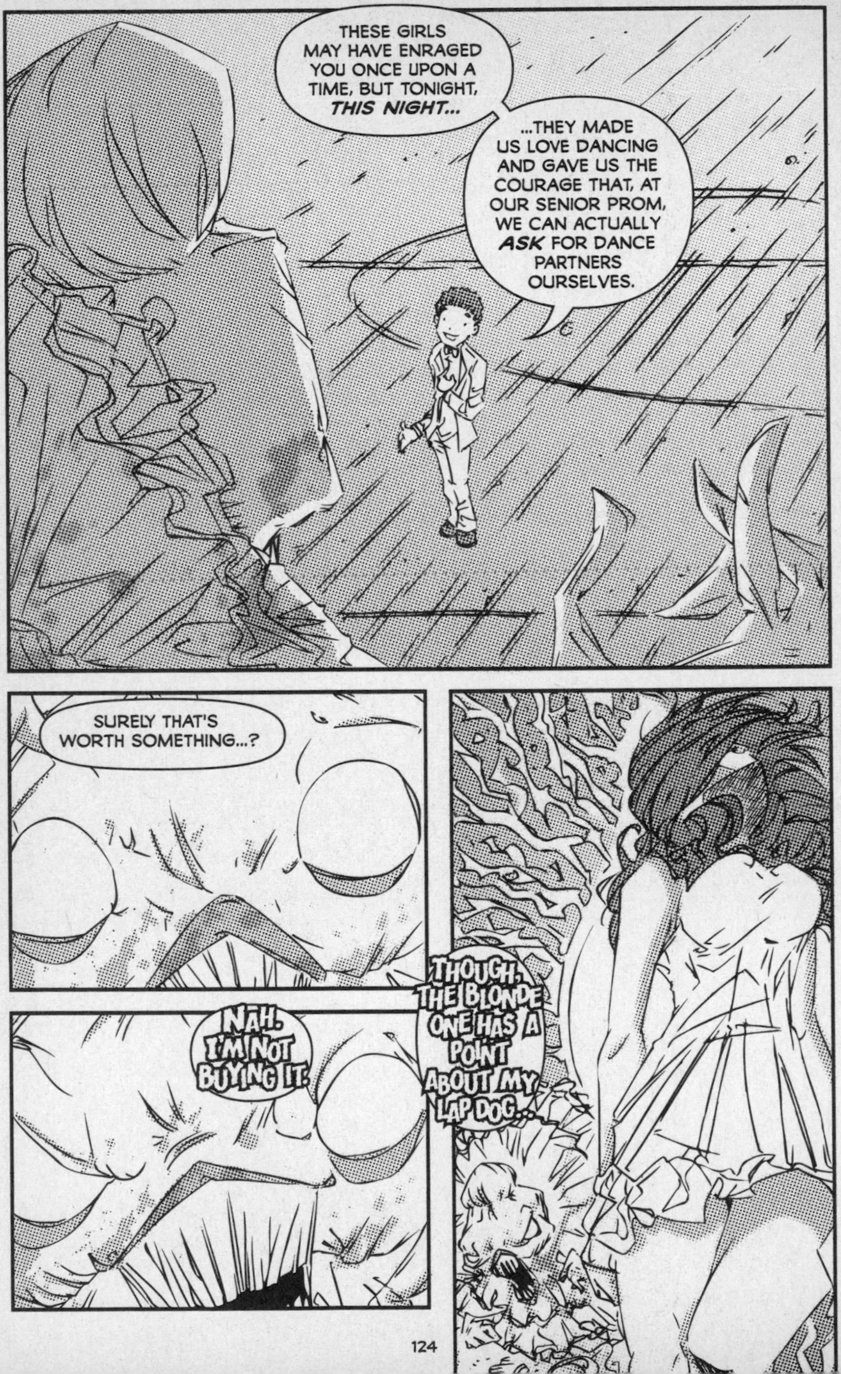
THESE GIRLS MAY HAVE ENRAGED YOU ONCE UPON A TIME, BUT TONIGHT, *THIS NIGHT...*
...THEY MADE US LOVE DANCING AND GAVE US THE COURAGE THAT, AT OUR SENIOR PROM, WE CAN ACTUALLY *ASK* FOR DANCE PARTNERS OURSELVES.
SURELY THAT'S WORTH SOMETHING...?
NAH. I'M NOT BUYING IT.
THOUGH, THE BLONDE ONE HAS A POINT ABOUT MY LAP DOG...

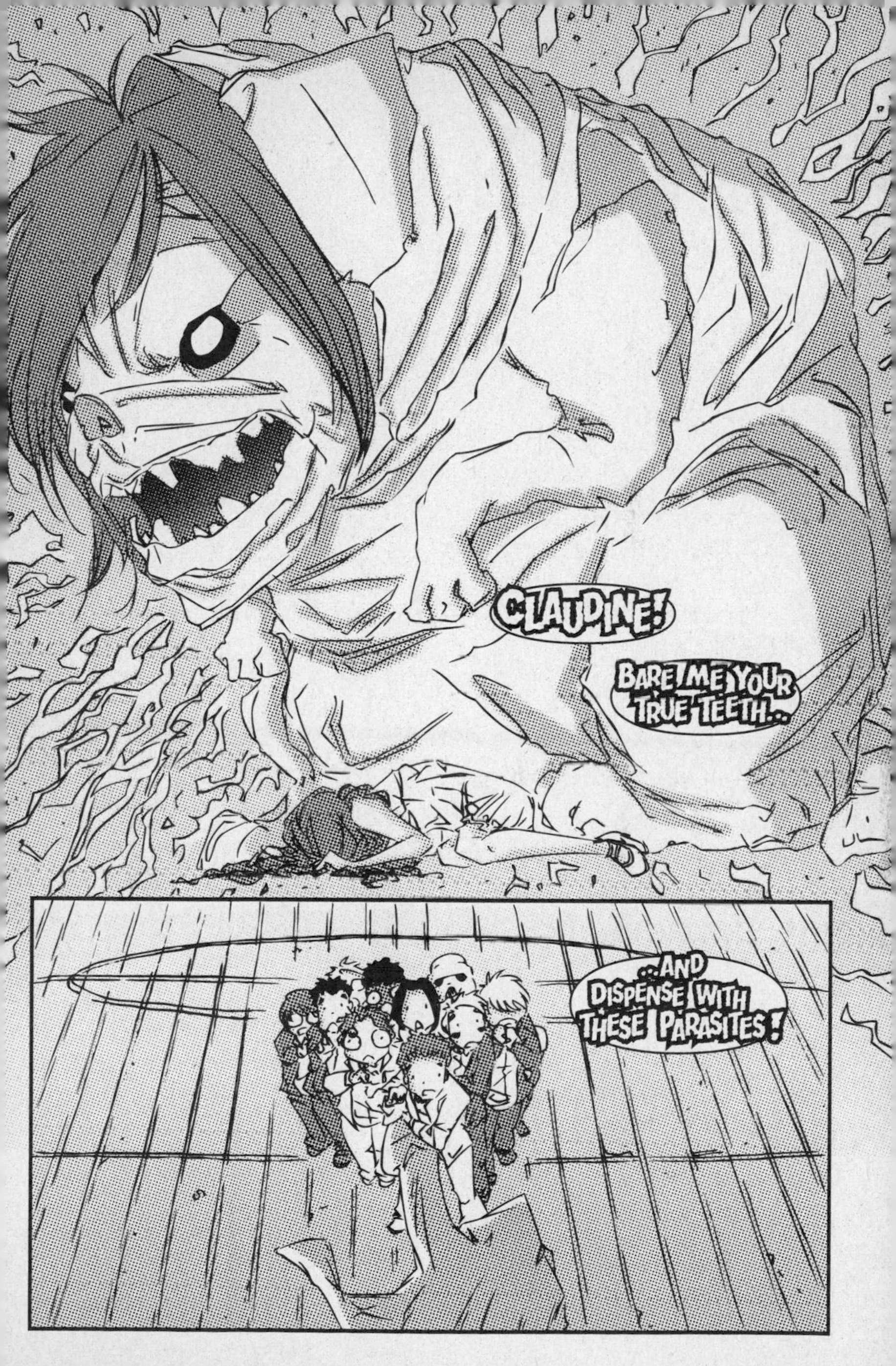
CLAUDINE!
BARE ME YOUR TRUE TEETH..
..AND DISPENSE WITH THESE PARASITES!

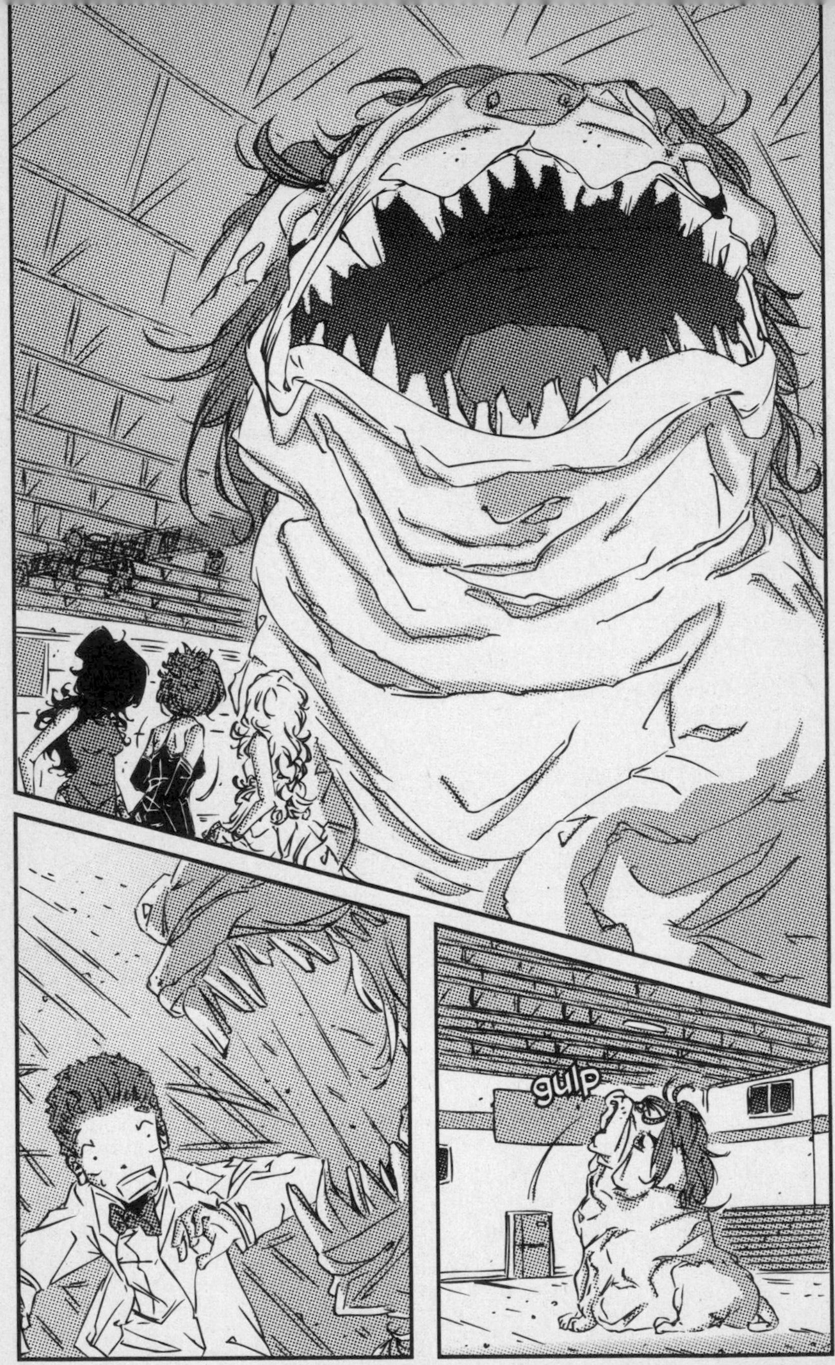
gulp

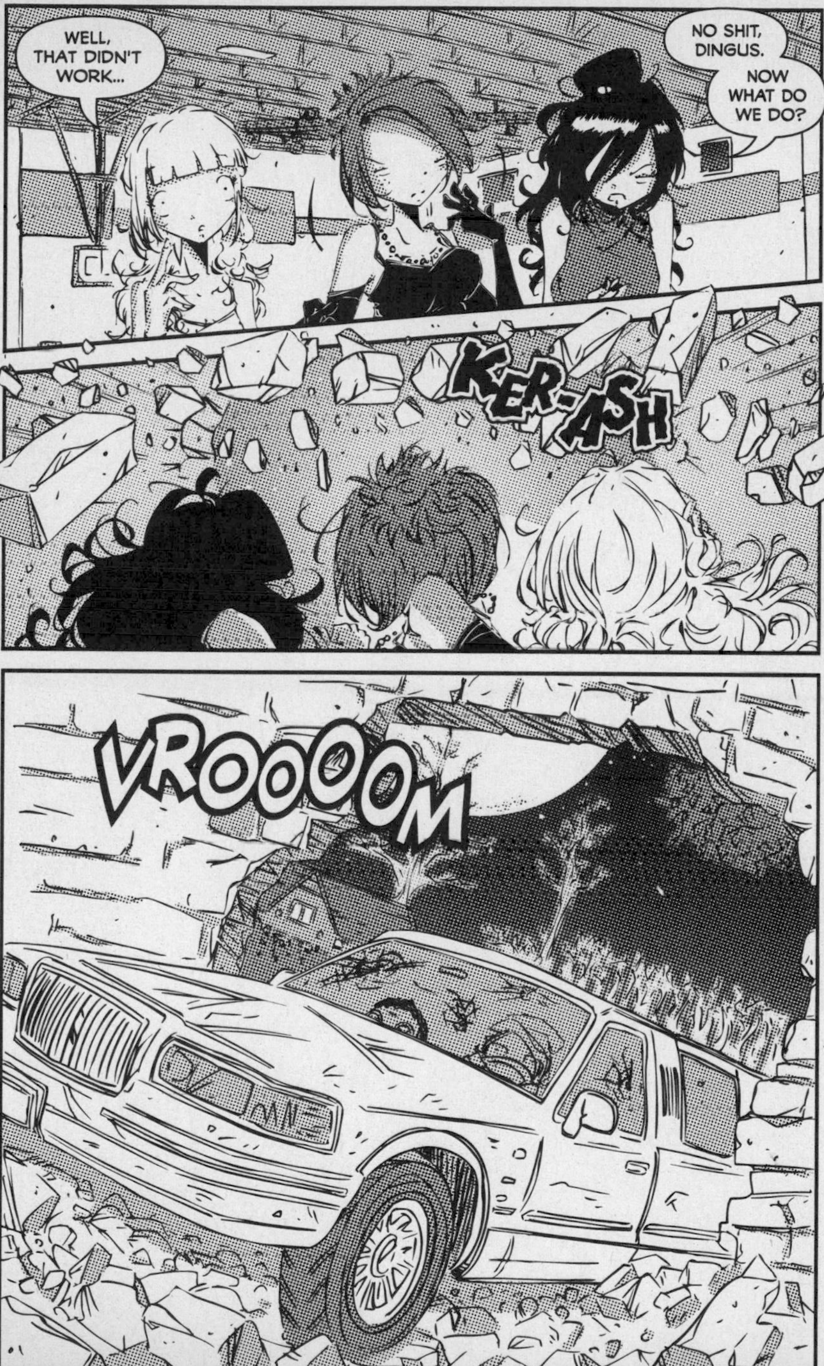
WELL, THAT DIDN'T WORK...
NO SHIT, DINGUS.
NOW WHAT DO WE DO?
KER-ASH
VROOOOM

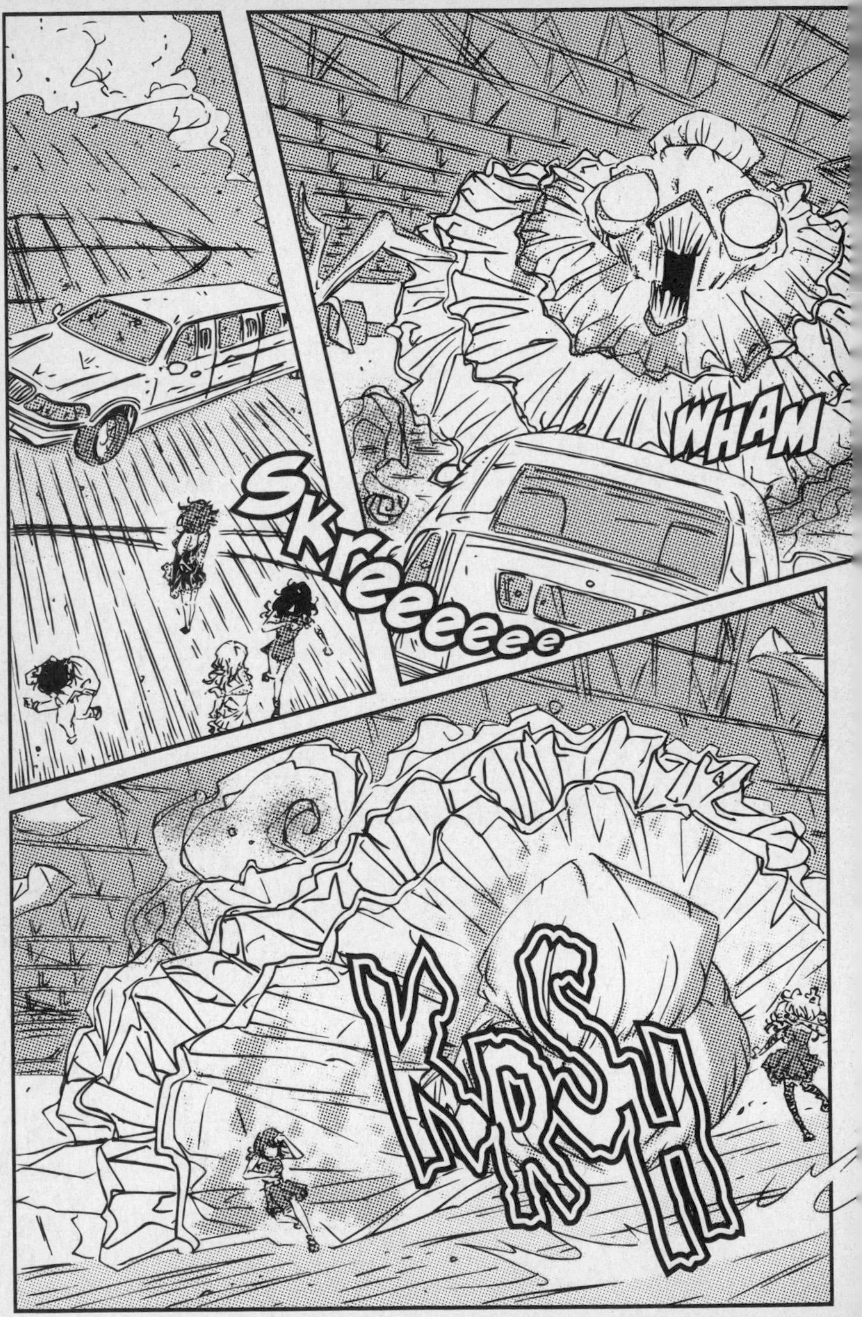
Skreeeeeee
WHAM
KRSH

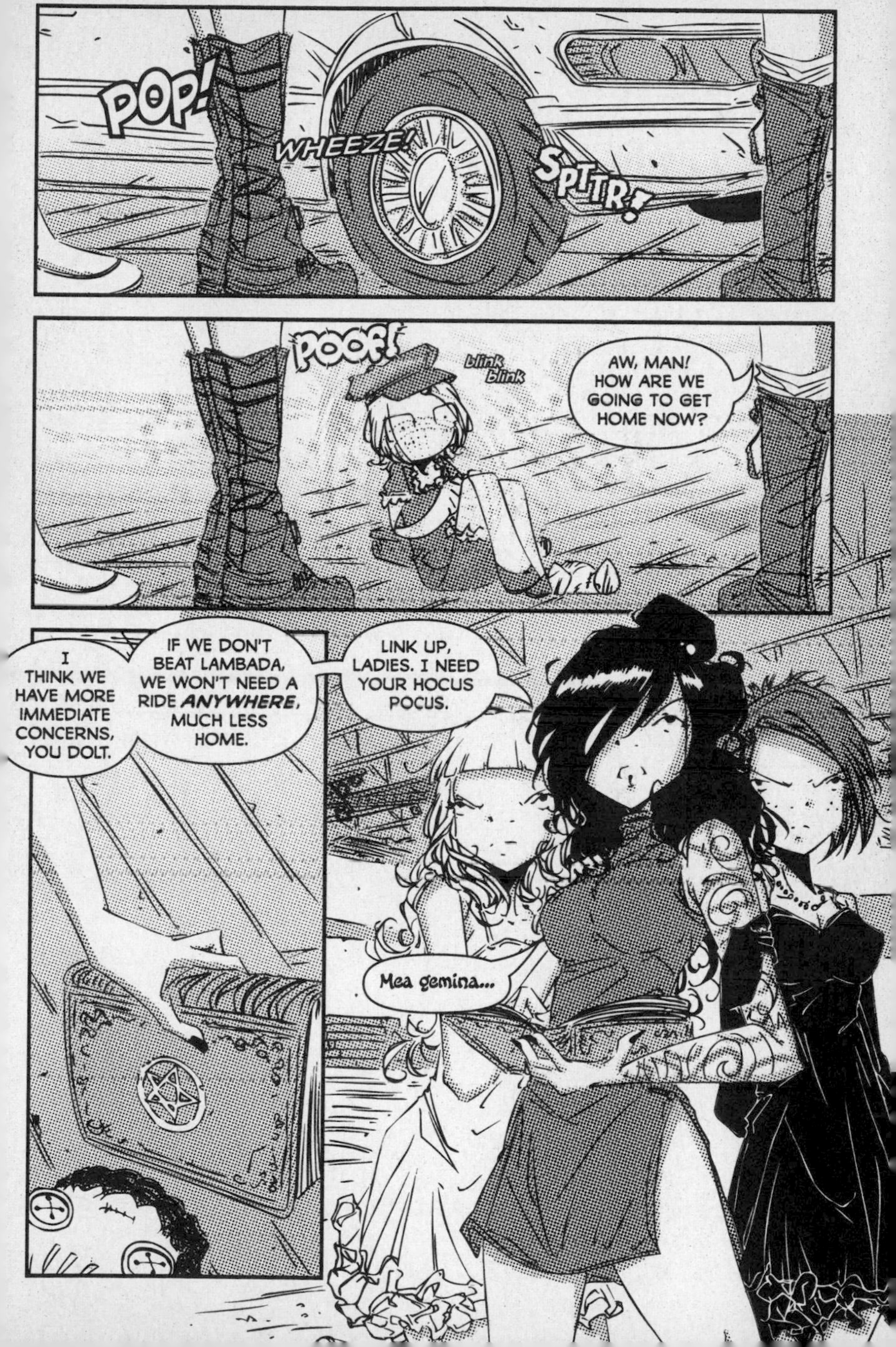
POP!
WHEEZE!
SPTTTR!
POOF!
blink blink
AW, MAN! HOW ARE WE GOING TO GET HOME NOW?
I THINK WE HAVE MORE IMMEDIATE CONCERNS, YOU DOLT.
IF WE DON'T BEAT LAMBADA, WE WON'T NEED A RIDE *ANYWHERE*, MUCH LESS HOME.
LINK UP, LADIES. I NEED YOUR HOCUS POCUS.
Mea gemina...

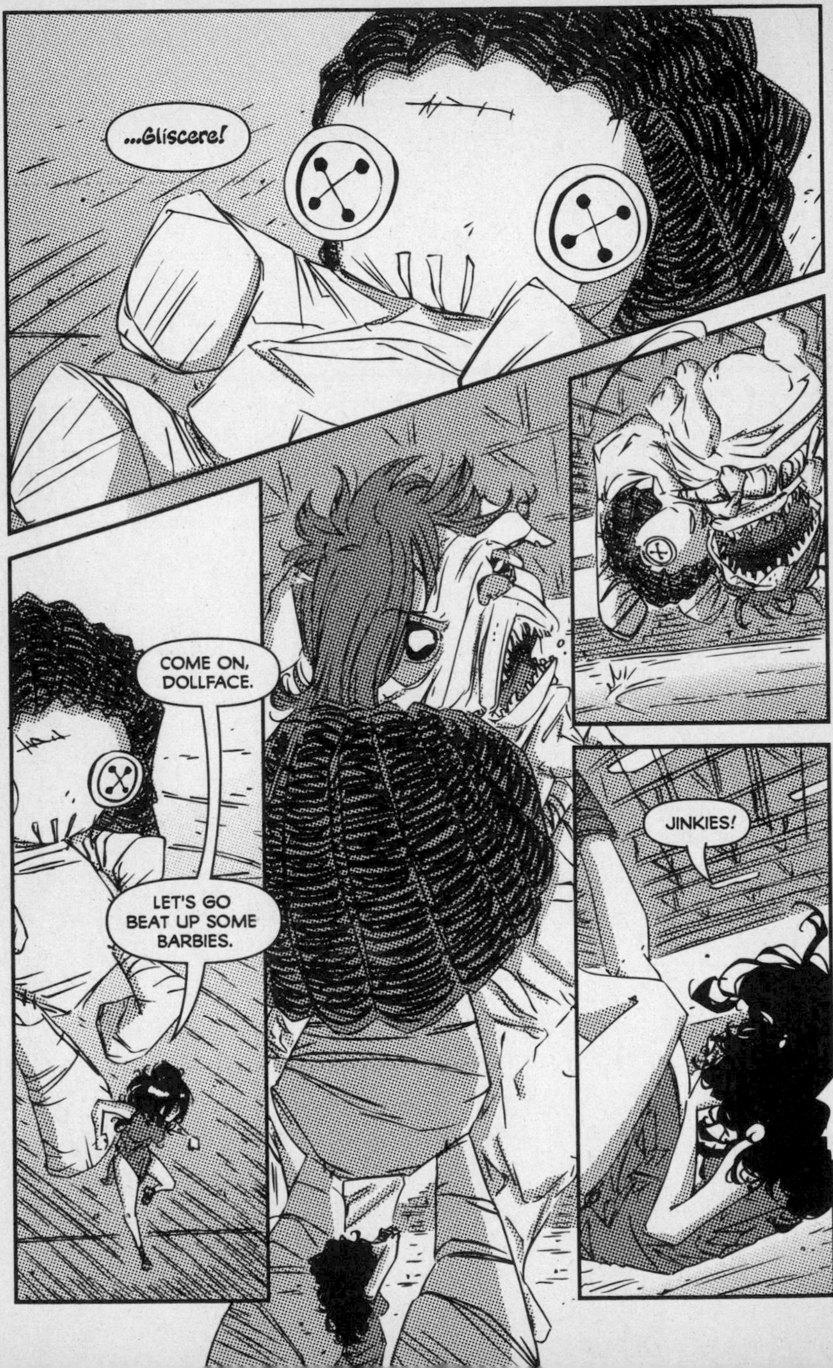
...Gliscere!
COME ON, DOLLFACE.
LET'S GO BEAT UP SOME BARBIES.
JINKIES!

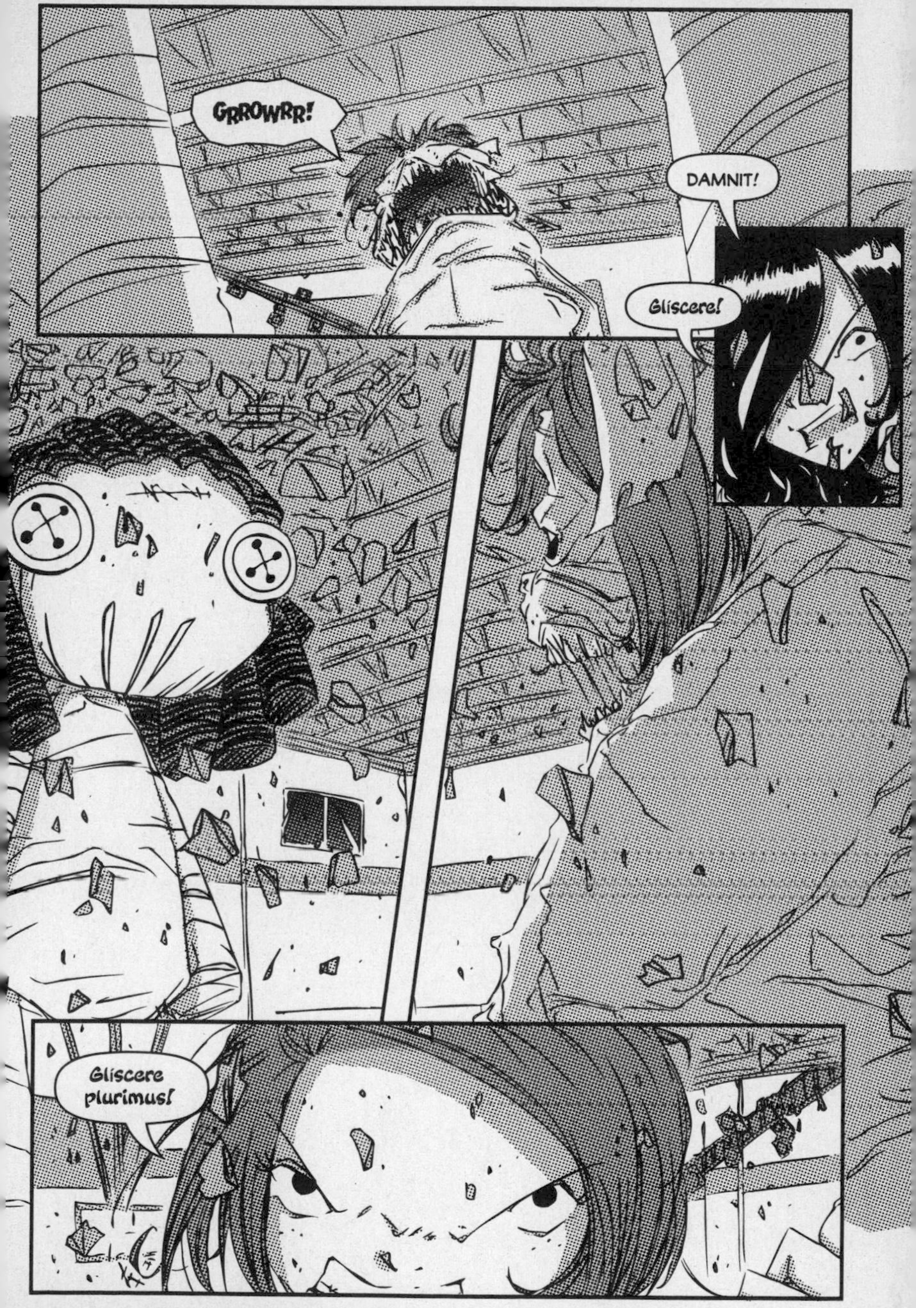
GRROWRR!
DAMNIT!
Gliscere!
Gliscere plurimus!

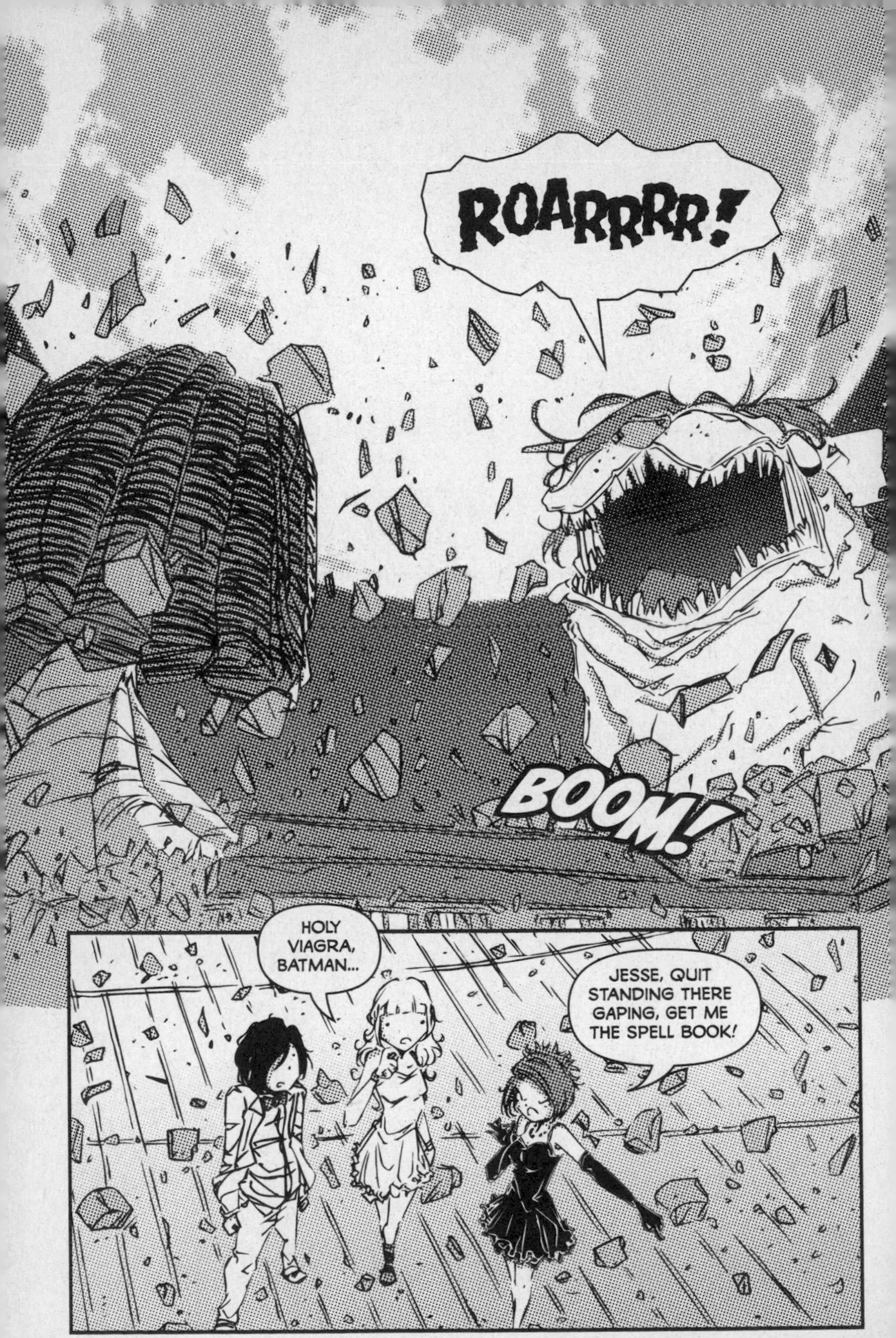
ROARRRRR!
BOOM!
HOLY VIAGRA, BATMAN...
JESSE, QUIT STANDING THERE GAPING, GET ME THE SPELL BOOK!

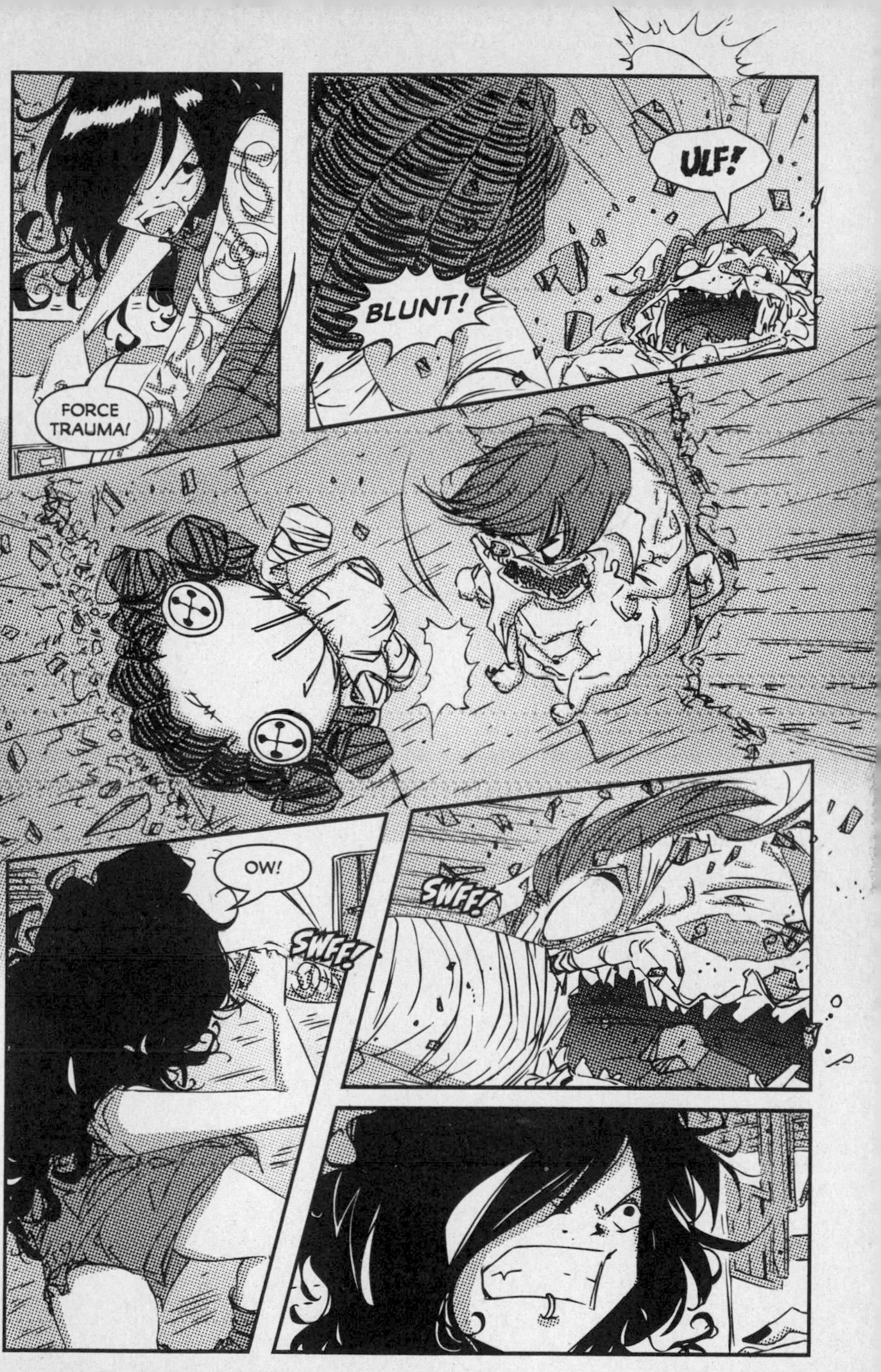
FORCE TRAUMA!
BLUNT!
ULF!
OW!
SWFF!
SWFF!

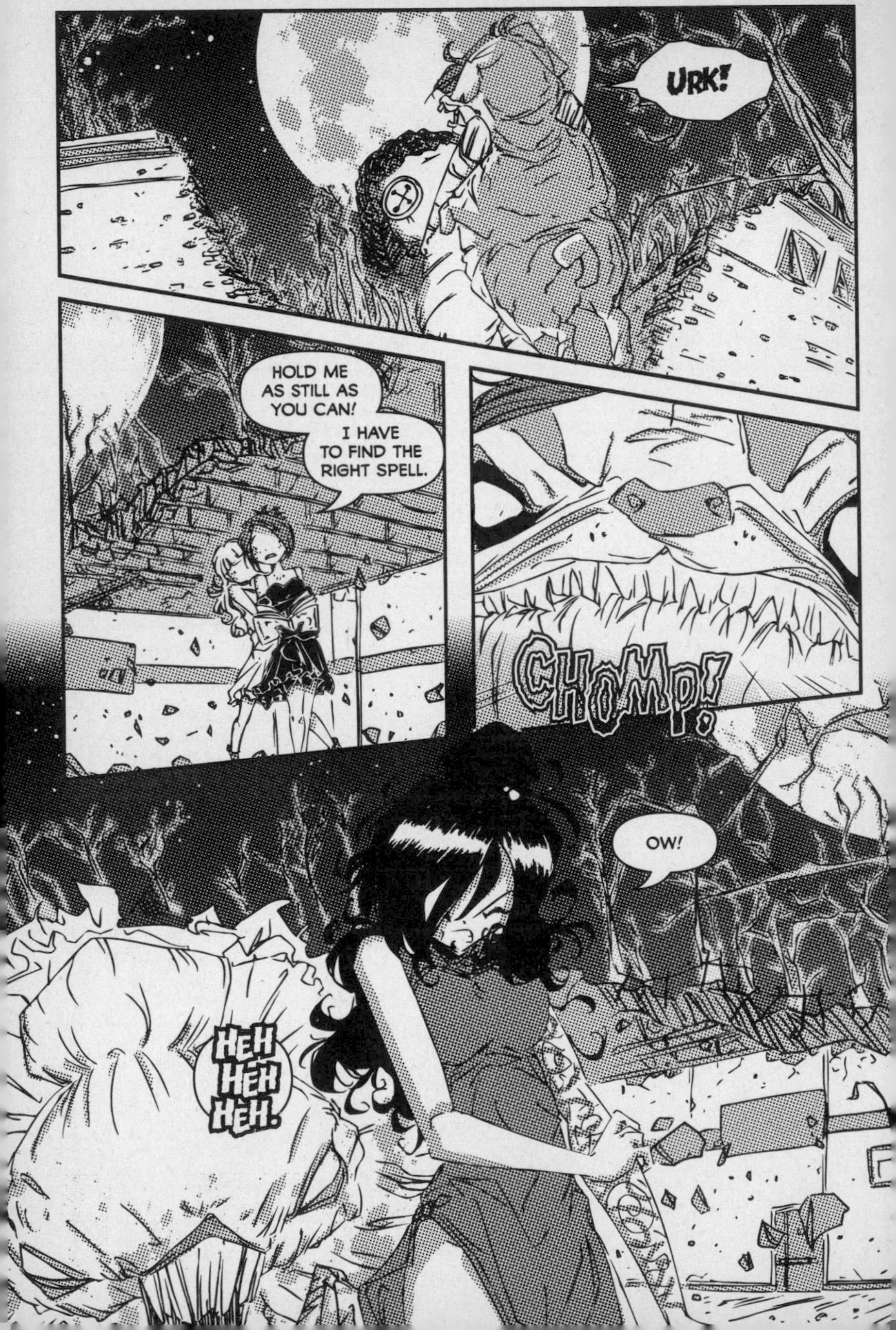
URK!
HOLD ME AS STILL AS YOU CAN!
I HAVE TO FIND THE RIGHT SPELL.
CHOMP!
OW!
HEH HEH HEH.

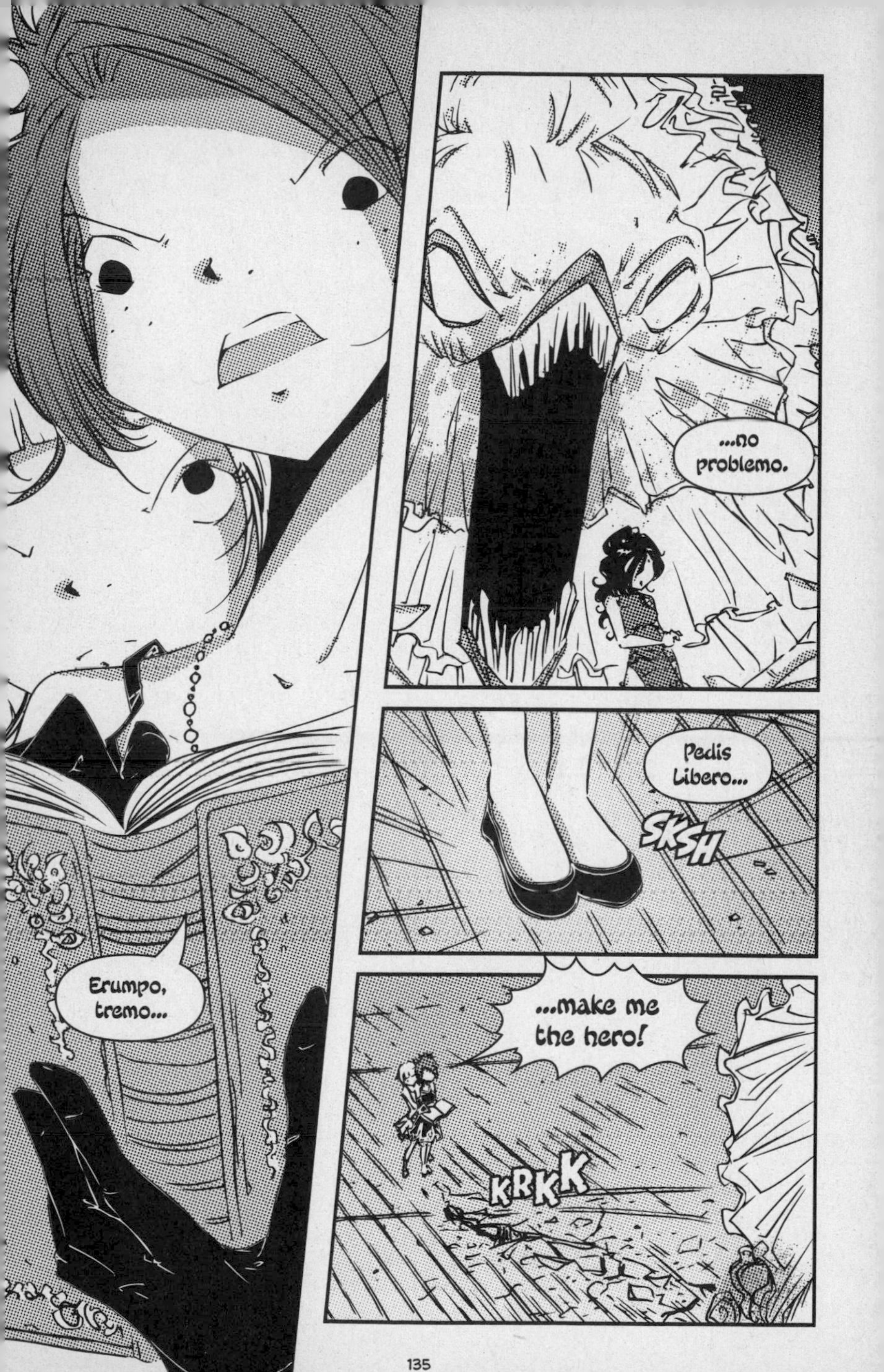

Erumpo,
tremo...
...no
problemo.
Pedis
Libero...
SKSH
...make me
the hero!
KRKK

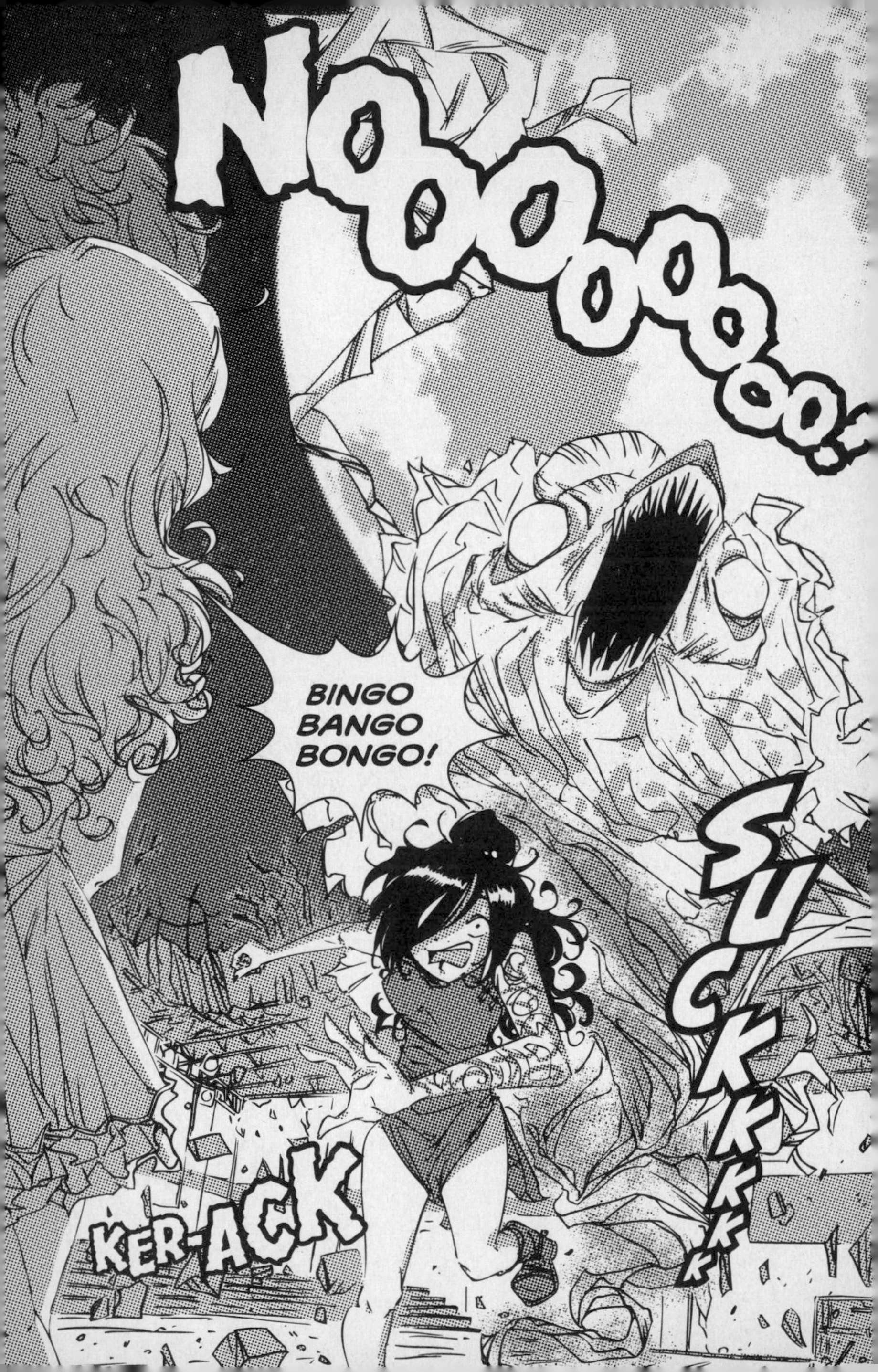
NOOOOOOOO!
BINGO BANGO BONGO!
SUCKKKKKK
KER-ACK

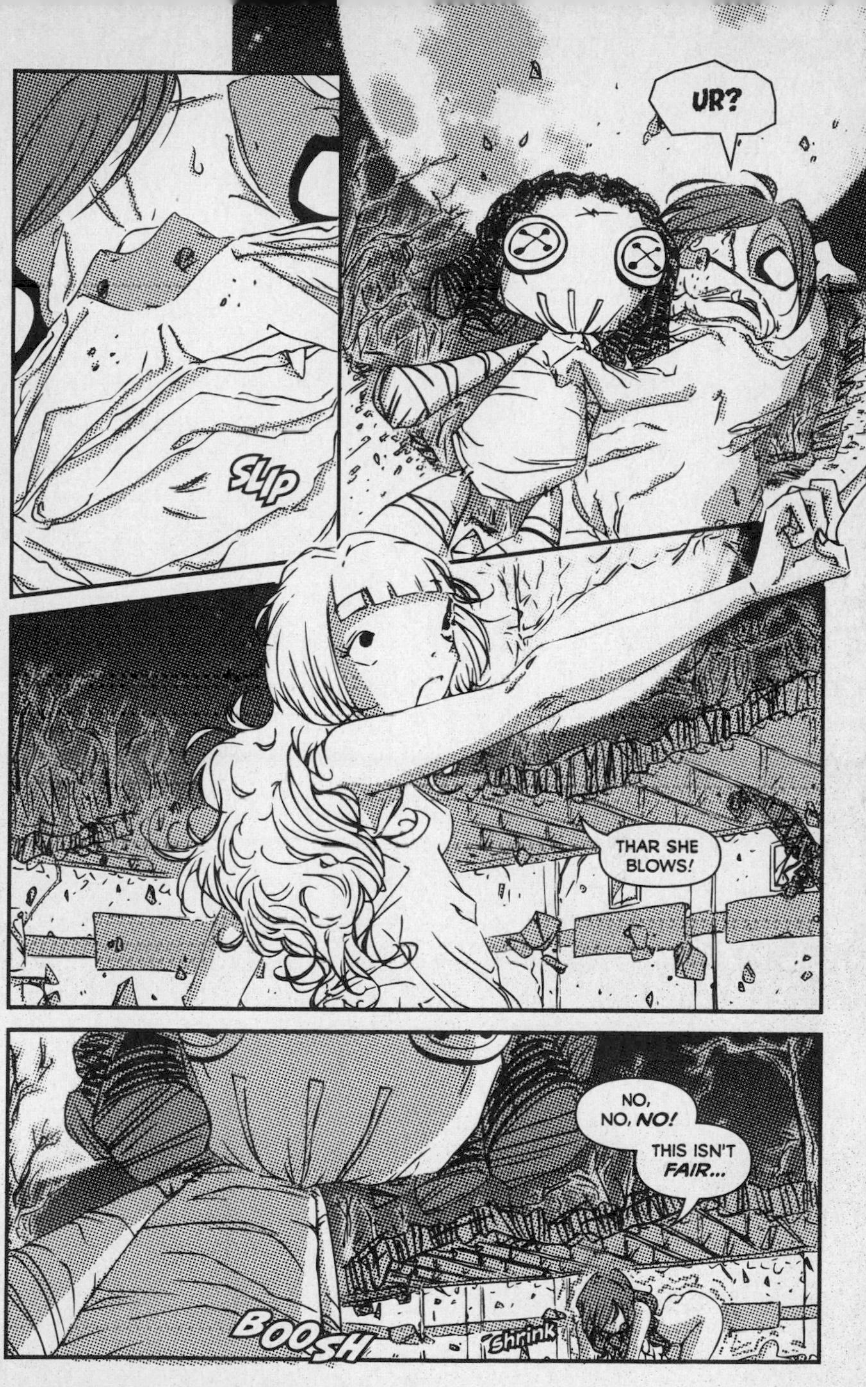
SLIP
UR?
THAR SHE BLOWS!
NO, NO, NO!
THIS ISN'T FAIR...
BOOSH
Shrink

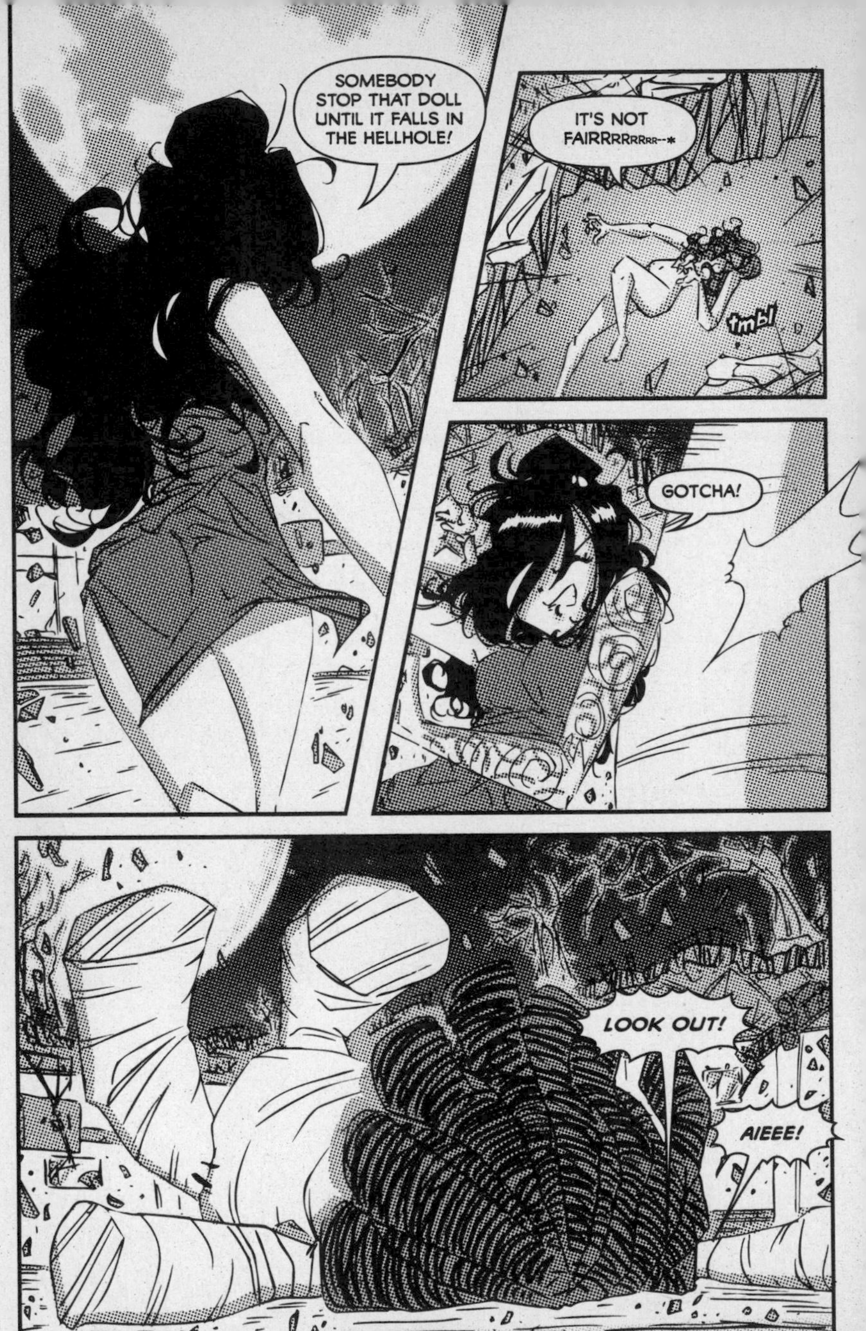
SOMEBODY STOP THAT DOLL UNTIL IT FALLS IN THE HELLHOLE!
IT'S NOT FAIRRRRRRRR--*
tmbl
GOTCHA!
LOOK OUT!
AIEEE!

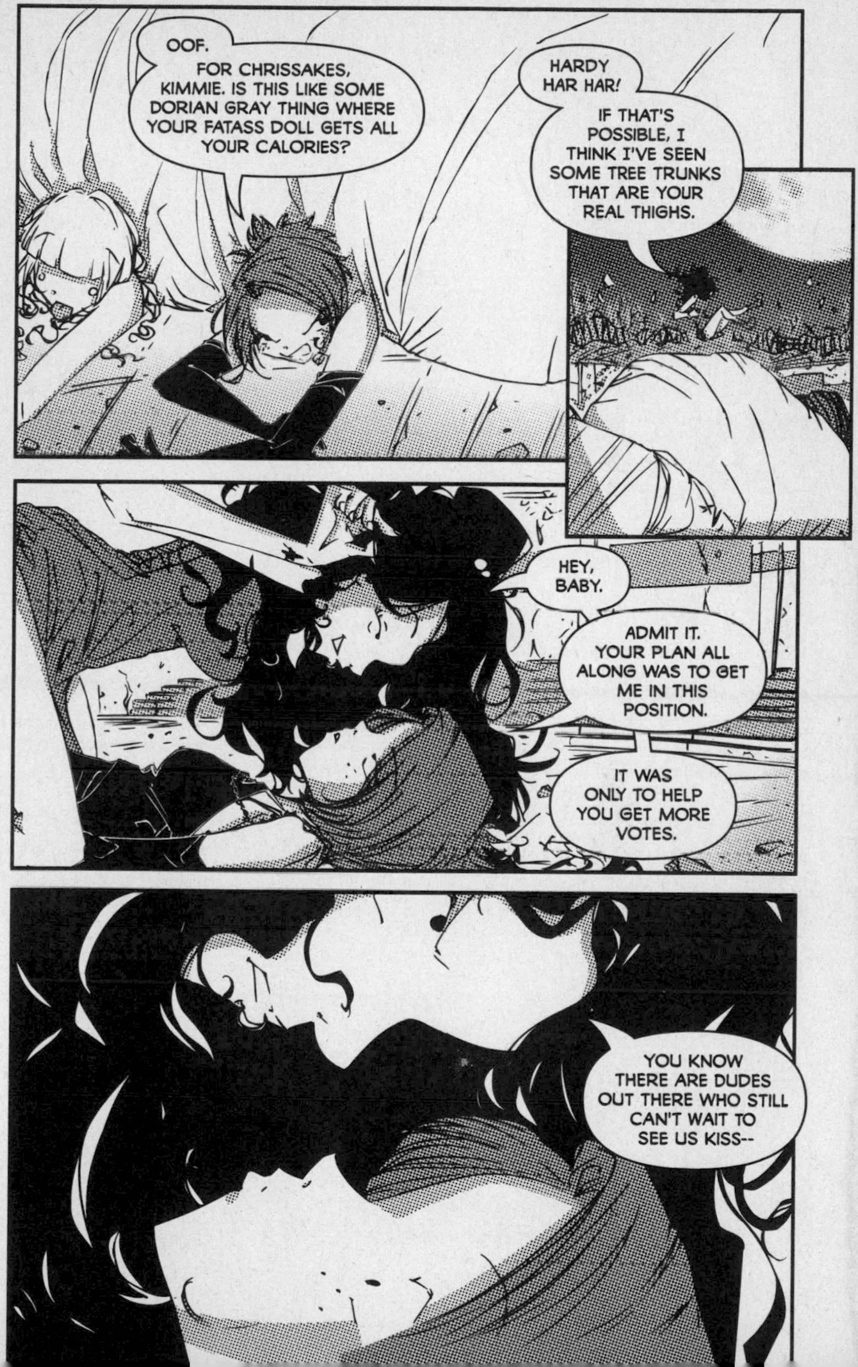
OOF.
FOR CHRISSAKES, KIMMIE. IS THIS LIKE SOME DORIAN GRAY THING WHERE YOUR FATASS DOLL GETS ALL YOUR CALORIES?
HARDY HAR HAR!
IF THAT'S POSSIBLE, I THINK I'VE SEEN SOME TREE TRUNKS THAT ARE YOUR REAL THIGHS.
HEY, BABY.
ADMIT IT. YOUR PLAN ALL ALONG WAS TO GET ME IN THIS POSITION.
IT WAS ONLY TO HELP YOU GET MORE VOTES.
YOU KNOW THERE ARE DUDES OUT THERE WHO STILL CAN'T WAIT TO SEE US KISS--

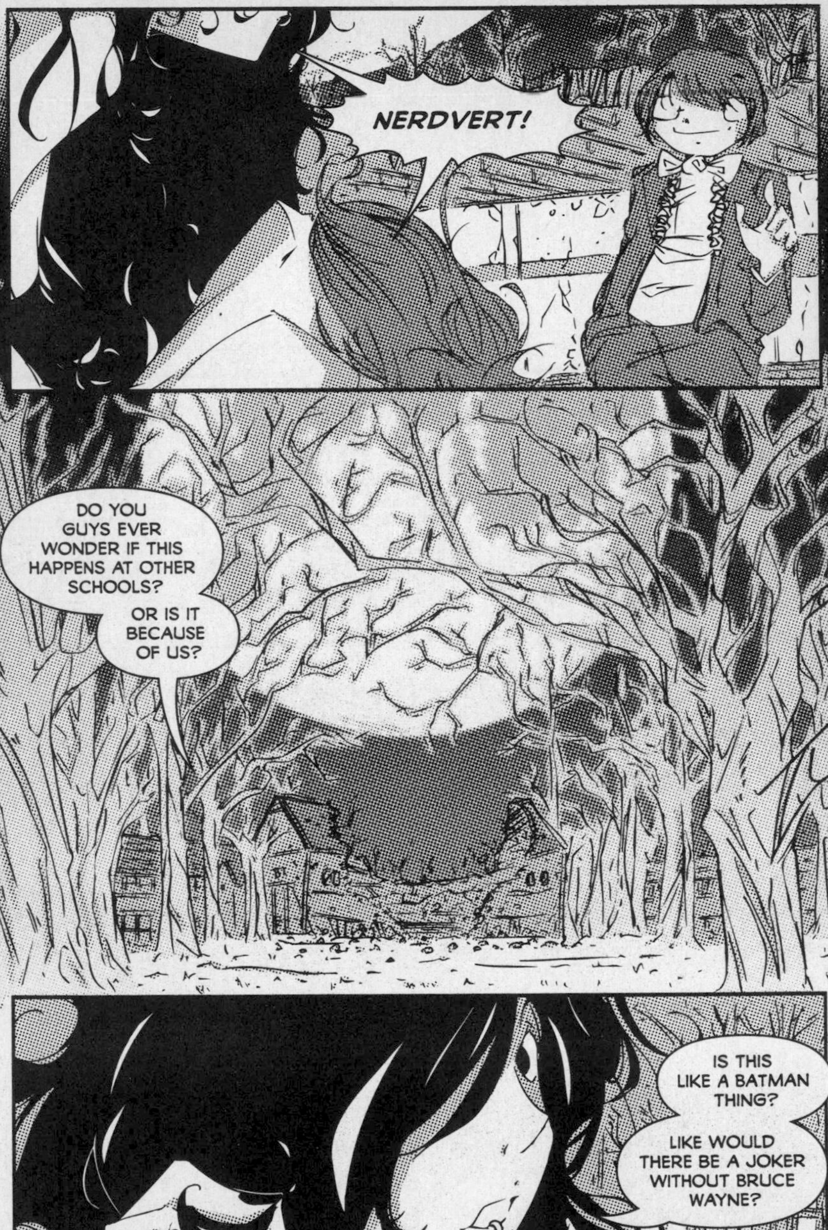
NERDVERT!
DO YOU GUYS EVER WONDER IF THIS HAPPENS AT OTHER SCHOOLS?
OR IS IT BECAUSE OF US?
IS THIS LIKE A BATMAN THING?
LIKE WOULD THERE BE A JOKER WITHOUT BRUCE WAYNE?

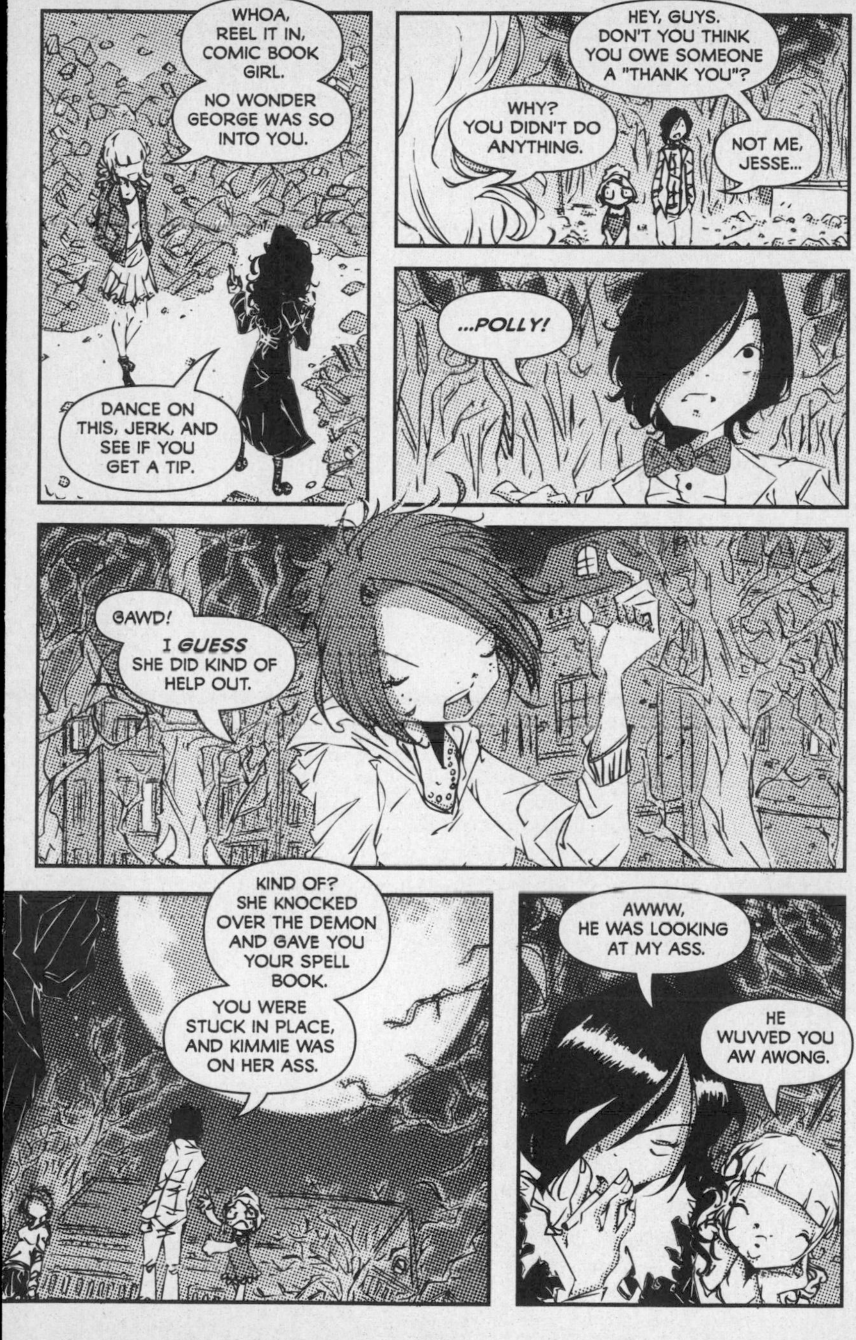
WHOA, REEL IT IN, COMIC BOOK GIRL.
NO WONDER GEORGE WAS SO INTO YOU.
DANCE ON THIS, JERK, AND SEE IF YOU GET A TIP.
HEY, GUYS. DON'T YOU THINK YOU OWE SOMEONE A "THANK YOU"?
WHY? YOU DIDN'T DO ANYTHING.
NOT ME, JESSE...
...POLLY!
GAWD!
I GUESS SHE DID KIND OF HELP OUT.
KIND OF? SHE KNOCKED OVER THE DEMON AND GAVE YOU YOUR SPELL BOOK.
YOU WERE STUCK IN PLACE, AND KIMMIE WAS ON HER ASS.
AWWW, HE WAS LOOKING AT MY ASS.
HE WUVVED YOU AW AWONG.

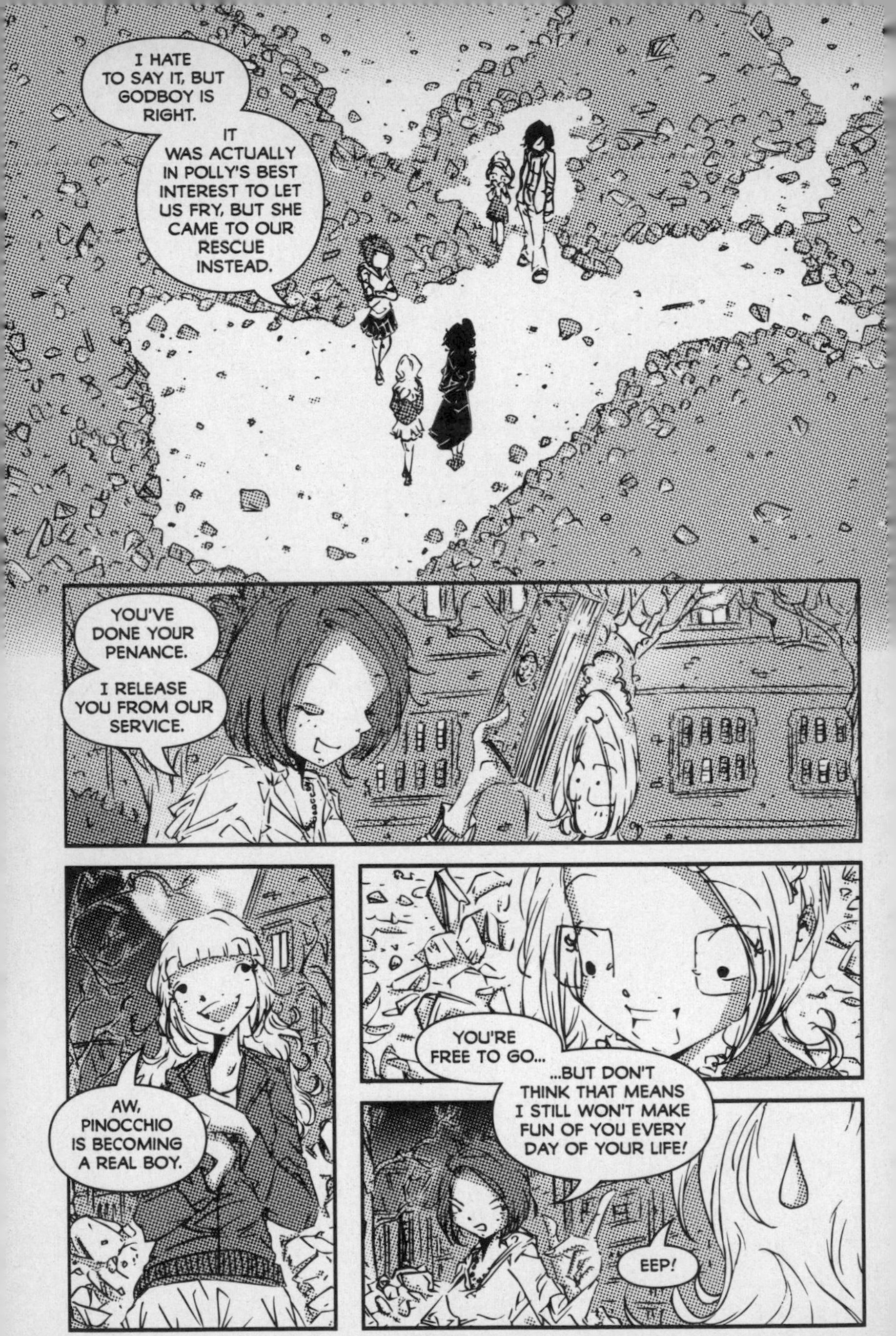
I HATE TO SAY IT, BUT GODBOY IS RIGHT.
IT WAS ACTUALLY IN POLLY'S BEST INTEREST TO LET US FRY, BUT SHE CAME TO OUR RESCUE INSTEAD.
YOU'VE DONE YOUR PENANCE.
I RELEASE YOU FROM OUR SERVICE.
AW, PINOCCHIO IS BECOMING A REAL BOY.
YOU'RE FREE TO GO...
...BUT DON'T THINK THAT MEANS I STILL WON'T MAKE FUN OF YOU EVERY DAY OF YOUR LIFE!
EEP!

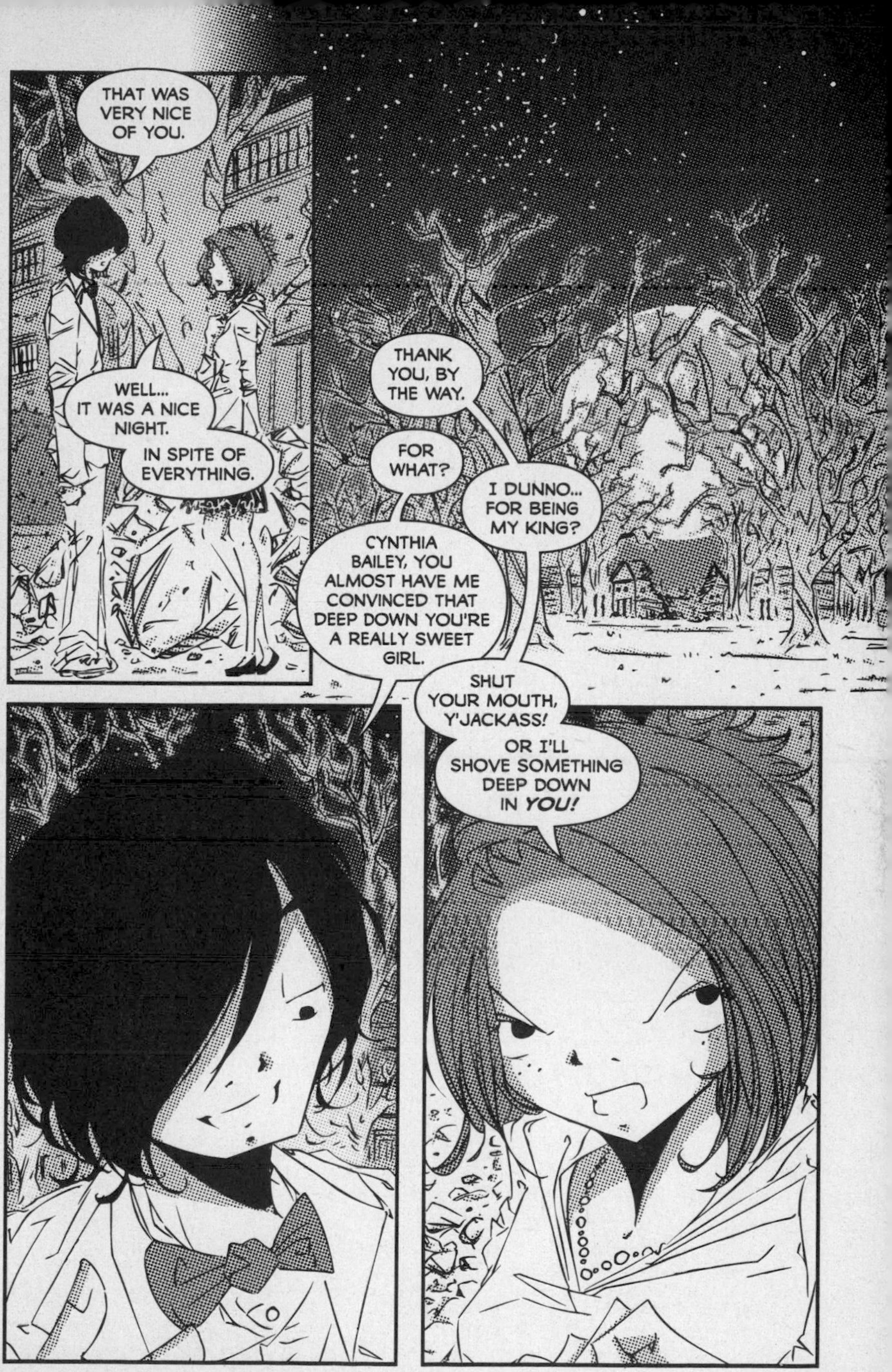
THAT WAS VERY NICE OF YOU.
WELL... IT WAS A NICE NIGHT.
IN SPITE OF EVERYTHING.
THANK YOU, BY THE WAY.
FOR WHAT?
I DUNNO... FOR BEING MY KING?
CYNTHIA BAILEY, YOU ALMOST HAVE ME CONVINCED THAT DEEP DOWN YOU'RE A REALLY SWEET GIRL.
SHUT YOUR MOUTH, Y'JACKASS!
OR I'LL SHOVE SOMETHING DEEP DOWN IN *YOU!*

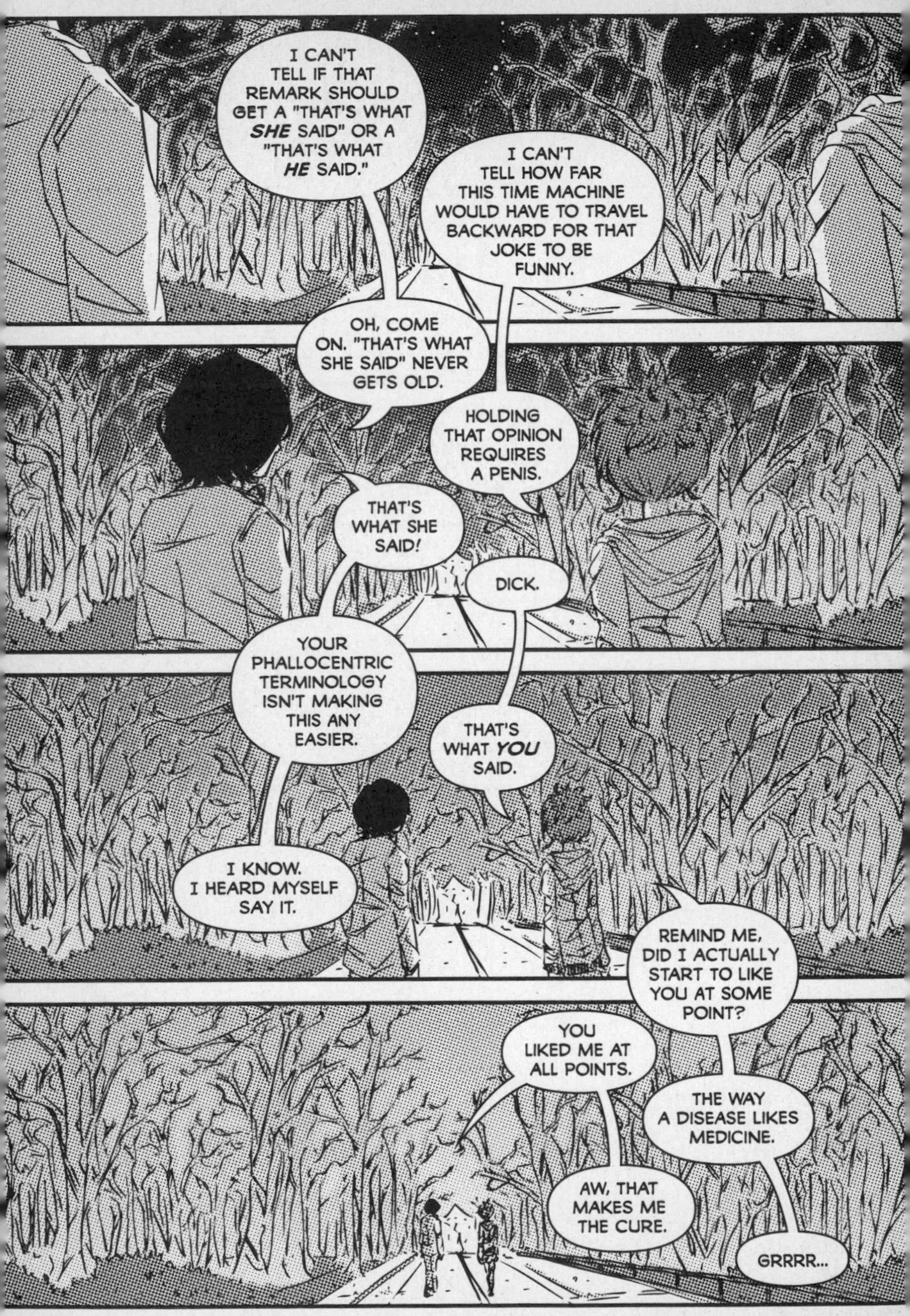

I CAN'T TELL IF THAT REMARK SHOULD GET A "THAT'S WHAT *SHE* SAID" OR A "THAT'S WHAT *HE* SAID."
I CAN'T TELL HOW FAR THIS TIME MACHINE WOULD HAVE TO TRAVEL BACKWARD FOR THAT JOKE TO BE FUNNY.
OH, COME ON. "THAT'S WHAT SHE SAID" NEVER GETS OLD.
HOLDING THAT OPINION REQUIRES A PENIS.
THAT'S WHAT SHE SAID!
DICK.
YOUR PHALLOCENTRIC TERMINOLOGY ISN'T MAKING THIS ANY EASIER.
THAT'S WHAT *YOU* SAID.
I KNOW. I HEARD MYSELF SAY IT.
REMIND ME, DID I ACTUALLY START TO LIKE YOU AT SOME POINT?
YOU LIKED ME AT ALL POINTS.
THE WAY A DISEASE LIKES MEDICINE.
AW, THAT MAKES ME THE CURE.
GRRRR...

Epilogue
"It Starts and Ends With You."

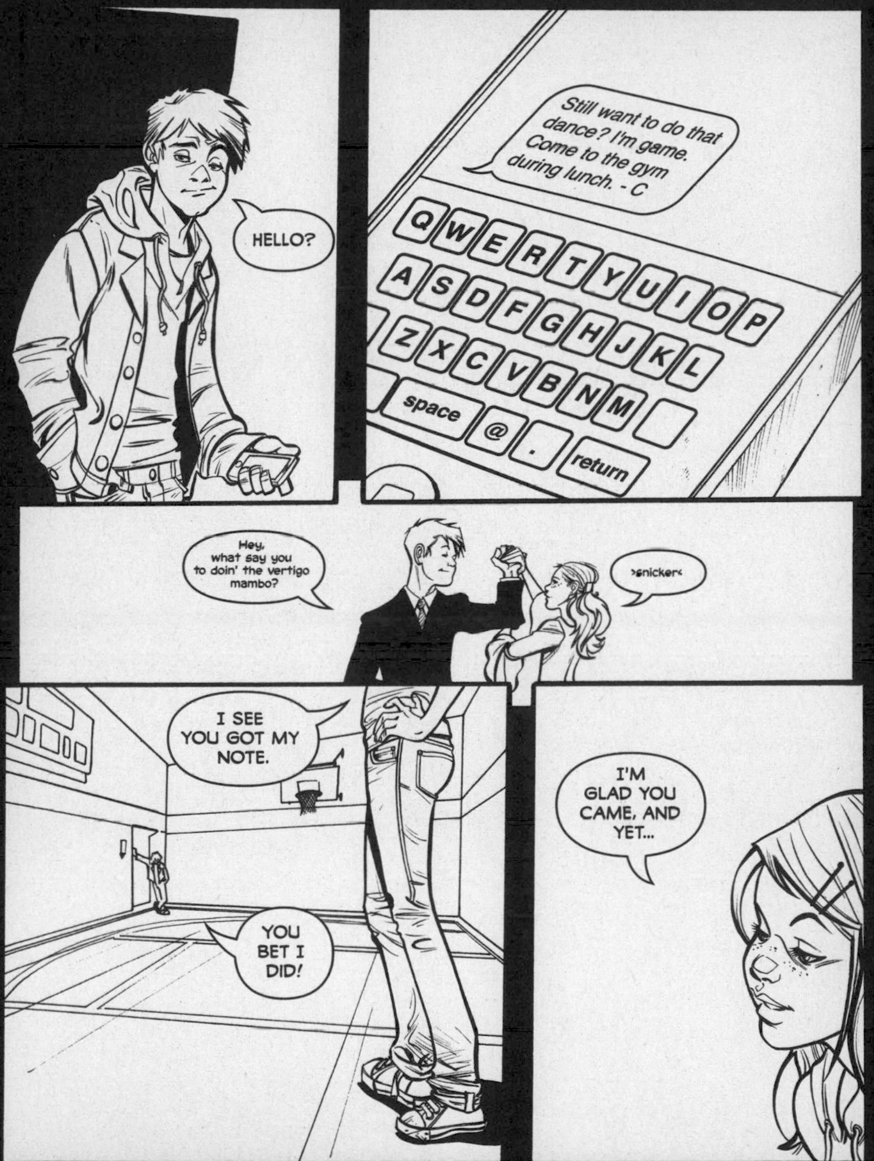
HELLO?
Still want to do that dance? I'm game. Come to the gym during lunch. - C
Q W E R T Y U I O P
A S D F G H J K L
Z X C V B N M
space @ . return
Hey, what say you to doin' the vertigo mambo?
>snicker<
I SEE YOU GOT MY NOTE.
YOU BET I DID!
I'M GLAD YOU CAME, AND YET...

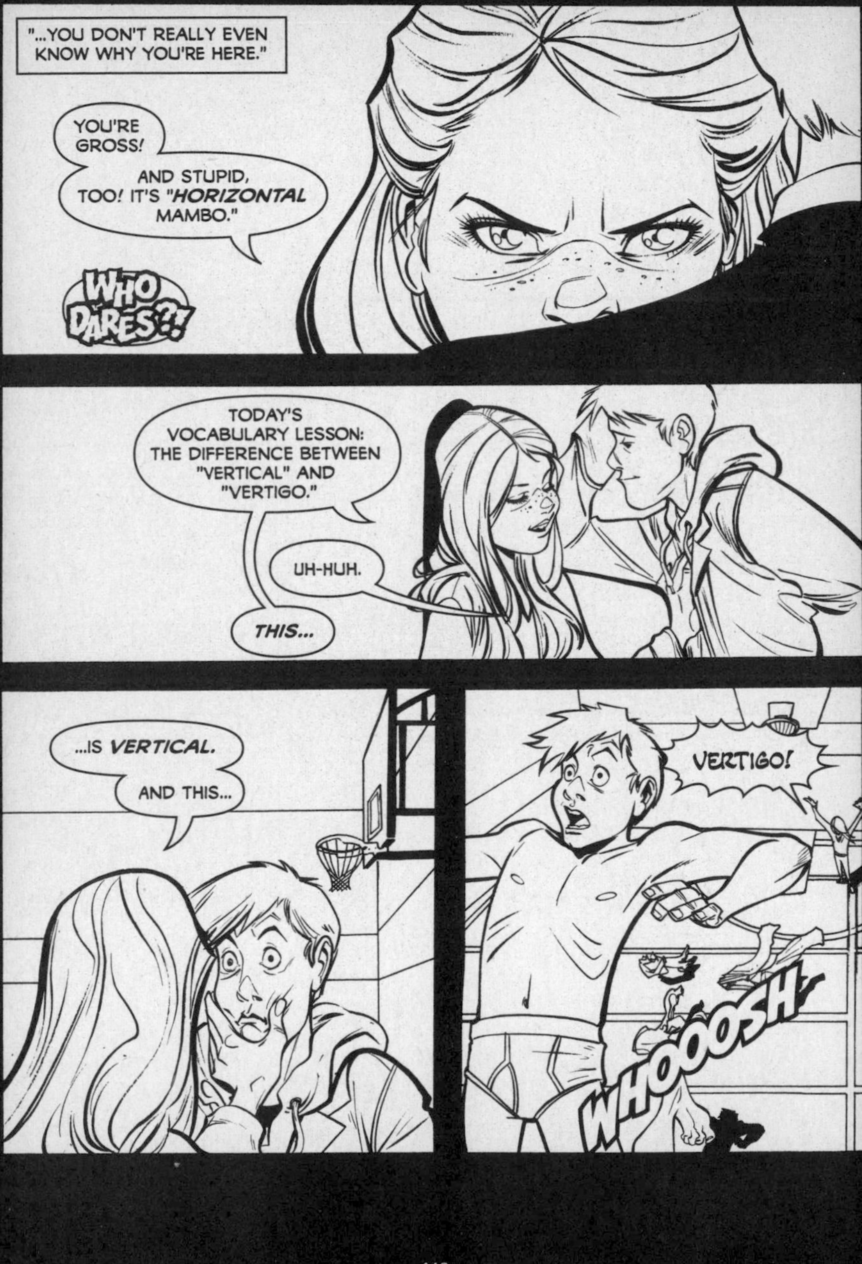
"...YOU DON'T REALLY EVEN KNOW WHY YOU'RE HERE."
YOU'RE GROSS!
AND STUPID, TOO! IT'S "HORIZONTAL MAMBO."
WHO DARES?!
TODAY'S VOCABULARY LESSON: THE DIFFERENCE BETWEEN "VERTICAL" AND "VERTIGO."
UH-HUH.
THIS...
...IS VERTICAL.
AND THIS...
VERTIGO!
WHOOOSH

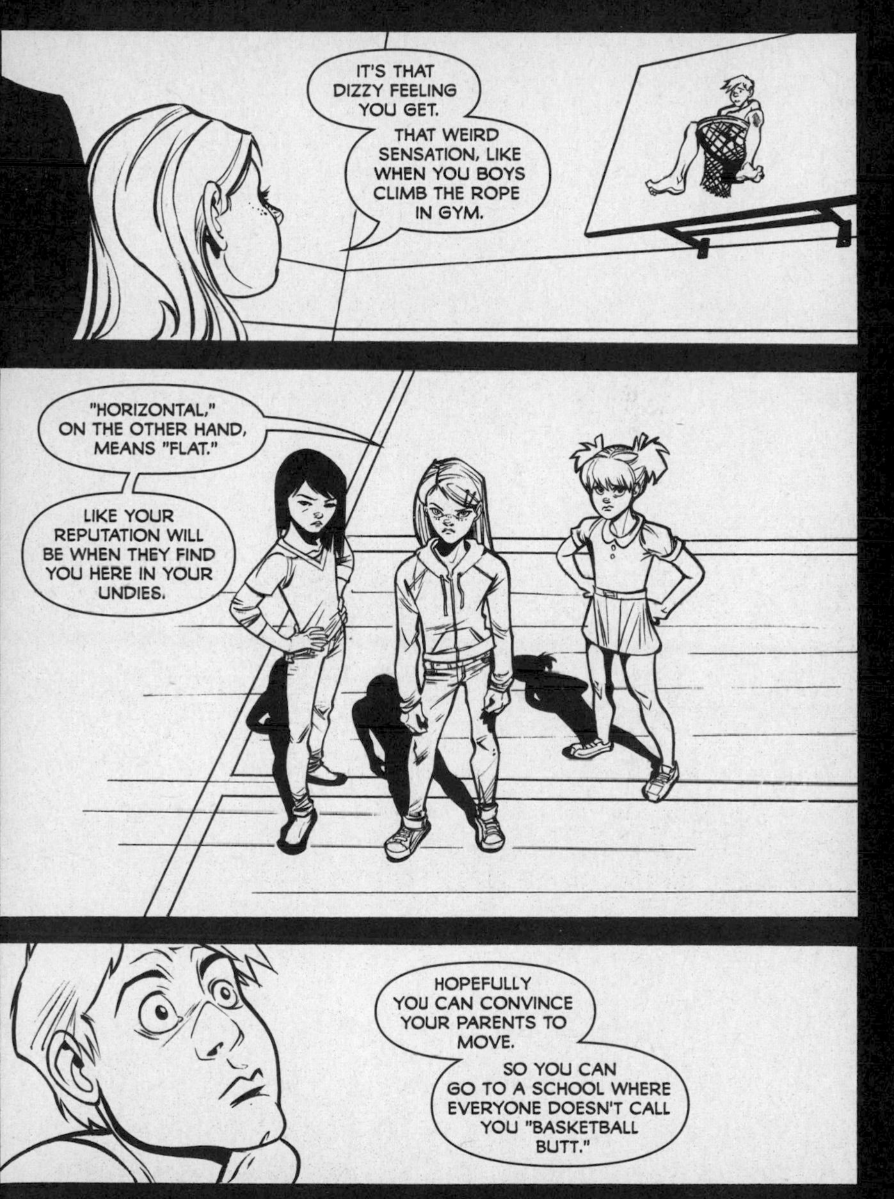
IT'S THAT DIZZY FEELING YOU GET.
THAT WEIRD SENSATION, LIKE WHEN YOU BOYS CLIMB THE ROPE IN GYM.
"HORIZONTAL," ON THE OTHER HAND, MEANS "FLAT."
LIKE YOUR REPUTATION WILL BE WHEN THEY FIND YOU HERE IN YOUR UNDIES.
HOPEFULLY YOU CAN CONVINCE YOUR PARENTS TO MOVE.
SO YOU CAN GO TO A SCHOOL WHERE EVERYONE DOESN'T CALL YOU "BASKETBALL BUTT."

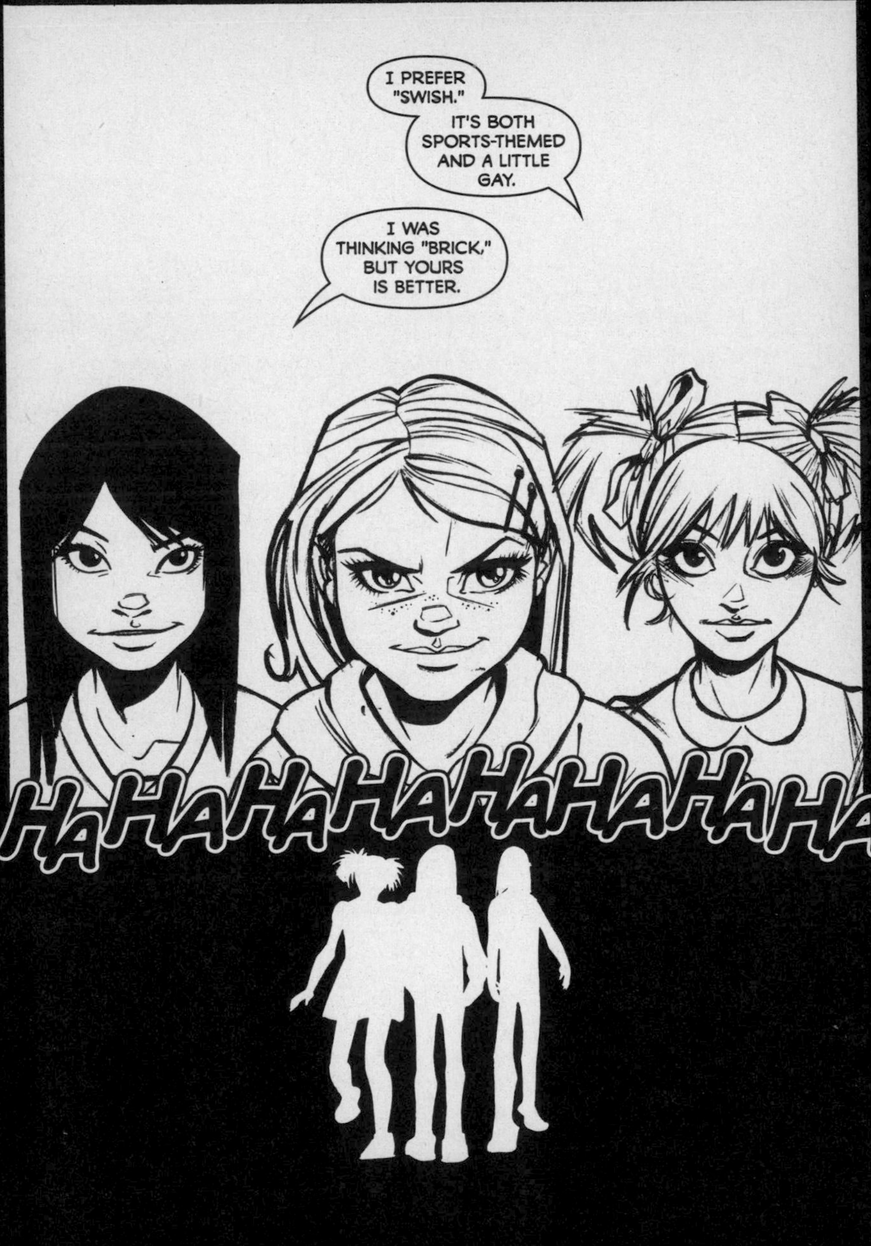
I PREFER "SWISH."
IT'S BOTH SPORTS-THEMED AND A LITTLE GAY.
I WAS THINKING "BRICK," BUT YOURS IS BETTER.
HAHAHAHAHAHAHAHAHAHAHA

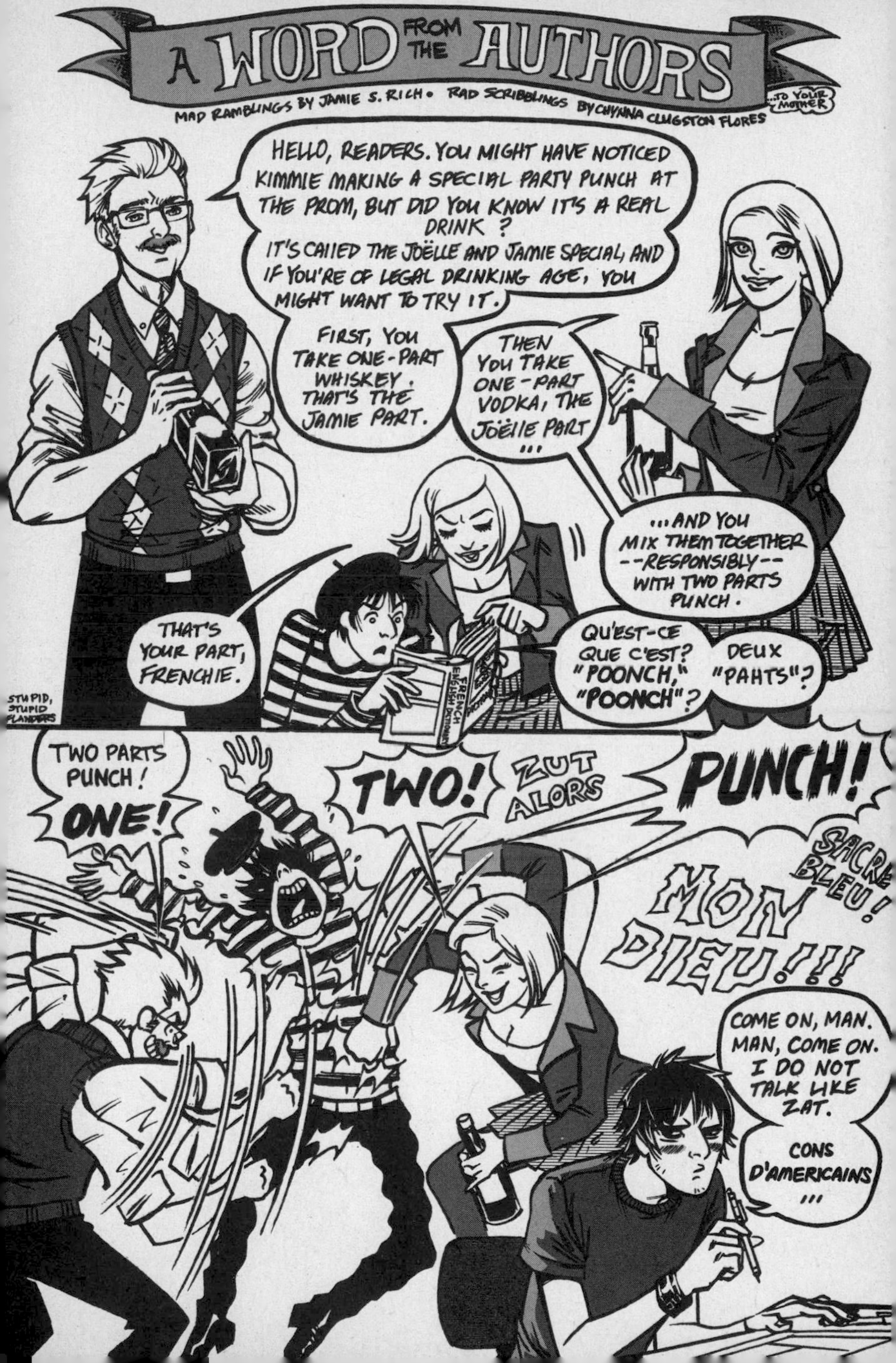

A WORD FROM THE AUTHORS
MAD RAMBLINGS BY JAMIE S. RICH • RAD SCRIBBLINGS BY CHYNNA CLUGSTON FLORES
...TO YOUR MOTHER
HELLO, READERS. YOU MIGHT HAVE NOTICED KIMMIE MAKING A SPECIAL PARTY PUNCH AT THE PROM, BUT DID YOU KNOW IT'S A REAL DRINK ? IT'S CALLED THE JOËLLE AND JAMIE SPECIAL, AND IF YOU'RE OF LEGAL DRINKING AGE, YOU MIGHT WANT TO TRY IT.
FIRST, YOU TAKE ONE-PART WHISKEY. THAT'S THE JAMIE PART.
THEN YOU TAKE ONE-PART VODKA, THE JOËLLE PART ...
...AND YOU MIX THEM TOGETHER --RESPONSIBLY-- WITH TWO PARTS PUNCH.
THAT'S YOUR PART, FRENCHIE.
FRENCH ENGLISH DICTIONARY
QU'EST-CE QUE C'EST? "POONCH," "POONCH"?
DEUX "PAHTS"?
STUPID, STUPID FLANDERS
TWO PARTS PUNCH!
ONE!
TWO!
ZUT ALORS
PUNCH!
SACRE BLEU!
MON DIEU!!!
COME ON, MAN. MAN, COME ON. I DO NOT TALK LIKE ZAT.
CONS D'AMERICAINS ...

OTHER TITLES FROM JAMIE S. RICH, JOËLLE JONES & NICOLAS HITORI DE

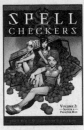

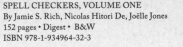

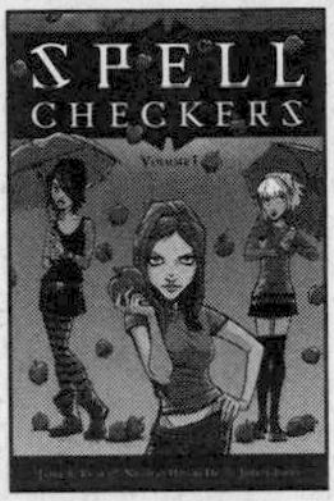

SPELL CHECKERS

SPELL CHECKERS
VOLUME 2:

SPELL CHECKERS, VOLUME ONE
By Jamie S. Rich, Nicolas Hitori De, Joëlle Jones
152 pages • Digest • B&W
ISBN 978-1-934964-32-3

SPELL CHECKERS, VOLUME TWO: SONS OF A PREACHER MAN
By Jamie S. Rich, Nicolas Hitori De, Joëlle Jones
156 Pages • Digest • B&W
ISBN 978-1-934964-72-9

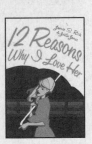

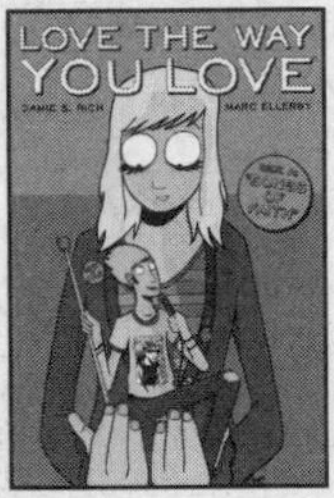

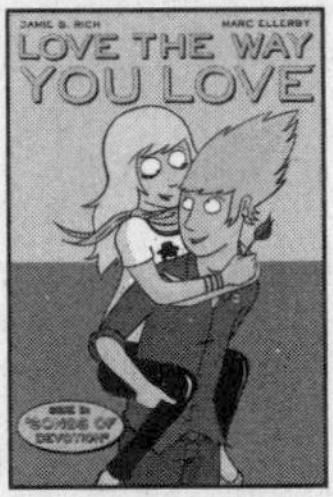

LOVE THE WAY YOU LOVE
JAMIE S. RICH
MARC ELLERBY

JAMIE S. RICH
MARC ELLERBY
LOVE THE WAY YOU LOVE

LOVE THE WAY YOU LOVE: SIDE A
By Jamie S. Rich & Marc Ellerby
200 Pages • Digest • B&W
ISBN 978-1-932664-66-9

LOVE THE WAY YOU LOVE: SIDE B
By Jamie S. Rich & Marc Ellerby
200 Pages • Digest • B&W
ISBN 978-1-932664-95-9

Jamie S. Rich & Joëlle Jones
12 Reasons Why I Love Her

YOU HAVE KILLED ME

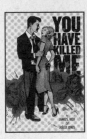

12 REASONS WHY I LOVE HER
By Jamie S. Rich & Joëlle Jones
144 Pages • 6"x9" Trade paperback • B&W
ISBN 978-1-932664-51-5

YOU HAVE KILLED ME
By Jamie S. Rich & Joëlle Jones
192 Pages • Hardcover • B&W
ISBN 978-1-932664-88-1

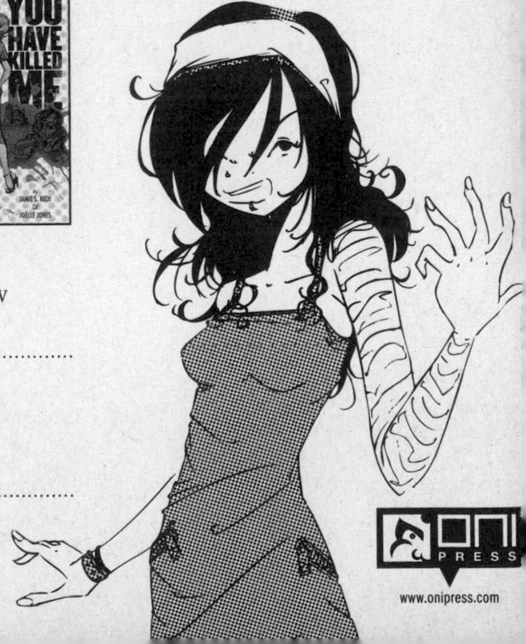

For more information on these and other fine Oni Press comic books and graphic novels, visit www.onipress.com. To find a comic specialty store in your area, call 1-888-COMICBOOK or visit www.comicshops.us.

ONI PRESS
www.onipress.com